Productivity and Jobs in a Globalised World

(HOW) CAN ALL REGIONS BENEFIT?

OECD
BETTER POLICIES FOR BETTER LIVES

Please cite this publication as:
OECD (2018), *Productivity and Jobs in a Globalised World: (How) Can All Regions Benefit?*, OECD Publishing, Paris.
http://dx.doi.org/10.1787/9789264293137-en

ISBN 978-92-64-29309-0 (print)
ISBN 978-92-64-29313-7 (PDF)

Photo credits: Cover © Parko Polo.

Corrigenda to OECD publications may be found on line at: *www.oecd.org/about/publishing/corrigenda.htm*.

Foreword

In recent years, the economic and social costs of persistent disparities in economic performance across regions have become apparent. National economic growth is limited by the lagging productivity growth in some regions. Within affected regions, persistently high unemployment and stagnating or declining wages create economic hardship and diminish people's confidence in a better future. As a consequence, there are populations in many OECD countries are increasingly discontent with the status quo and, not surprisingly, there is a geographic pattern to much of this discontent.

Helping all regions identify opportunities in globalisation is essential, and ensuring countries remain open to globalisation will require greater success in addressing regional divides within. The costs and benefits from trade are unevenly distributed across regions. Whereas in most regions the benefits from trade have far outweighed the costs, some regions have mainly experienced its downsides. In those regions, old industries have been harmed severely by foreign competition and large numbers of workers have lost their jobs. Furthermore, adjustment processes have been very slow and in many of those regions the jobs have not returned. In the future, unemployment might be exacerbated as jobs become increasingly automated.

To reduce such spatial disparities, policy makers need to address low productivity growth in economically lagging regions. Raising labour productivity is not only essential for long-term economic prosperity but also the only way to ensure sustainable wage growth. Beyond economic output and income levels, productivity matters for many other dimensions of well-being. It is, for example, directly linked to the resources that are available for investments in health care or environmental protection.

This report assesses the regional and national framework conditions that are conducive for the "catching up" of lagging regions and examines how tradable sectors, clusters and well-functioning cities contribute to this process. The analysis is complemented by concrete policy lessons and examples on how to harness the opportunities provided by a globalised world and effectively address the challenges that it brings. Put differently, this report is asking the question: How can all regions benefit?

This publication contributes to the broader work programme of the OECD Regional Development Policy Committee. It was approved by the Committee on 13 December 2017 under the COTE CFE/RDPC(2017)7 after discussion of the final report at its 38th Session on 7-8 December 2017 and of intermediate findings in earlier sessions of the Committee and its Working Party on Territorial Indicators.

Acknowledgements

This report was produced by the Centre for Entrepreneurship, SMEs, Regions and Cities led by Lamia Kamal-Chaoui, Director.

It is part of the project "Sound Macroeconomic Framework Conditions, Structural Reforms and Convergence in Less-developed Regions", which benefitted from financial support of the European Commission – Directorate-General for Regional and Urban Policy and from comments and input by Lewis Dijkstra (Head of Economic Analysis Sector).

The project was co-ordinated by Karen Maguire and Alexander Lembcke. The report was co-ordinated by Alexander Lembcke and prepared under the supervision of Karen Maguire and Rüdiger Ahrend with guidance from Joaquim Oliveira Martins. It was drafted by Alexander Lembcke (Chapters 1, 2 and 4), Abel Schumann (Chapter 3), and Lorena Figueiredo (Chapter 5). Eric Gonnard provided statistical support. Contributions and data from Wen Chen (University of Groningen), Sabine D'Costa (University of Westminster), Christian Ketels (BCG Henderson Institute Stockholm), Bart Los (University of Groningen), Sergiy Protsiv (Stanford University) and Clara Wolf supported this work and are gratefully acknowledged.

The OECD Secretariat extends its thanks and appreciation to the countries and regions that have collaborated in the five case studies that supported the work and are published separately. Specifically, the Secretariat thanks the delegates of Greece, Poland, Portugal, Romania and Spain to the OECD Regional Development Policy Committee and the regions of Andalusia (Spain), Central Macedonia (Greece), Central and North Portugal, South East Romania and Warmian Masuria (Poland).

The Secretariat also thanks the delegates to the OECD Regional Development Policy Committee and its Working Parties, as well as the participants in workshops at OECD, the European Commission (DG for Regional and Urban Policy and Joint Research Centre), the European Commission, and at the 2017 conferences of the European Regional Science Association and the Regional Studies Association for valuable comments on earlier versions of (parts of) the report.

Andrew Brenner provided editorial assistance, Julie Harris prepared the manuscript for publication and Pauline Arbel, Cicely Dupont-Nivore and Pilar Philip supported the production process.

Table of contents

Tables

Figures

Boxes

Abbreviations and acronyms

ANRT	National Association for Technological Research (France)
BIF	Baltic Institute of Finland
EGF	European Globalisation Adjustment Fund
EPL	Employment Protection Legislation
EU	European Union
GDP	Gross domestic product
GVA	Gross value added
GVCs	Global value chains
ICT	Information and communication technologies
KORUS	U.S.-Korea Trade Agreement
MAR-externalities	Marshall-Arrow-Romer-externalities
MIP	European Macroeconomic Imbalance Procedure
NUTS 2/3	EU Nomenclature of territorial units for statistics (level 2/3)
OSHA Act	Outer Space and High-Altitude Activities Act (New Zealand)
POWER	Partnerships for Opportunity and Workforce and Economic Revitalization (United States)
R&D	Research and development
RTOs	Research and technology organisations
SACI	Society-Academia Collaboration for Innovation (Japan)
SMEs	Small and medium-sized enterprises
TAA	Trade Adjustment Assistance (United States)
TAAF	Trade Adjustment Assistance for Firms (United States)
TL2/TL3	OECD Territorial Level 2/3
TREDEA	Tampere Region Economic Development Agency (Finland)
WTO	World Trade Organisation

Executive summary

When considered at the scale of the OECD area, economic inequality across regions declined since the turn of the millennium. Between 2000 and 2015, inequality in regional GDP declined by 15% across the OECD and by 25% across Europe, driven by the catching up of regions in countries with comparatively lower income. However, in many OECD countries the economic disparities between the regions *within* the same country grew substantially over the same time period.

Some of the regions that fell further behind with respect to the peers in their country exhibited persistently low economic growth rates, others followed unsustainable growth models that were exposed by the global financial crisis and its aftermath. Many regions that appeared to be in the process of catching up, but relied on an expansion of non-tradable sectors, such as retail services or construction, experienced rapid declines that wiped out the gains from previously high growth rates. As of 2015, per capita GDP levels in almost two-fifths of OECD regions (135 out of 350) were still below their pre-crisis peak.

Productivity growth is a key factor in ensuring economic prosperity and setting regions on a path towards more inclusive societies. In part, the link arises as sustainable wage growth needs to be supported by productivity growth. Flexible exchange rates can compensate for a growing gap between wages and productivity, but in a single-currency area or across the regions in a country a growing gap between wages and productivity in some regions results instead in rising unit labour costs and accruing imbalances in regional competitiveness. Estimates for Europe suggest that a 1 percentage point increase in the growth rate of regional unit labour costs is, on average, associated with a 0.3 percentage point decrease in per capita gross value added growth and 0.4 percentage point decrease in per capita exports in the region.

Growing gaps within countries in terms of productivity may come at the cost of higher income inequalities. On average, productivity growth is slightly higher in countries where productivity frontier regions outperformed others. However, inter-regional inequality in these countries – as measured by the Gini coefficient of per capita GDP – increased by more than 15% over the 2000-14 period, while it remained constant in those where lagging regions were catching up. The most productive regions are also highly persistent over time and in most countries the productivity leader is typically the capital region.

Two characteristics stand out among regions that successfully narrowed productivity gaps. The first is the proximity to well-functioning cities and the links between the cities with their surrounding rural areas. The second, and main focus of this report, is a strong reliance of the regional economy on tradable sectors. Tradable sectors are those that produce goods and services that could potentially be traded and are therefore exposed to international competition, irrespective of whether trade actually takes place or not. Manufacturing is still at the core of tradable sectors, but tradable services are gaining ground and already accounted for 15% of total regional output in 2013. In many well-performing regions, tradable services were the fastest growing sector, on average

2.5% per year in terms of gross value added between 2000 and 2013. Yet, not all regions take advantage of this potential. In European regions with low levels of income or low levels of growth, tradable services expanded by only 1% per year.

There is a misconception that a greater share of economic activity in tradable sectors increases economic vulnerability. No doubt, in some regions external trade competition has caused extensive economic restructuring, especially where regions were highly specialised in specific sectors. But, as a whole, the tradable sector is not more susceptible to economic shocks than the non-tradable sector. It is over-reliance on the non-tradable sector that creates risks for a region's long-term economic performance. The 10% of regions with the largest shifts towards the non-tradable sector before the crisis also experienced the strongest employment losses after the crisis, with an average decline in employment of 2.9% annually.

Any strategy that helps regions benefit from an increasingly globalised world and supports the development of their tradable sectors needs to be multi-faceted. Regions are different and regional policy approaches need to be tailored to their different conditions and specific circumstances. To this end, policies should follow three core principles:

- They should be well co-ordinated across the territory and policy fields.
- They should identify and build on local strengths.
- They should help regions overcome barriers to knowledge and innovation diffusion.

However, a "silo approach" to regional policy is still a common occurrence. For example, trade adjustment programmes that aim to provide laid-off workers with new skills are often disconnected from those that support firms and entrepreneurs. Skill development and utilisation policies need to be linked with wider regional economic development strategies and support for labour mobility where necessary. Likewise, policy should be co-ordinated across the territory and account for the actual extent of the economic and social ties within and across regions. Particularly leveraging the potential of urban areas requires that their links with rural areas and other cities are taken into account.

A second common pitfall to regional economic development is to attract firms through tax exemptions, financial incentives, flexible regulations or similar measures risking a "race to the bottom" for what is often only a moderate impetus to wider regional development. Building on local strengths can take the form of "niche" sectors that exploit locational advantages, strategic diversification in related sectors through a range of policies, including clusters and harnesses the skills and knowledge of the local workforce.

As productivity growth across the OECD stalls, efforts to support the diffusion of knowledge from the most innovative firms and regions to other firms and regions can unlock growth potential. Public authorities can contribute to the diffusion process. Innovation agencies and business support centres can help small businesses implement effective production and management practices; these can be combined with other assistance, such as advice on how to enter foreign markets. Finally, effective university-industry collaboration is another tool to create and spread innovation.

Chapter 1. The elusive quest for regional convergence?

This chapter outlines trends in regional productivity growth and job creation (and destruction) over the past 15 years. Both convergence and divergence are evident across OECD countries and this chapter highlights the trade-offs that countries and regions face in terms of inequality, growth and job creation. A particular focus in this chapter is on economic trends before and since the global 2007-08 crisis and why some regions might have been more strongly affected than others.

Chapter synopsis

Economic integration and global trade have created great opportunities to improve lives for many people and in many regions. Average income levels in the OECD have continuously risen over the last 20 years and only the global crisis that began in 2007-08 put the economic expansion to a (brief) halt. Disparities in terms of per capita GDP and in labour productivity have declined, driven by a catching up of countries and regions with the lowest income levels.

But not all people and all regions have benefited. In many countries the gap between the region(s) with the highest labour productivity and other regions has widened between 2000 and 2014. This growing divide is not a result of the global 2007-08 crisis, though the crisis revealed unsustainable growth models that some regions followed. Even 7-8 years after the onset of the crisis its marks are still evident across OECD regions. By 2015, real per capita GDP in 135 out of 350 large (TL2) OECD regions remained below 2007-08 levels. Most of the regions that are still struggling with the aftermath of the crisis are located in Europe, with rapid recovery concentrated in Germany and in Europe's east, as well as in the northern regions of Scandinavia.

Inequalities often persist over long periods of time. In 14 out of 19 European countries with at least 5 NUTS 2 regions, the most productive region was the same in all years between 1995 and 2014. Regions with large cities and those rich in natural resources are the most productive in the OECD. But the potential to "catch up" is present in all types of region and many have found ways to narrow the gap to their country's frontier. Across OECD countries regional productivity growth follows mainly two models: countries where regions' catching up drives overall productivity growth and countries where the most productive region dominates and the economic strength becomes increasingly concentrated.

Combining dynamic growth of the most productive "frontier" regions with catching up of those that are lagging behind proves a challenge. The regional frontier is, on average, less dynamic in countries where "catching up" was predominant than in countries where the most productive region(s) were pulling away. The lack of catching up comes at a cost. Per capita GDP inequality, measured by the Gini coefficient remained stable across regions in countries where regions managed to "catch up" to their country's frontier in terms of labour productivity. In contrast inequality increased in countries where the frontier regions kept pulling away from other regions.

Raising productivity is not only essential to curtail growing economic disparities it is also essential to sustain individual well-being. Sustainable wage growth, and thereby growth in living standards, requires that productivity keeps pace with wage increases. As ageing becomes increasingly pervasive, regions need to find ways to compensate for a declining workforce to ensure prosperity does not decline. But even in regions with growing productivity, inclusive gains from growth are by no means automatic and a key policy challenge remains to ensure a fair distribution of the benefits created by economic growth. While in boom periods between 1980 and 2014 more than 40% of OECD regions combined productivity and employment growth, about the same percentage of regions experienced productivity growth at the expense of employment growth in the recessions that followed.

The quest for regional convergence

Countries undertake tremendous effort and often spend considerable resources in trying to balance aggregate economic development and supporting growth in all regions. But divides are often entrenched. It seems that the "quest for convergence", i.e. the catching up of lesser performing regions to a national or global frontier, seems ever elusive.[1] The challenge is not unique to a single country. The United States face a growing "great divide" that opens between innovative, educated and growing metro areas on the one hand and those struggling to keep up on the other.[2] In Europe, countries have faced a reversal of convergence in the wake of the 2007-08 global crisis, with regions that were able, before the crisis, to narrow their gap to the European average before falling back again. Across the OECD, trends are pointing to a growing divide between well-performing and lagging regions.

Notwithstanding the existence of economic cycles, economic theory would suggest that in the long term regions that are lagging behind their peers have the capacity to "catch up" to those leading regions.[3] Lagging regions' lower levels of economic output are often associated with structural deficits, such as insufficient basic infrastructure, transport connectivity or low skill levels in the workforce. But the gap to leading regions also constitutes a possible advantage, deemed "the advantage of backwardness" in many economic textbooks. In less-developed regions, capital investment, skill development and the adoption of technologies from more advanced regions all offer significant growth and catching-up potential.

But in reality there is often little evidence for an advantage of backwardness in lagging regions. For example, Île-de-France, the region containing the metropolitan area of Paris, experienced faster economic growth than all other French mainland regions. This success widened an already substantial gap between the region and the rest of the country. Île-de-France produced 53% more GDP per inhabitant than the second richest region in 2000 and this gap has grown to 66% over the last 15 years. In part, gaps are due to differences in local economic assets and economic forces.[4] A region located in a central position surrounded by large markets or close to a large city will find it easier to attract business and residents. A remote rural region that is rich in (coveted) natural resources will be better off than a region without such resources. Often these assets, which contribute to economic development, are tied to a place and hard to create or change through policy.

However, even factors than can be affected by policy are often hard to disassociate from the place where they are located. A top-tier university operates in a specific city (or even neighbourhood), a successful technology cluster develops in a certain place, and the location of major transport infrastructure, e.g. ports or airports, also changes rarely. Some of these place-specific factors contribute to virtuous cycles. The investment of a high-tech company in a research campus might incentivise other firms to locate complementary research facilities in the area, creating demand for high-skilled jobs, which, in turn, results in demand for personal services, high quality housing and local amenities and an incentive for firms and local governments to invest. Whether major investments can create and sustain development without initial impetus or complementary policies is less clear.[5] Even with virtuous cycles, progress is often slow and dependent on past success.

As local growth potential depends on local assets and can follow virtuous cycles, inequalities are not expected to completely disappear. However, when disparities become entrenched or worsen it is sometimes symptomatic of regions failing to leverage their "advantage of backwardness". The OECD Regional Outlook 2016 (OECD, 2016[1]) highlights the growing disparity in labour productivity within countries as a key policy challenge, as the most productive regions are pulling further away from other regions. This is worrying as growth in productivity is essential for economic growth, improving living standards and increasing well-being.[6]

Gaps between OECD countries are narrowing, but they persist across regions

Closing interregional gaps is a key policy objective in many countries. Often policies focus on economic convergence, i.e. the reduction in the gap between more prosperous regions and those lagging behind in terms of per capita income (typically measured by gross domestic product, GDP). Examples include the European Union (EU)'s Regional "Cohesion Policy", Korea's aim for "balanced economic development" or Turkey's efforts to reduce regional and rural-urban disparities.[7] Support is typically provided to regions that are lagging behind the more prosperous parts of a country (or the EU), helping them to develop a better socio-economic foundation, improve competitiveness or attract investment.

Economic convergence is often not the sole focus of regional policy. Increasingly, wider concepts, such as well-being, are at the fore of convergence considerations. For example, the goals of the Europe 2020 Strategy cover a wide range of social, innovation and environmental goals that are supported through European Cohesion Policy.[8] Similarly, in the Region of Southern Denmark, a comprehensive set of well-being indicators has been developed that aim to enhance the "good life" of people in the region. This initiative also supports its multi-year Regional Growth and Development Strategy and guides policy decisions.[9]

Overall economic inequality declined, but within-country inequality did not follow

Inequality across European regions in terms of per capita GDP has declined since the mid-1990s.[10] Inequality, measured by the Theil Index, followed a steady downward trend from 1995 until the 2007-08 crisis (Box 1.1). Since the crisis, inequality remained fairly constant until 2015, the last year with available data. The positive trend towards greater cohesion masks significant diversity among regional growth paths within countries.

Disparities within countries have remained large in many countries and have even grown in some. The overall decline in inequality in terms of per capita GDP since 1995, as measured by the Theil Index, was purely driven by declining inequality across countries. Inequality within countries, i.e. inequality between their regions, even increased over the 1995-2015 period (Box 1.1). The pattern is not only evident for Europe, but across the OECD (OECD, 2016[1]). For OECD regions, however, the decline in overall inequality was slower than in Europe and the contribution of inequality across countries to total inequality remains larger than the contribution from interregional inequality within countries.[11]

Box 1.1. Regional disparities are declining across countries but not within them

Since 1995, inequality between European regions, as measured by the Theil index, has declined by about one third (Figure 1.1). In 1995, nearly 75% of total inequality in Europe in terms of per capita GDP came from differing levels of income among EU countries. Regional disparities within countries contributed only about 25%. By 2007, faster growth in countries with lower per capita income had reduced the gap with other European countries. This led to a decline in inequality across countries. In fact, inequality between countries was cut in half. Over the same period, inequality within countries rose by about 20%. These opposing trends mean that since the 2007-08 crisis about 50% of inequality in Europe has been due to disparities across regions within the individual countries.

Labour productivity (measured as GDP per worker) mimics the change in per capita GDP inequality (Figure 1.1). A decline in disparities between countries is met with persistent inequality within countries, albeit the contribution of cross-country differences to inequality remains larger than within-country productivity differences. Unlike inequality in terms of per capita GDP, productivity continued its convergence trend even through the 2007-08 crisis and the subsequent recession.

Figure 1.1. In Europe, inequality across regions is now as high as inequality across countries

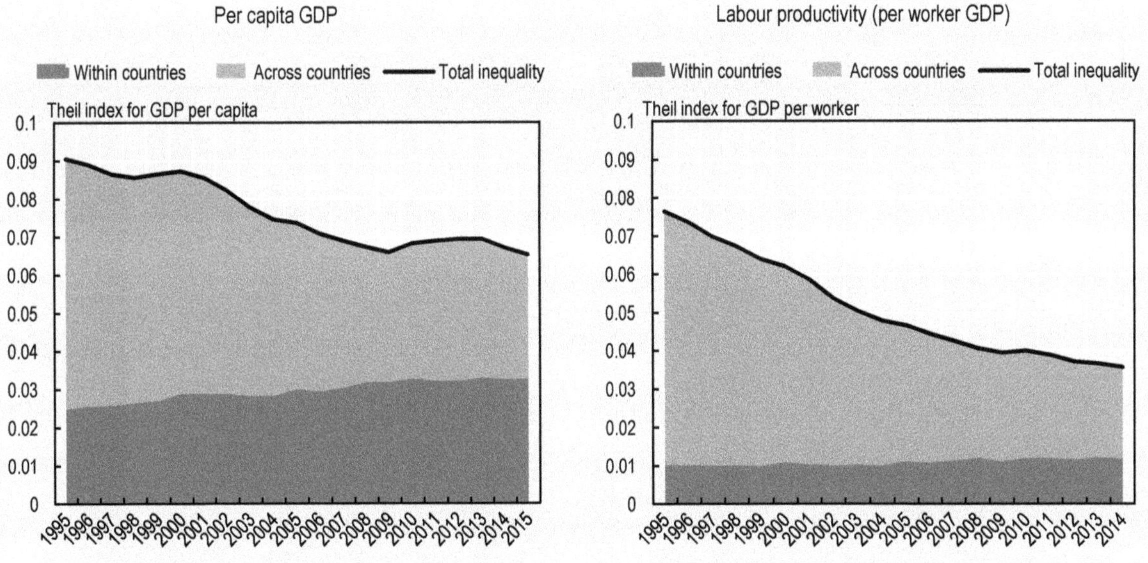

Note: Data refers to regional GDP per capita expressed in constant 2010 USD PPP. Data for the period 1995-99 represent estimates based on SNA93. Data for 2000-2015 and for large (TL2) regions in 21 countries: Austria, Belgium, Bulgaria, Czech Republic, Germany, Denmark, Spain, Finland, France, United Kingdom, Greece, Hungary, Ireland, Italy, Netherlands, Poland, Portugal, Romania, Slovak Republic, Slovenia and Sweden. Countries with only one TL2 region are excluded: Estonia, Malta, Lithuania, Luxembourg and Latvia. Due to a break in series for Irish GDP in 2015, 2014 data have been used for 2015.

Source: Calculations based on OECD Regional Statistics [Database].

StatLink http://dx.doi.org/10.1787/888933707513

"Low-income" regions leverage their growth potential

The decline in overall inequality is driven by a catching up of countries and regions with the lowest income levels. For 363 large (TL2) OECD regions and comparable regions in Bulgaria and Romania, growth over the 2000-15 period was negatively associated with initial income. Over the 2000-15 period, regions with the lowest income levels at the beginning of the period were able to capitalise on their "advantage of backwardness" (Figure 1.2).[12] Per capita GDP in regions in Bulgaria, Hungary, Poland, the Slovak Republic or Romania grew in excess of 3% per year, in many cases even reaching annual average growth rates of around 4%. To put this into perspective, at a growth rate of 4% the per capita output of a region doubles in less than 20 years. Within the OECD, Chilean and some Mexican regions were able to match similarly high growth rates over the same period.

Figure 1.2. Convergence is driven by the poorest "low-income" regions

Per capita GDP and per capita GDP growth, 2000-15

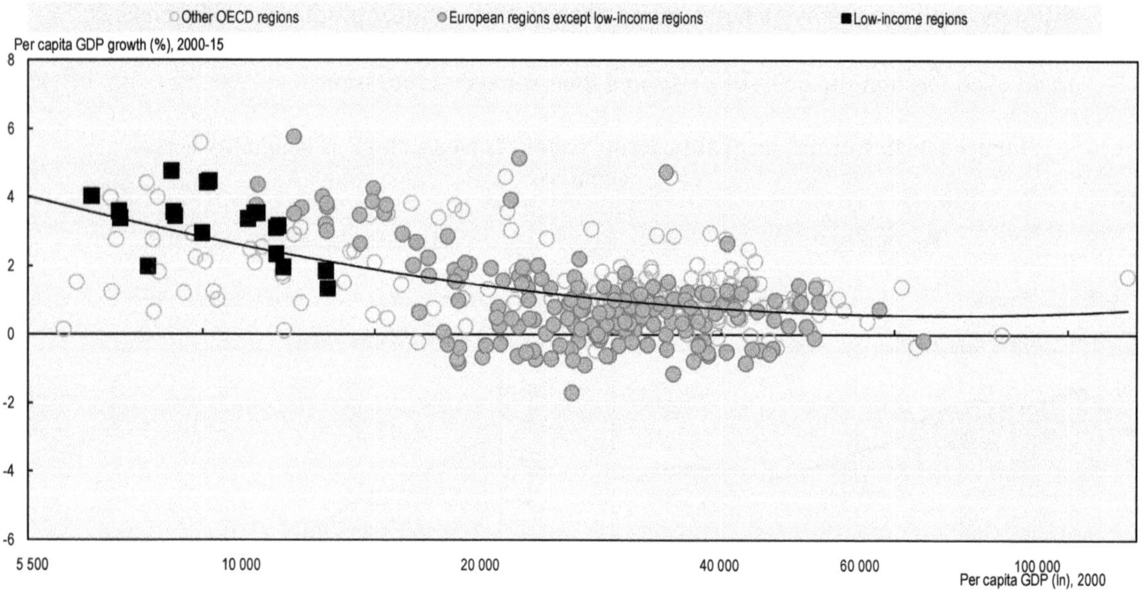

Note: Data refers to regional GDP per capita expressed in constant 2010 USD PPP. Data for 2000-15 and for 363 large (TL2) regions in 30 countries (AU, AT, BE, CA, CL, CZ, DK, FI, FR, DE, EL, HU, IE, IT, JP, KR, ME, NL, NZ, NO, PL, PT, SK, SI, ES, SE, UK, US, BG, RO). Low-income regions are EU regions with less than 50% of EU-average per capita GDP in 2000 (full list in Annex Table 1.A.1).
Source: Calculations based on OECD Regional Statistics [Database].

StatLink http://dx.doi.org/10.1787/888933707532

Some European regions seem to fall into a "middle income trap"

Convergence is rarely a smooth process. It often includes prolonged periods of low growth. In development economics, the idea of a "middle income trap" has been proposed as growth slowdowns seem to follow the successful transition of many low- to middle-income countries.[13] In Europe and the OECD, convergence was driven by rapid growth before the 2007-08 crisis. During the pre-crisis period, growth was not limited to the regions with the lowest per capita GDP levels, but also sustained by many regions with intermediate income levels, (e.g. by Greek or Spanish regions). But many of the

OECD's "middle" income regions, with per capita GDP above USD 20 000 in 2010 prices and purchasing power parities, have stagnated or even declined since the 2007-08 crisis (Figure 1.3).

The regional middle income trap is partly driven by slow growth in some countries that fall into the middle income range within the OECD. For Europe, these are mainly "low-growth" regions in the south of Europe.[14] Another reason is the lack of catching up within countries. In Italy and Spain, for example, the negative correlation between growth and initial level of per capita GDP – indicating the catching up of less affluent regions to the more prosperous ones – turns positive for the 2008-15 period. This means that less-developed regions in these countries were not only unable to narrow the gap, but they even lost ground against more affluent parts of the country.

Figure 1.3. A middle income trap ensnared "low-growth" regions after the 2007-08 crisis

Per capita GDP and per capita GDP growth, 2008-15

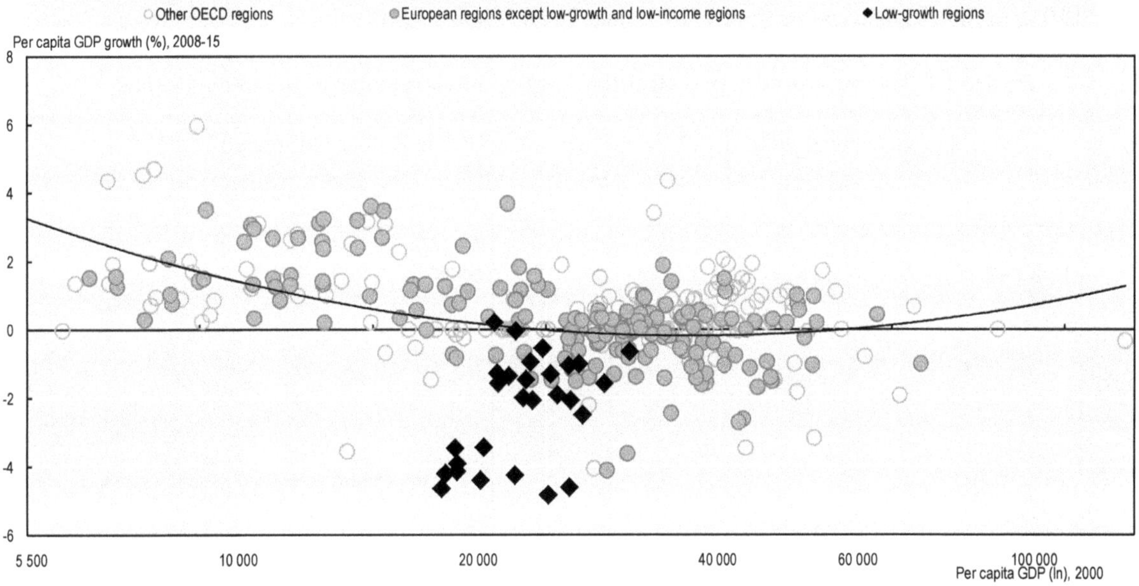

Note: Notes: Data refers to regional GDP per capita expressed in constant 2010 USD PPP. Data for 2008-15 and for 363 large (TL2) regions in 30 countries (AU, AT, BE, CA, CL, CZ, DK, FI, FR, DE, EL, HU, IE, IT, JP, KR, ME, NL, NZ, NO, PL, PT, SK, SI, ES, SE, UK, US, BG, RO). Low-growth regions are EU regions with less than 90% of the EU-average per capita GDP in 2000 (less-developed and transition regions) that grew less than the EU-average over the 2000-13 period (full list in Annex Table 1.A.1).
Source: Calculations based on OECD Regional Statistics [Database].

StatLink http://dx.doi.org/10.1787/888933707551

Not all gaps will close, but persistent and growing differences raise concerns

Differences in prosperity of regions and places within a country have always been a reality. Prague was the most productive region in the Czech Republic in the 1990s and remains the most productive region in 2014, as does Stockholm in Sweden. In 14 out of 19 European countries with at least 5 NUTS 2 regions, the most productive region was the same in all years between 1995 and 2014.[15] These differences are unlikely to completely disappear. As already mentioned, regions have different endowments in factors that support growth, as well as different types of economic activity. For example, knowledge-intensive services are often concentrated in large cities.

The underlying factors and regional assets that matter most in supporting growth can change over time. Proximity of suppliers and producers was a major factor in firm location choices until transport costs declined. Resources that were highly valued 30 years ago are not the same as those most sought after today. In addition, decisions made by individuals and policy makers sometimes affect growth drivers. Where to move, where to start a new business or where to invest are conscious decisions that are greatly affected by the policy environment in a region.

Gaps are therefore not set in stone, change can occur and new frontier regions can emerge. Even without complete "catching up", gaps between the most productive region and the rest of the country can narrow. Whereas Stockholm produced about 40% more output per worker in the 1990s than other parts of the country, progress in other regions has cut the lead to about 30%. The Czech Republic experienced the opposite trend with the productivity gap between Prague and the rest of the country growing from about 110% in the 1990s to more than 150% since 2010 (Figure 1.4).

Figure 1.4. The most productive "frontier" region often remains at the top over time

Labour productivity in TL2 regions (per worker GDP in EUR at 2005 prices)

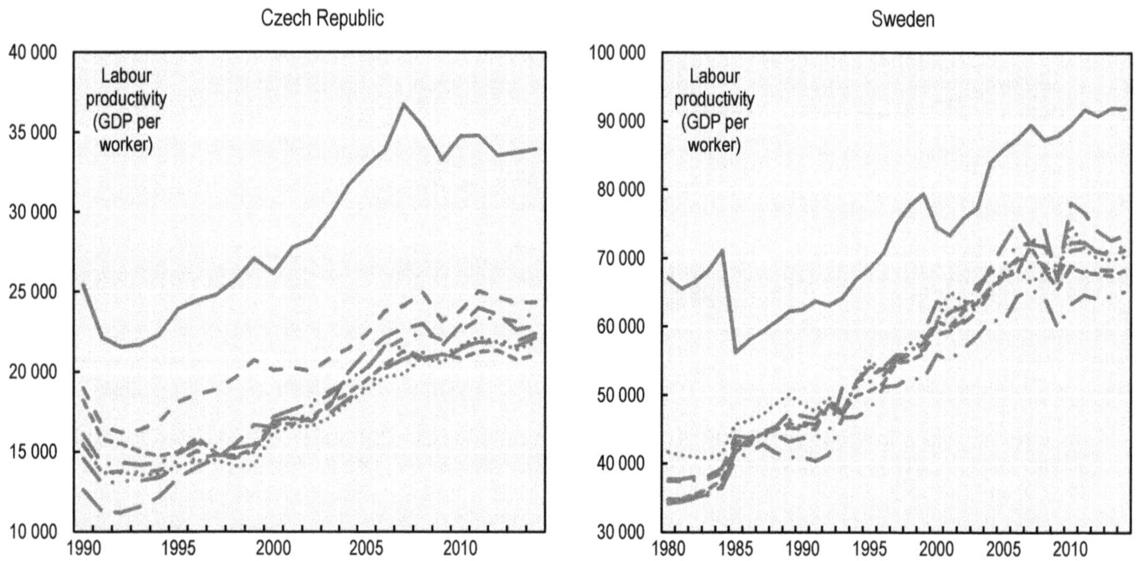

Source: Calculations based on Cambridge Econometrics (2017) European Regional Database [Database].

StatLink http://dx.doi.org/10.1787/888933707570

The challenge when economic inequalities become entrenched is that they become self-perpetuating. Income levels, employment and wealth are lower in the north of the United Kingdom than in the south (McCann, 2016[2]). In the United States, the returns to education, divorce rates, crime rates and even life expectancy are growing further apart between dynamic and growing metro areas and those that are losing ground.[16] A strategy that relies on budgetary transfers from better-performing regions to others will not address the root cause of the problem. Without narrowing the economic gaps, especially productivity gaps, it is unlikely that living standards can be sustainably raised.

Catching up is possible, but is often a long-term effort

Bavaria in Germany is one of the regions that successfully narrowed the gap to Germany's most productive "frontier" regions over the 2000-14 period. Productivity in the region grew faster than in Hamburg and Hesse.[17] The strong position of Bavaria today is in stark contrast to the situation in the middle of the 20th century. Between 1950 and the mid-1980s, the Federal State was a net recipient of fiscal transfers from other parts of Western Germany that compensate for low tax revenues. By the mid-1990s, Bavaria's was providing a net contribution to the system of horizontal transfers (BMF, 2012[3]). Between 2000 and 2014 labour productivity in Bavaria grew at about three times the rate in Germany's frontier, but even if current trends continue it will take until 2030 for Bavaria to completely close the gap.[18]

These slow changes are a common feature. In the United States, the greater Los Angeles area and San Francisco Bay Area followed markedly different trends. In terms of median household income the Bay Area (San Jose, San Francisco and Oakland) was the most prosperous in the United States in the 1970s and has remained among the top-income regions. Conversely the southern Californian greater metro area around Los Angeles-Long Beach-Riverside, which started at the same level as the Bay Area in 1970, has experienced a continuous decline compared to its peer areas, and over time this gap has begun to widen at an increasingly fast pace. While the region was ranked 4th among US Metropolitan Statistical Areas in 1970, its position had dropped to 25th by 2009.[19]

Local assets differ and contribute to regional economic gaps

Productivity or income gaps reflect, in part, differences in local fundamental assets. Resource-rich or fertile soil, an accessible and protected bay, a central location within a country and even climatic conditions are all local advantages that can be turned into growth opportunities. They are geophysical advantages and are often slow to change and difficult to alter, at least positively. In the subfield of economic geography, these advantages are called "first nature" assets.[20]

Whether "first nature" assets constitute an advantage can also change over time. The importance of an accessible port may have waned over the centuries as land-based transport became cheaper and maritime freight transport required increasingly larger ports. Conversely, the demand for certain metals or minerals has risen as new technologies and production methods require different materials than were used in the past.[21] The value of "first nature" advantages is therefore something that has changed fundamentally over the years, changing the value of some assets or the costs associated with them. Innovation can play an important role in this context. In one example, hydraulic fracturing ("fracking") paved the way for the commercial exploitation of oil and gas reserves in areas where costs were previously too high.

Using natural resources can, however, come at significant costs and for different reasons. The depletion of natural resources results in a more finite opportunity to use them as an economic growth asset. The environmental and health impacts of fracking are still hotly debated; indeed, exploitation of natural resources sometimes comes with other costs. Even economically abundant natural resources can stifle growth. When resource extraction arises as a natural advantage for the area, development of other sectors is often limited. Wages and demand are driven by the productive resource-intensive industry, making it difficult for firms in other sectors to develop and to diversify the economy. The local economy remains, therefore, highly dependent on the extractive sector, the global demand and supply of its main product and the (finite) availability of reserves in the region.

While some local assets are determined by nature, others depend on human actions

There are also regional disparities driven by "second nature" advantages, which are created through human intervention. People's choices of where to live and work, firm location decisions, or public policies typically contribute to these "second-nature" advantages. Not only policies that are set at the local level, but also country-wide "structural" policies (c.f. Chapter 4). The location of capital cities, selection of sites for academic institutions and the placement of large plants are choices favouring certain places over others. These choices are necessary. Separating an institution or a firm across space is usually costly at best and often unviable. Importantly, the cost associated with distributing activities is not only a direct cost associated with the split, e.g. through increased transport, communications and shipment costs between locations. A split can also result in the loss of benefits that come from formal and informal interactions that are facilitated by being located close to colleagues.

The benefit from concentrating activities derives, in part, from "positive economies of scale". As firms become larger they can sustain more specialised functions, e.g. a marketing department or a research and development team for new products or processes. Bulk purchases of raw materials and other inputs reduce the average price per unit. Firms can also share some administrative functions and utilisation of capital investment across a larger workforce, e.g. a server for the company network or human resource activities.

Usually the gains from positive economies of scale are limited, e.g. gains from specialisation are balanced by higher co-ordination costs. Similarly, the benefits of expanding production and serving a larger market may be outweighed by the increase in transportation costs.[22] The latter is evident, for example, among building material manufacturers. Transport costs constitute a major part of the total cost of their products, e.g. for concrete. The result is that most building materials are rarely shipped over long distances and the largest companies in the sector have thousands of production sites.[23]

Another benefit of concentrating activity in a specific place is external to the firm. As economic activity becomes embedded in an area, the interaction and links across firms and workers create mutual benefits. Co-location of suppliers and customers reduces transport costs and facilitates communication. A larger pool of workers in an area makes it easier for firms to find employees with the right skill set and for workers to find a job that suits them. More formal or incidental interaction in places that are denser and concentrated in terms of economic activity makes it easier for knowledge to be shared and spread. These "agglomeration benefits" create a virtuous circle, as more workers are attracted to the opportunities created by the firms in an area. Over time, it becomes more attractive for firms to locate there and vice versa (c.f. Chapter 2).

Regions with large metropolitan areas or resource-intensive economies are among the most productive in the OECD

Both first and second nature advantages can support high levels of labour productivity. In OECD countries, the most productive regions are mostly those with either a thriving extractive sector, e.g. Alberta in Canada or Antofagasta in Chile or a large (often capital) city.[24] For example, Greater London in the United Kingdom, Île-de-France that contains the Paris metropolitan area, or Istanbul in Turkey lead the productivity rankings in their countries, as do Stockholm in Sweden and Prague in the Czech Republic. A caveat in these comparisons is that city regions are often "underbound", covering only part of the full economic area surrounding the city (Box 1.2). Even in comparisons based on a functional definition however, workers are more productive in larger urban areas.[25]

Box 1.2. Regional boundaries: Administrative or functional realities?

Administrative boundaries typically do not depict economic realities

A difficulty in comparing productivity at the regional level is that the administrative or statistical boundaries of a region do not necessarily coincide with the functional boundaries of the local economic area. This is particularly the case for regions that cover cities that are at the core of a metropolitan area. The region of Greater London, for example, covers only a small part of the London metropolitan area according to the EU-OECD definition. Conversely, the Île-de-France region is actually a good approximation of the metropolitan area of Paris. Economic activities located in the densely-populated core are typically also the most productive. Therefore, "underbounded" city regions tend to have higher productivity and per capita output levels than those that cover both the urban core and the whole commuting zone.

Functional boundaries to capture economic links

To overcome the limitations of non-comparable administrative boundaries, the EU-OECD definition for functional urban areas uses population in densely-populated and contiguous 1km² grid cells to determine the spatial delineation of urban centres with at least 50 000 inhabitants. These urban centres are then matched to small local administrative or statistical areas, such as municipalities or census tracts, which then allows urban centres and low-density areas to be connected via commuting flows to the urban centre. The resulting "functional urban areas" capture the daily reality of worker flows and include the dense urban centre as well as the linked less-densely populated commuting zone.

Source: OECD (2012) *Redefining "Urban": A New Way to Measure Metropolitan Areas*, OECD Publishing, Paris, http://dx.doi.org/10.1787/9789264174108-en.

While larger cities and resource-rich regions are the most productive regions, all types of regions have some growth potential and most can find ways to narrow the gap with their country's frontier. Considering productivity growth in 1 380 small regions in OECD countries and beyond shows more intermediate and predominantly rural regions among those that managed to narrow the gap vis-à-vis the most productive region(s) in their country, rather than predominantly urban ones.[26] The potential for catching up is present in all types of regions, but the levers to unlock and sustain growth are quite distinct as economic models and local fundamental conditions differ significantly between regions.

Figure 1.5. Frontier regions tend to be urban, but catching up can happen anywhere

Distribution of type of regions in the frontier and among regions catching up, diverging and keeping pace

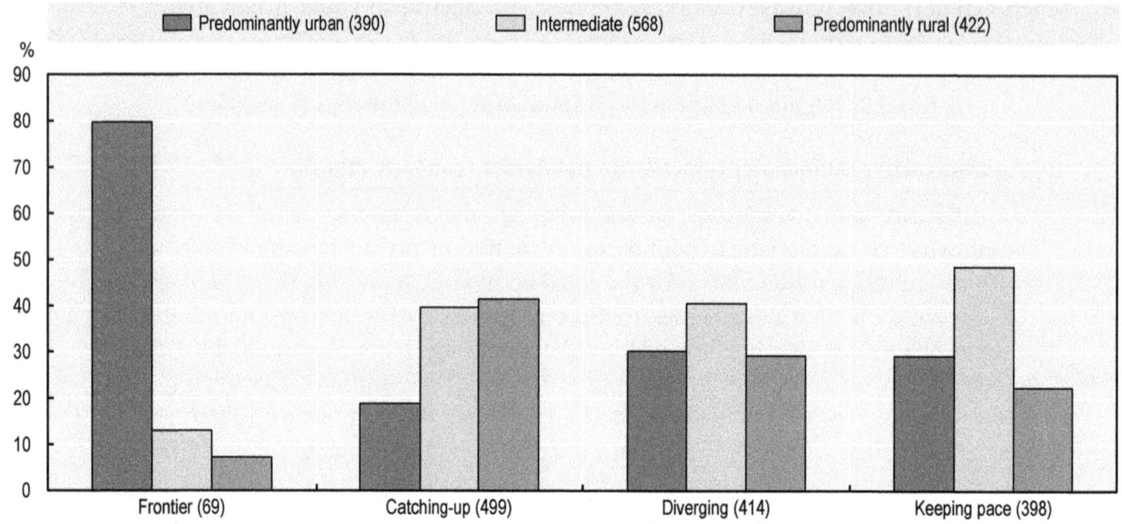

Note: Bars indicate the share of regions within each group that are predominantly urban, intermediate or predominantly rural. Numbers in parentheses indicate the number of small (TL3) regions in the group. Frontier regions are the most productive regions in a country in terms of GDP per worker (labour productivity) that account for at least 10% of total employment. Regions catching up to/diverging from the frontier are those in which labour productivity grew by 5% (over a normalised period of 15 years) more/less than in the frontier region(s) of the country over the relevant period, with regions "keeping pace" falling in that range. The period covered is 2000 to 2014. The 29 countries included are: Austria, Belgium, Czech Republic, Denmark, Estonia, Finland, France, Germany, Greece, Hungary, Ireland, Italy, Korea, Latvia, Luxembourg, Netherlands, New Zealand, Norway, Poland, Portugal, Slovak Republic, Slovenia, Spain, Sweden, Switzerland and United Kingdom from OECD countries plus Bulgaria, Lithuania and Romania.
Source: Calculations based on OECD Regional Statistics [Database].

StatLink http://dx.doi.org/10.1787/888933707589

Outmigration and ageing create challenges for all types of regions

Demographic shifts and people's decision to move can affect local fundamentals. An increase in the elderly – non-working age – population changes the local structure of supply and demand. Once retired workers start drawing on their pensions, they reduce their investments in capital and increase their consumption.[27] This affects wages and the cost of capital, but it also shifts the structure of demand. Local services such as health care or household services become more important as the local population ages. Even before retirement however, the decisions workers take as they age affect the regional economy. While older workers tend to be more experienced and therefore more productive, they also have less incentive to acquire new skills or knowledge. As the retirement age approaches, the period in which a worker can utilise their skills becomes incrementally shorter, which means the benefits of lifelong learning become increasingly limited.

Population ageing limits future growth in OECD countries and regions

Ageing is pervasive in all types of regions in OECD countries. Elderly dependency ratios, i.e. the ratio between the resident population that is 65 years or older and those of working age (15-64), grew by more than 25% between 2001 and 2015. In addition, there can be pressure for local economies resulting from low fertility rates and (out)migration trends. Such pressures tend to be stronger in predominantly rural regions (small regions, TL3). The difference in elderly dependency ratios between predominantly rural and predominantly urban regions exceeds 10 percentage points in nine countries, more than one-fourth of OECD countries (Figure 1.6).[28] While predominantly urban regions in Japan have to adapt to support nearly 4 elderly people for every 10 people of working age, it is more than 5 in predominantly rural regions of Japan. While elderly dependency rates in Japan exceed those in other OECD countries, many European countries and regions are coming close to Japanese dependency ratios. Predominantly rural regions in Spain, the United Kingdom, the Netherlands, Portugal, Sweden and Greece, the six countries following Japan, all have dependency rates of close to or even above 4 in 10.

Figure 1.6. Demographic pressures are unevenly distributed

Elderly dependency ratio by type of region and country, 2015

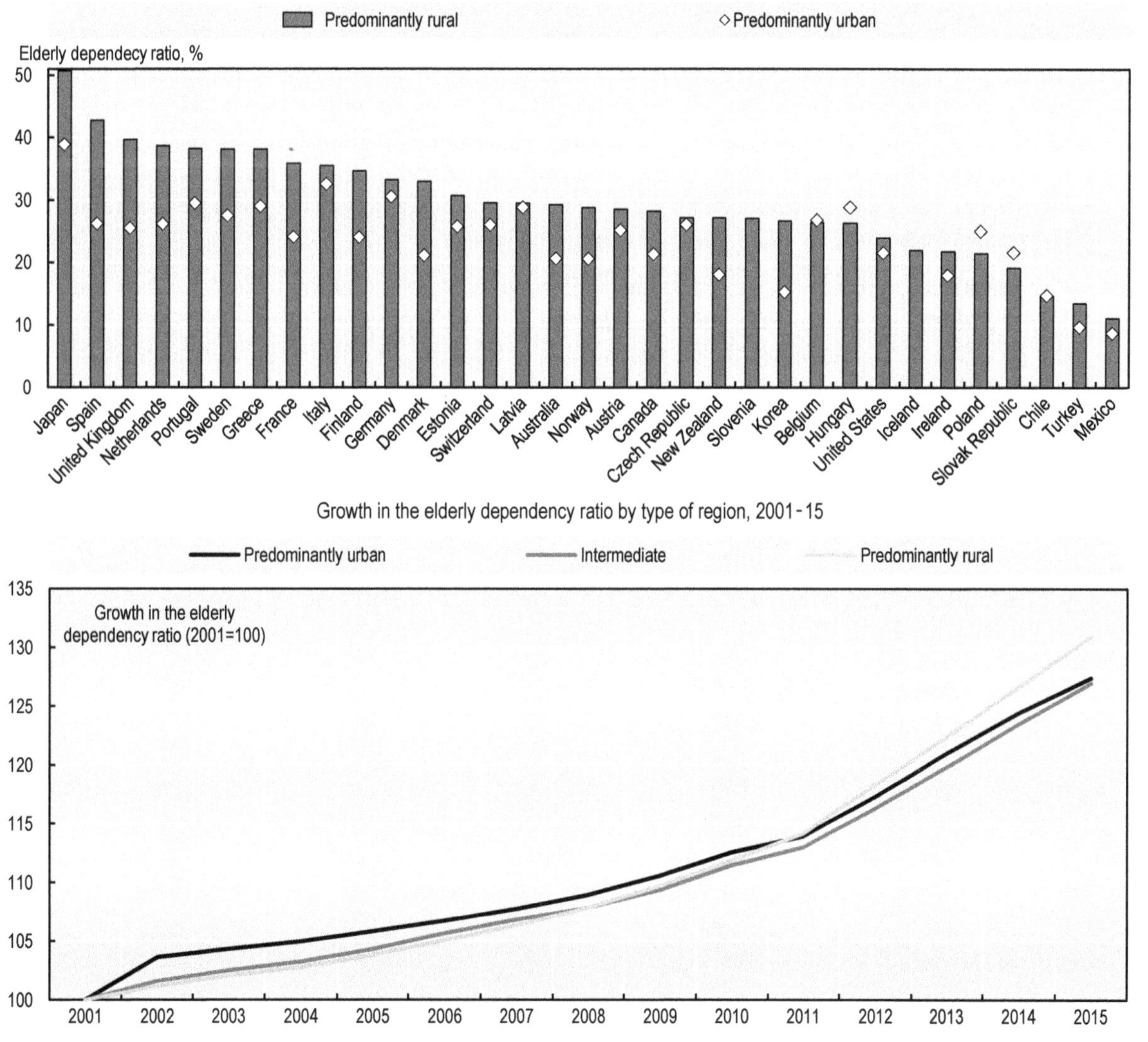

Note: Elderly dependency ratio defined as the ratio of 65+ year olds and the 15-64 year old population in a small (TL3) region. Data for countries (upper panel) refers to 2015 or closest year available with countries ranked the elderly dependency ratio in predominantly rural regions. In the lower panel, data on growth of the elderly dependency ratio depicts the the unweighted average of the elderly dependency by type of region.

Source: OECD Regional Statistics [Database]

StatLink http://dx.doi.org/10.1787/888933707608

Ageing can lead to a shrinking local labour market and present a potential fiscal challenge for regions that will need to rely more on transfers than on collecting local taxes. Moreover, providing services for the elderly and young can place pressure on an already thin labour market in low-density areas. A focus on local support services means that workers move into sectors that tend to have low levels of productivity, reducing average productivity in the region, especially in low-density areas where economies of scale cannot be achieved (e.g. the number of home visits a doctor or nurse can manage is less in a rural environment with longer distances between patients than in an urban setting). With sufficient transport links, policies can try to address the supply of certain services by enhancing links between urban and rural areas, at least for those rural areas that are located close to cities.

Outmigration amplifies the challenges for rural regions and smaller cities

At the regional level, the demographic shift is sometimes amplified by the outflow of young and more mobile workers towards different regions or even different countries. Moving is costly, both in terms of direct costs associated with moving one's home, but also in terms of non-pecuniary costs such as weakened local networks and family ties. Given the wide discrepancy in economic opportunities, mobility of workers is nonetheless often seen as too low. But outflows, in particular from lagging regions, are significant and even within regions many small towns and villages are losing population as people concentrate in and around (the main) cities.

Urbanisation is growing fastest outside of Europe.[29] Africa, Asia and the Americas are leading global trends towards greater urbanisation. In Europe, the urbanisation rate, i.e. the percentage of people in urban areas is fairly stable. But in Europe, as well as in other parts of the OECD, the importance of concentration of population in the largest cities – metropolitan areas with 500 000 or more inhabitants – is increasing (Figure 1.7). In Australia, Japan and Korea more than 70% of the total population lived in a metro area in 2014, an increase of 4 percentage points compared to 2000. In American and European OECD countries, the increase was more modest, about 2 percentage points in Canada, Chile, Mexico and the United States and slightly more than 1 percentage point in Europe.[30]

Figure 1.7. The move towards metropolitan areas

Percentage of total population in the OECD areas living in metropolitan areas with at least 500 000 inhabitants, 2000-14

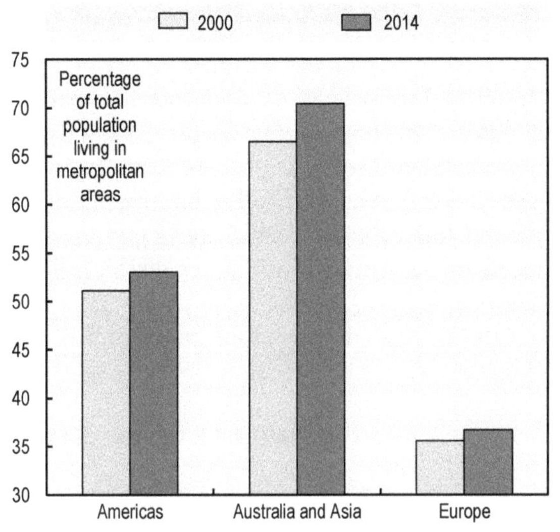

Note: Population in metropolitan areas in the EU-OECD definition with at least 500 000 inhabitants in 2000. Countries included are CAN, CHL, MEX, USA (Americas); AUS, JPN, KOR (Australia and Asia); AUT, BEL, CHE, CZE, DEU, DNK, EST, ESP, FIN, FRA, GBR, HUN, IRL, ITA, NLD, NOR, POL, PRT, SVN, SVK, SWE (Europe)
Source: OECD Metropolitan areas [Database].

StatLink http://dx.doi.org/10.1787/888933707627

The global 2007-08 crisis uncovered some unsustainable growth models

Nearly all regions grew in terms of per capita GDP during the first years of the new millennium. Until the 2007-08 crisis, only 4 out of 350 OECD regions (TL2) had experienced decline. Adding Romanian and Bulgarian regions, per capita GDP in half of the 364 regions grew by 16% or more between 2000 and 2007/08.[31] Between 2007/08 and 2015, the picture changed significantly. The median growth rate, i.e. the rate that 50% of the regions exceed and the other 50% do not reach, is just 4%. Economic prosperity in half of OECD regions seven or eight years after the initial shock was just barely above crisis levels (Figure 1.8Figure).

Many regions struggle to return to growth since the 2007-08 crisis, most of them in Europe

Before the crisis, 61% of the TL2 regions with above median growth rates were European regions, since the crisis these regions account for only 44%, well below the total percentage of European regions in the sample (59%). While regions in the Americas (Canada, Chile, Mexico and the United States) and Asia/Oceania (Australia, Korea, Japan and New Zealand) recorded slow growth as well, European regions were overrepresented.

This is particularly true when consistently low growth is considered. Nearly 80% of regions with below-median growth rate both before 2007 and after 2008 are European regions (lower left hand square of Figure 1.8).[32] These regions are predominantly regions in Europe's south. Regions in Italy, Portugal and parts of Spain, but also the Brussels

Region in Belgium and most French regions, except Île-de-France (Annex Figure 1.A.2). Outside of Europe they include regions like Colorado and Georgia in the United States or Chiapas and Quintana Roo in the south of Mexico.

Some "low-growth regions" have actually gone through a phase of rapid growth followed by rapid decline

The "middle income trap" in Europe has its root cause in persistently slow growth in some regions. But for others, the trap sprung as the 2007-08 crisis revealed that their growth models were not sustainable. Per capita GDP in these regions grew before the crisis, often by more than 2% per year. But following the initial shock, per capita output contracted rapidly. Over the full 2000-14 period, these regions appear to have stagnated, but what they experienced was a period of rapid expansion followed by an equally long period of contraction and stagnation (regions close to the solid black line in Figure 1.8). Andalusia in Spain and Central Macedonia in Greece exemplify the growth experience in these types of region (Figure 1.9).

Figure 1.8. Rapid growth before the 2007-08 crisis was not always sustainable

Per capita GDP growth before and since the 2007-08 crisis

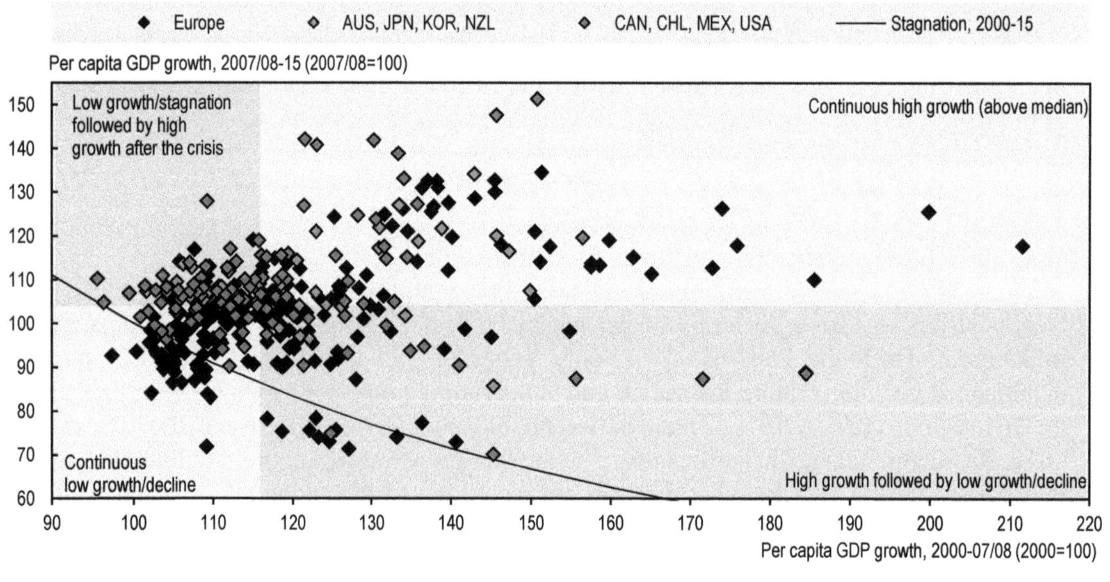

Note: Real per capita GDP growth in large (TL2) regions from 2000 (or closest year available) to 2007-08 (lower value) and from 2007-08 (higher value) to 2015 or closest year available. Shaded quadrants depict the above/below median value growth (median for 2000-07/08: 115.9; 2007/08-15: 104.1). The solid black line indicates the growth rates that led to stagnation between 2000 and 2015, i.e. the decline after the 2007-08 crisis offsets the growth from before the crisis. Europe includes European OECD regions, as well as Bulgarian and Romanian regions.

Source: Calculations based on OECD Regional Statistics [Database]

StatLink http://dx.doi.org/10.1787/888933707646

Figure 1.9. Seven year cycles of growth and decline in Andalusia (Spain) and Central Macedonia (Greece)

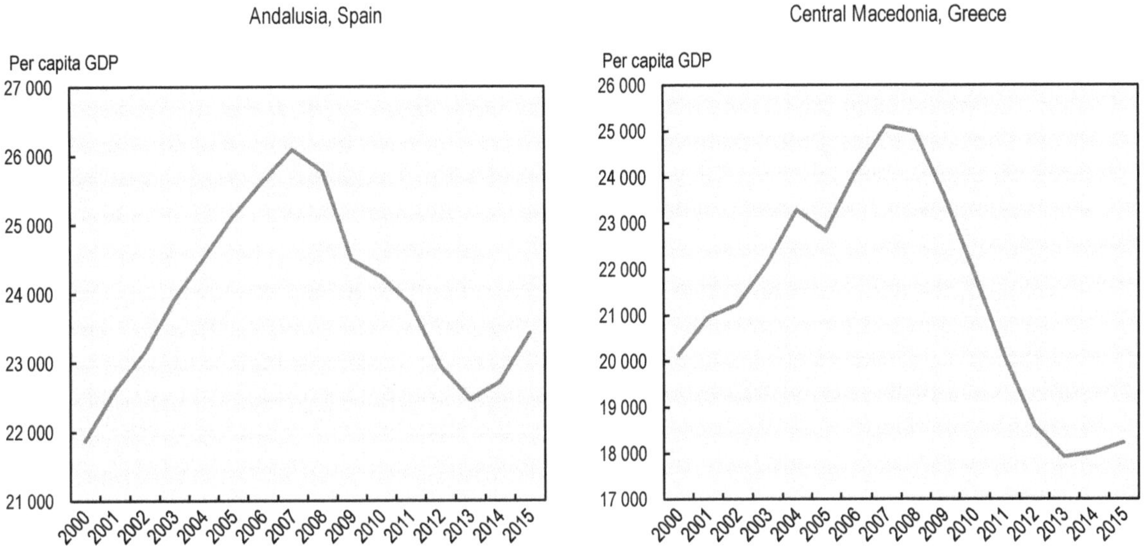

Note: Data refers to national and regional GDP per capita expressed in constant 2010 USD PPP.
Source: OECD (forthcoming) Reigniting growth in Andalusia (Spain): a case study; OECD (forthcoming) Reigniting growth in Central Macedonia (Greece): a case study; and OECD Regional Statistics [Database]

StatLink http://dx.doi.org/10.1787/888933707665

Most Greek and many Spanish regions followed similar growth paths as those of Central Macedonia and Andalusia, but rapid growth that was not sustained after the 2007-08 crisis was not limited to the two countries. All Finnish regions experienced a brief recovery after the initial shock of the 2007-08 crisis, but continued to contract after 2011. Central Hungary grew by more than 40% before the crisis and has stagnated since, with per capita GDP increasing by less than 4% between 2007-08 and 2015. Both the east and the west of Slovenia followed similar trends, as did Ireland's Border, Midland and Western regions and the archipelagos Madeira and Azores in Portugal. Outside of Europe, several rural and resource-intensive economies, such as Alberta in Canada, Antofagasta in Chile, Campeche in Mexico or the Taranaki regions in New Zealand, joined the group of regions that declined after rapid pre-crisis expansion.

Growth returned quickly in parts of Europe and the OECD

Some regions were barely affected by the crisis and others emerged from the crisis with fresh growth momentum. Polish regions avoided a recession, although growth has slowed since the 2007-08 crisis. The four large (TL2) regions in the Slovak Republic experienced a drop in per capita GDP in 2009, but returned to growth right after. Not all regions in Europe's east, however, were as quick to return to pre-crisis levels. Central Hungary, the West region in Romania, Central Bohemia and Moravia-Silesia in the Czech Republic, as well as Bulgaria's regions, grew at about median rates, but were a far cry from their robust pre-crisis growth rates. Outside of Europe the picture is more diverse. Korean regions retained solid growth between 2007-08 and 2015, albeit with a high dispersion. The growth rate in Chungcheong, the fastest growing region in Korea was, at 34%, double that of the slowest growing regions, the Capital Region (Seoul) and Gyeongnam Region. Most Chilean regions continued to support the country's course towards economic convergence and some of the US states managed to recover from the crisis and grow by 10% or more between 2007-08 and 2015.[33]

No single factor is likely to explain success or failure in returning to growth

The diversity in growth paths of successful and struggling regions suggests that different factors contributed to regions' economic success – or the lack thereof. Resource-intensive economies had mixed growth paths, some regions lagging far behind their country's most prosperous and productive regions were able to narrow the gap, others fell further behind, and regions with large cities tended to perform well in some countries, but less so in others.

Combined, the pattern suggests that there are drivers that are specific to the regions and those that are common across all regions in the country (see also Chapter 2). The experience of Greek regions, those in Spain, Portugal or Ireland cannot be considered independent of the overall framework set by the structural policies in their country, the measures targeted towards fiscal consolidation in the aftermath of the euro area crisis or the macroeconomic trends that followed the introduction of a common currency in Europe.

The global 2007-08 crisis and the euro area crisis left their mark on Europe's regions

Despite the positive experience of many regions, a large percentage of regions have not recovered to pre-crisis levels of economic prosperity. By 2015, real per capita GDP in 135 out of 350 large (TL2) OECD regions remained below 2007-08 levels. Most of the regions that are still struggling with the aftermath of the crisis are located in Europe, with rapid recovery concentrated in Germany and in Europe's east, as well as in the northern regions of Scandinavia (Figure 1.10).

The lack of full recovery is not just concentrated in Europe. Outside of Europe, regions that have failed to recoup lost growth are diverse and include regions that are economically more advanced within their countries, e.g. Queensland in Australia, regions with important export-oriented sectors, such as Baja California in Mexico, or with strong tourism sectors, such as Nevada in the United States, resource-rich regions, such as Canada's Northwest Territories, Campeche in Mexico, or Alaska in the United States, as well as regions that have the lowest levels of economic development, e.g. Tasmania in Australia, or Alabama and Mississippi in the United States.

Figure 1.10. Real per capita GDP has started to recover, but many regions remain below pre-crisis levels

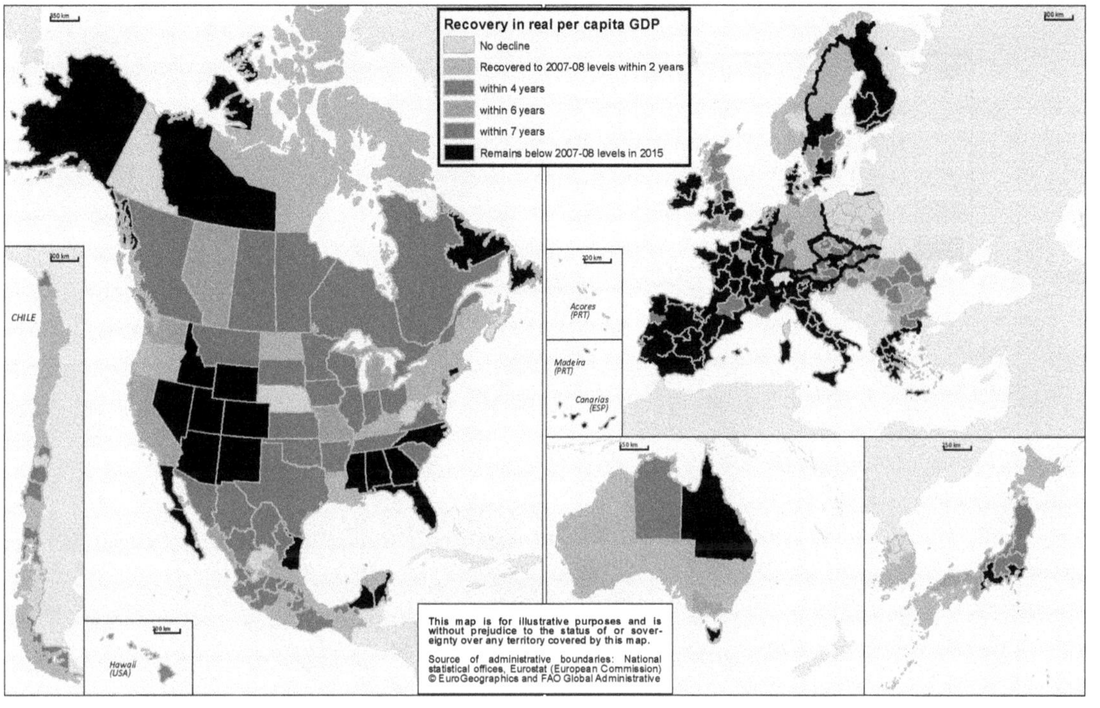

Note: The year refers to the first year that per capita GDP recovered to at least 2007-08 levels after the recession that was triggered by the 2007-08 crisis. Light grey areas indicate missing data.
Source: Calculations based on OECD Regional Statistics [Database].

StatLink http://dx.doi.org/10.1787/888933707684

Investment remains low in many parts of Europe

Real per capita GDP is not the only economic indicator that has not returned to pre-crisis levels, capital investment, for example, exceeded pre-crisis levels in only about one-third of 253 European regions (NUTS 2) in 2014.[34] In some regions, the situation was even more dramatic. In more than 20% of the regions, investment in 2014 was below levels seen in the 1990s. Real gross fixed capital formation, measured in constant 2005 prices, was at levels that had been surpassed in the mid-1990s in most Greek and southern Italian regions. This slack performance was not confined to Europe's south. In 2014, investment levels in Dutch, Finnish or French regions, as well as parts of northern England – among others – trailed those in the early 2000s. Germany's eastern regions are notable as they seem to be as strongly affected by the crisis as Europe's south. Unlike other regions, investment followed a general downward trend in most of eastern Germany between 1994 and 2007.

Figure 1.11. Investment was set back by more than a decade in many regions

Gross fixed capital formation in 2014 measured in constant 2005 EUR compared to GFCF in previous years

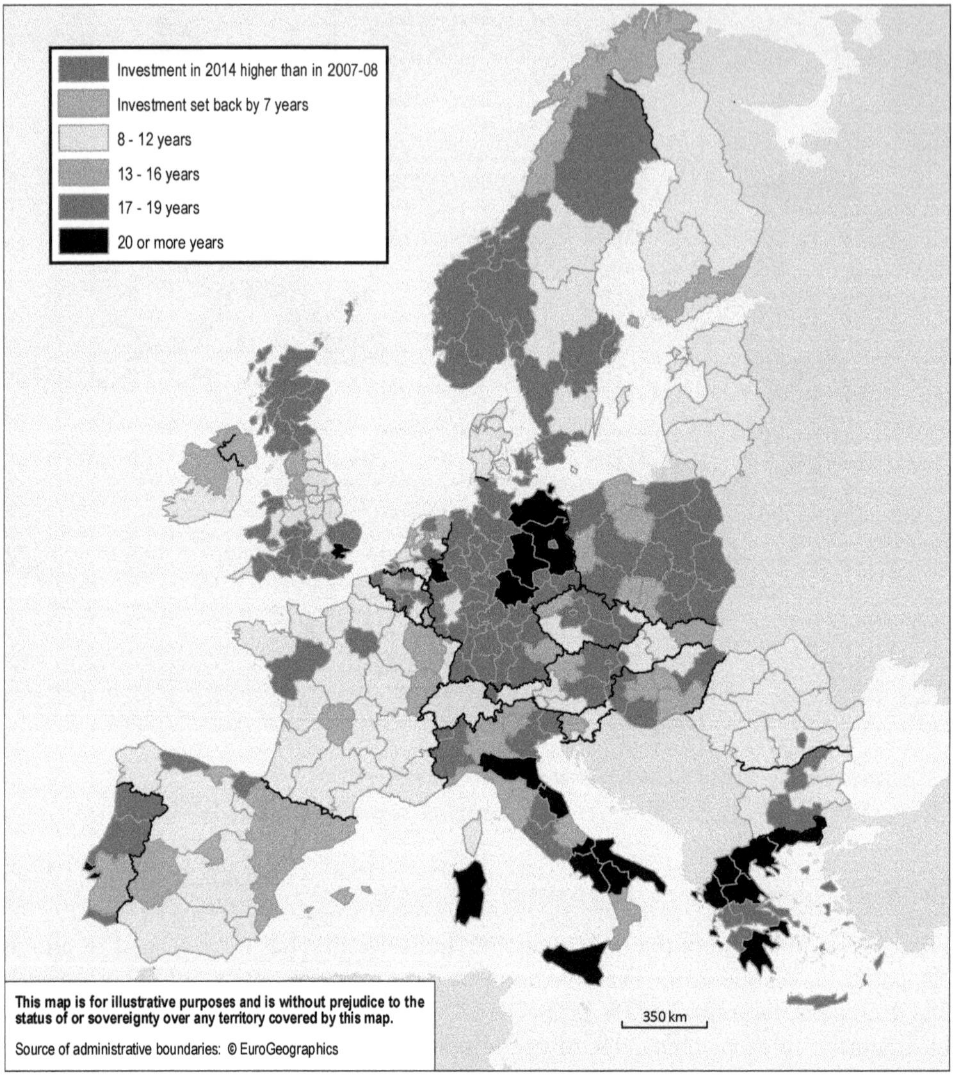

Note: Regions in dark blue had higher levels of GFCF in 2014 than in 2007 or 2008. Light blue regions had levels in 2014 that were lower than in 2007 or 2008, but higher than in previous years. The grey hues and year bands indicate the number of years that had higher investment than that of 2014.
Source: Calculations based on Cambridge Econometrics (2017) European Regional Database [Database].

StatLink http://dx.doi.org/10.1787/888933707703

Private investment in OECD countries declined drastically in the wake of the 2007-08 crisis, with public investment falling from 2010 onwards. For private investment, year-on-year growth started to rebound in 2014, but public investment has continued its decline. Falling public investment is not only due to limits on overall public expenditures. As a percentage of total government expenditure, public investment declined from around 9.0-9.5% in the decade preceding the 2007-08 crisis to just 7.7% in 2014. While better governance, improvements in institutional quality and capacity to leverage private investment can improve the efficiency and effectiveness of public investment, the continued decline raises the concern of increasing underinvestment.[35] With capital accumulation as one of the key drivers of growth,[36] a prolonged slowdown in investment raises the spectre of protracted stagnation and regions becoming permanently stuck in a "middle income trap".

Economic growth and, in some cases, productivity may suffer if there are investments for which the social return would easily outweigh the risk, but which are not undertaken by private investors. Such missing investment can result from the fact that benefits from investments can accrue not only to the investing firm, but also to other firms and residents. If the investing firm is unable to internalise this positive externality, e.g. by charging other firms for these benefits, the private returns to the firm from an investment might be insufficient and it decides to forego the investment. Typically, such cases occur if investments create substantial network effects or large spillovers. In order to overcome the co-ordination problem associated with such investments, public involvement is needed (Box 1.3).

Box 1.3. Public investment

The assumption that all returns from physical and human capital benefit only the firm that paid for the investment or the worker who undertook the training is unrealistic. Investing in transport infrastructure or the creation of a public university can create major benefits for the local economy. For some firms, benefits from these public investments can be huge: for instance, farmers or manufacturing firms can reap significant direct benefits from the development of transport infrastructure, as they can ship their products more cheaply, reach a larger market and can also import more easily inputs for their production process. The total value of agricultural land in the United States at the end of the expansion of the railway network in the late 19th century would have been 60% less without the expansion (Donaldson and Hornbeck, 2016[41]). Other firms may benefit less from such public investment, and even among manufacturers the gains from new infrastructure usually vary.

Total benefits of major investments can easily outweigh their costs, yet these projects are not undertaken by the private sector. This arises typically if there is a large number of beneficiaries and co-ordinating them or capture the value the investment creates for them is difficult. The role of the public sector is therefore crucial in areas where investment can create significant public benefits such as major transport infrastructure and other areas. Research and innovation in one firm can create positive spillovers for other firms in the area. As new technology or products become available, firms can learn from the example and build on these innovations. This might benefit the initial innovating firm (e.g. through patent license fees), but many benefits may arise without directly rewarding the initial innovator. Such spillovers can be highly localised and not extend beyond regional or even local borders.

Within Silicon Valley, innovating firms in different technological fields operate in close proximity. They seem to cover small, distinct but overlapping technological zones. In general, knowledge spillovers, measured by the rate of patent citations, decline rapidly with distance. For the United States, the citation rate halves in postal codes that are located 25-30 kilometres away from the initial patent compared to postal codes in the direct vicinity (Kerr and Kominers, 2015[51]). The reason is that proximity supports two channels through which knowledge spreads. 1) Firms learn from the example and knowledge gained by others, and 2) inventors move between firms or even into newly created businesses, as documented by Matray (2014[61]) or the United States.

Sources: Donaldson and Hornbeck (2016[41]), Kerr and Kominers (2015[51]) and Matray (2014[61]).

Productivity growth is necessary for sustained improvements in living conditions

The economic wealth of a nation is determined by its resources, its physical capital and by its working population that combines resources and capital to produce goods and services. Labour productivity is the amount of goods and services a worker can produce given a set of resources and time and essential in determining the overall income in a country. Indeed, across OECD countries, a large part of the difference in per capita income is due to differences in labour productivity. This affects workers directly, as the increasing dispersion in average wages is associated with growing differences in wages paid by more and those paid by less productive firms.[37] Labour productivity is not about using more time or effort, it is not about "working harder": Instead it is about making the best use of the available resources, it is about "working smarter".

Raising productivity is not only essential for overall economic growth, it also determines individual well-being. Sustainable wage growth, and thereby growth in living standards, requires that productivity keep pace with wage increases. The willingness (and capacity) of a firm to compensate their workers depends – to a large degree – on their productivity.[38] Of course, inclusive gains from growth are by no means automatic and a key policy challenge remains to ensure a fair distribution of the benefits created by economic growth.[39]

As pressures from an ageing workforce mount and efficiency gains are required to limit the strain on natural resources and the environment, higher productivity growth is becoming increasingly essential to sustain public budgets and to help regions escape the "middle income trap".

Employment and productivity growth are often difficult to reconcile

Different measures can lead to labour productivity growth. In firms, investment in training and new skill acquisition can make workers more effective or efficient, new processes or new ways of working in teams can raise the productivity of the workforce or new machinery or tools can reduce the time and effort workers have to spend for a given output. Productivity growth is "labour saving", i.e. fewer workers or fewer hours are required to produce the same amount of output. But productivity increases are not necessarily associated with job losses. If increased productivity leads to lower prices and increased demand for the product, firms and regional employment might expand along with increasing demand.

Another channel that increases productivity is to abandon the least productive activities, or to terminate the least productive jobs. If the economy is booming and demand is high, even firms with relatively low levels of productivity can find a niche and operate profitably. But if the economy slows down, the pressure for less productive firms to improve their productivity rises. If they fail to do so, they face the choice between accruing losses and closing down. This might affect the firm in aggregate or just certain parts of the business or certain jobs.[40] Firms might cut the parts of their business that are less productive and focus on their core activities. At the regional level, this also means that some firms will cease to operate and some people will lose their jobs. But since it is the least productive firms and jobs, this can result in increased regional productivity; although some people might be worse off, at least in the short term.

The relationship between employment and productivity growth in Europe is indeed negative in the aggregate. In regions with higher productivity growth, employment is expanding, on average, more slowly or sometimes not at all (Figure 1.12). The negative relationship between productivity and employment growth has been fairly stable since the 1980s. No matter what year is selected, employment and productivity growth are negatively associated. But beyond the average, the data show massive dispersion of growth experiences, with many regions showing that productivity growth does not have to be combined with job losses.

Figure 1.12. Productivity grows, on average, faster in regions that experienced job losses

Year-on-year growth in labour productivity (real per worker GDP) and employment in Europe's small (NUTS3) regions, 1981-2014

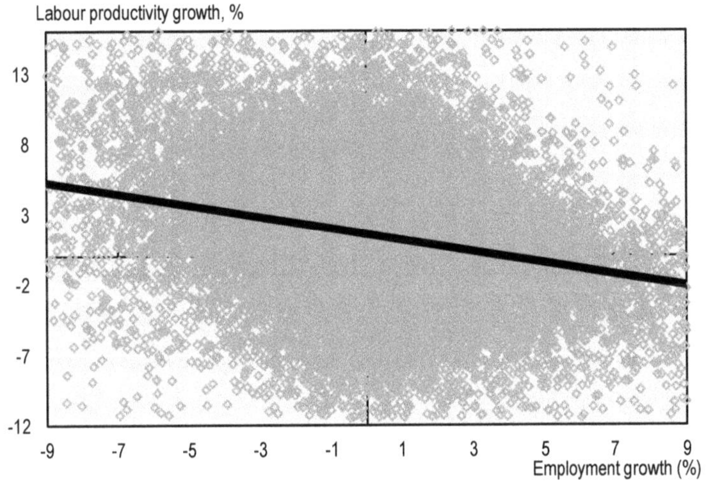

Note: Each diamond corresponds to the year-on-year growth rate in labour productivity (per worker GDP in EUR at constant 2005 prices) and employment in small (NUTS 3) regions in Europe. Extreme observations (bottom and top percentile) are excluded. Trend lines depict the linear fit in the indicated year.
Source: Calculations based on Cambridge Econometrics (2017).

StatLink http://dx.doi.org/10.1787/888933707722

Some regions manage to create a win-win of productivity and employment growth

A large percentage of regions manage to combine productivity and employment growth, with the share of successful regions depending on the business cycle. In the years of economic expansion, the percentage of European regions (NUTS 3) that combined productivity and employment growth exceeded 40% in the late-1980s, late-1990s and mid-2000s. Conversely, employment declined in more than 40% of Europe's regions that experienced productivity growth after the recession of the early-1980s, early-1990s, early-2000s and the global crisis of 2007-08 (Figure 1.13).[41]

The adjustments during recession years are economically and socially costly. Often they follow after periods when an increasing number of regions saw an increase in employment at the cost of reducing average productivity in the region. These jobs might be associated with flourishing sales in more productive sectors and indicate growing demand for local services, to take just one example, but they might also indicate growing inertia in the reallocation of capital and jobs from less to more productive firms.[42]

Figure 1.13. Many regions combine employment and productivity growth

Percentage of small (NUTS3) European regions with positive/negative year-on-year employment and labour productivity growth

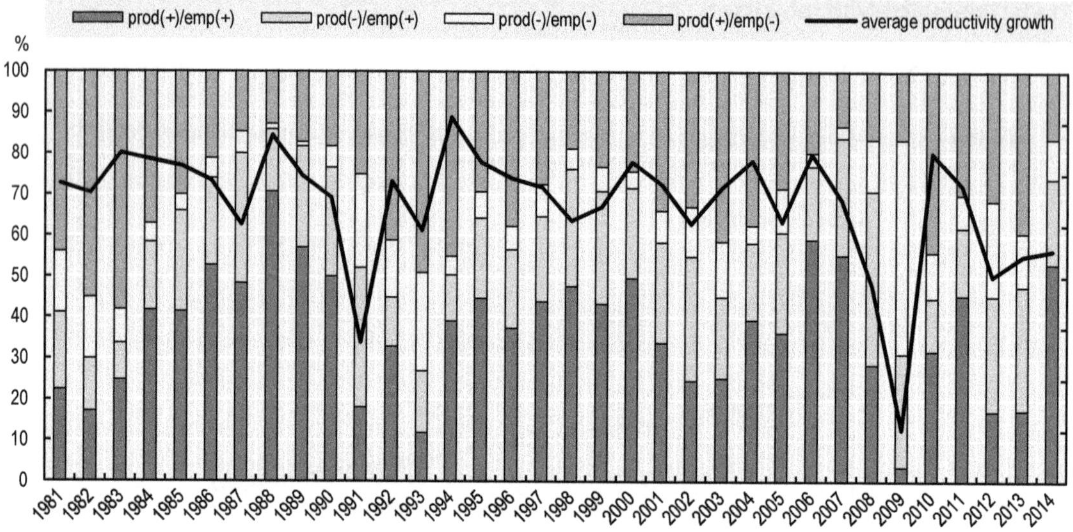

Note: Small (NUTS 3) regions in Europe are classified based on positive/negative year-on-year growth rates in labour productivity (per worker GDP in EUR at constant 2005 prices) and employment. Average productivity growth is the unweighted average across regions.

Source: Calculations based on Cambridge Econometrics (2017).

StatLink http://dx.doi.org/10.1787/888933707741

Box 1.4. Business cycles in the euro area and the United States

The euro area and the United States followed similar business cycles. The recession at the beginning of the 1980s was followed by an expansion until the early 1990s. The subsequent recession (Figure 1.14) came later to Europe than in the United States, but lasted longer. The recession following the burst of the dot-com bubble in the early 2000s affected parts of the euro area (e.g. Germany and France), but was less evident at the aggregate level. The global financial crisis of 2007-08 led to lasting recessions both in the euro area and the United States. In Europe, the short-lived recovery was followed by the sovereign debt crisis that kept many European economies in recession for several consecutive years.

Figure 1.14. Quarters of recession in the United States and the euro area

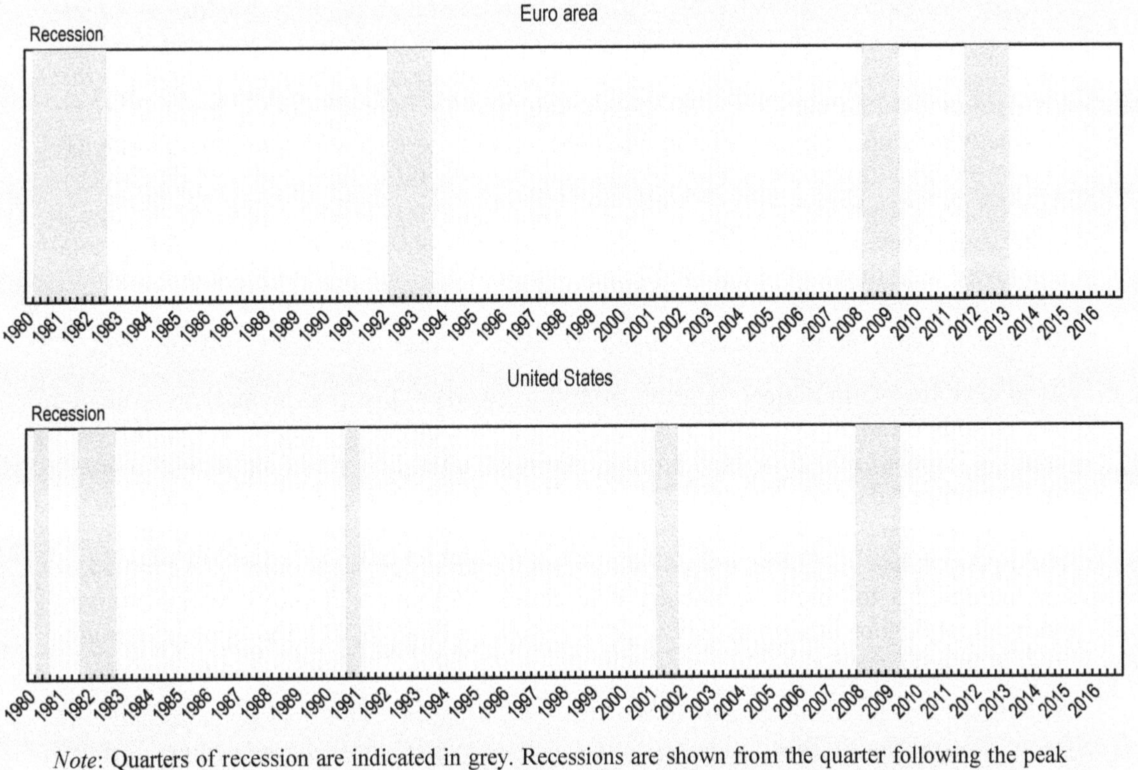

Note: Quarters of recession are indicated in grey. Recessions are shown from the quarter following the peak through the quarter of the trough (i.e. the peak is not included in the recession shading, but the trough is).

Sources: CEPR, *Euro Area Business Cycle Dating Committee*, http://cepr.org/content/euro-area-business-cycle-dating-committee (accessed 30 October 2017) and NBER, *US Business Cycle Expansions and Contractions*, www.nber.org/cycles.html (accessed 30 October 2017).

StatLink http://dx.doi.org/10.1787/888933707760

The employment benefits of productivity growth are rarely immediate

Taking a long-term view, both productivity and employment tend to increase as the wealth and prosperity of countries grow. But creating employment benefits through productivity growth is not automatic.[43] Investment in physical and human capital can help harness the potential for employment creation and overcome the short-term trade-off between productivity and employment growth.[44] As the capital stock deepens the productivity of additional hires increases as well. Similarly, an increase in worker skills raises their productivity and therefore employability in the more productive environment.

How quickly benefits materialise depends on the ability of the local economy to adjust. Capital locked in underperforming firms may have accumulated over years and barriers to its reallocation can hinder productivity growth. Recent research suggests that insolvency regimes that reduce barriers to corporate restructuring and the personal cost incurred by entrepreneurs and equity holders associated with firm failure may reduce the capital that is sunk in firms that fail to create profits large enough to cover the cost of their capital.[45] Internal restructuring and an expansion of incumbent firms, but perhaps more importantly expedient ways of entering and exiting the market, are the channels through which better insolvency regimes result in the reduction of sunk capital.

Setting framework conditions that favour the creation of new firms and the capacity of fast-growing firms to leverage their growth spurt can be particularly promising. Young firms tend to contribute disproportionately to employment growth (Criscuolo, Gal and Menon, 2014[7]) and among the young it is the small fraction of high-growth firms that drives growth (Calvino, Criscuolo and Menon, 2015[8]). In the United States, half of the productivity benefits from shifts in employment from less to more productive firms are driven by firms that are less than 10 years old, among these firms, 40% of the effect is through the expansion of employment in young high growth firms. The contribution is quite large given that firms that are less than 10 years old account for only 19% of total employment (Haltiwanger et al., 2017[9]).

Structural adjustment following the 2007-08 crisis was followed by job growth

A positive long-term outlook is little comfort for workers that find themselves without a job. Whether and how rapidly productivity growth can be leveraged for employment creation in subsequent periods varies between years (Box 1.5). Empirical estimates based on 30 years of data for European TL3 regions that take initial regional conditions and country and time aggregate effects into account, show that productivity growth in the previous year has little or no impact on job creation during boom periods.[46] In contrast, in the periods that followed the two major recessions in Europe, employment growth was, on average, higher in regions where productivity grew more. But the positive stimulus differs between the recession of the 1990s and recent global 2007-08 and euro area crises.

The major structural adjustments in the aftermath of the recent global financial and euro area crises seem to have ultimately created employment growth momentum through productivity growth in Europe. In regions where productivity grew more, jobs were created in the following year, while regions that experienced productivity decline were also struggling in terms of employment (Box 1.5). This positive stimulus is 3-5 times stronger than it was in the 1980s and 1990s. An increase in productivity by 10 percentage points in the previous year is associated with 1 percentage point higher employment growth in the current year for the period between 2009 and 2015 in OECD regions and 0.7 percentage points in European regions (until 2014). Productivity decline in the same order of magnitude is, however, associated with 0.7 and 0.4 percentage points lower employment growth, respectively.

A possible explanation for the strong positive effect in recent years is that, in the run-up to the 2007-08 crisis, investment in some European countries seems to have favoured less productive over more productive firms.[47] The inertia created by a build-up of misallocated capital might have been corrected by the crisis and the reforms that followed.[48] The impact of the Great Recession following the 2007-08 crisis on job creation differs also in the United States. The "cleansing" effect of a recession normally forces less productive firms to close up shop and employment is subsequently reallocated from less to more productive firms. This pattern was less marked during the Great Recession as employment creation – in particular among young firms – was relatively slow compared to prior recessions.[49]

Box 1.5. Productivity growth, productivity decline and employment

More jobs are created in more productive regions and those with higher population growth

Employment grows, on average, faster in more productive regions in a country. Taking into account 1) current population growth, 2) a measure of (potential) supply of workers, and 3) the employment rate as a proxy for the "slack" in the local labour market, the estimate suggests that for each 10% difference in labour productivity between two regions in a country, employment growth is between 0.1 and 0.2 percentage points higher in the more productive region. The estimated impact is stable and highly statistically significant across different time periods considered (Table 1.1).

Given the productivity divides in some countries, expected differential in employment growth can be substantial. Labour productivity in Italy's most productive province, the city of Milan, was more than 40% higher than in the region of southern Italy's largest city, Naples. This difference implies that employment is expected to grow by more than half of a percentage point faster in Milan than in Naples.

The impact is further amplified as more productive regions also have higher population growth. Population growth, in turn, translates into employment growth at a rate of about 1 to 2, i.e. a 1% increase in the population in a region is associated with roughly half of a percent increase in employment. This holds for EU and OECD countries.

Productivity growth is followed by job growth, but only after the 2007-08 crisis

Productivity growth is often associated with a decline in employment. Using data for the last 30 years, productivity and employment growth are, at least on average, negatively correlated. This means that regions where productivity grew faster were growing slower or even declining in total employment. But this contemporaneous pattern might miss the adjustment in the sectors and firms that can generate subsequent employment growth.

Data from the early 1980s onwards shows little evidence of an employment boost following productivity growth in the previous period. To the contrary, the period between the early 1980s and the new millennium shows a positive impact of productivity decline on employment growth (I and IV in Table 1.1). A 10 percentage point decline in productivity in the previous year is associated with 0.5 percentage point higher employment growth in the current year for the pre-2000 period. A further breakdown shows that this relationship is driven by developments in the 1980s and early 1990s and disappears as the 1992-93 recession hit.

Unlike before the 1992-93 recession, there seems to be no association between productivity growth and job growth before the 2007-08 crisis (II and V in Table 1.1). The adjustments, which are evident in the data, followed the massive shock to the labour market that took place through the crisis years and beyond. Those regions where productivity have grown since 2009 have, on average, also created more jobs, whereas regions that experienced productivity decline were also declining in terms of employment (VI and VII in Table 1.1).

Table 1.1. Employment dynamics in NUTS 3/TL3 regions

Multivariate regressions with employment growth in year t as the dependent variable

	(I)	(II)	(II)	(IV)	(V)	(VI)	(VII)
ln(Productivity in t-1)	0.02***	0.02***	0.02***	0.01***	0.02***	0.02***	0.01***
	(0.001)	(0.002)	(0.002)	(0.001)	(0.002)	(0.002)	(0.003)
Productivity growth	0.01	0.00	0.05***	0.02*	-0.00	0.07***	0.10***
(t-1)	(0.004)	(0.009)	(0.008)	(0.008)	(0.013)	(0.013)	(0.016)
Productivity decline				-0.05***	0.02	0.04*	0.07***
(t-1)				(0.011)	(0.021)	(0.014)	(0.015)
Population growth	0.45***	0.44***	0.27***	0.42***	0.44***	0.28***	0.41***
(t)	(0.018)	(0.048)	(0.035)	(0.022)	(0.048)	(0.035)	(0.047)
Employment rate	-0.02***	-0.02***	-0.01***	-0.02***	-0.02***	-0.01***	-0.00***
(t-2)	(0.002)	(0.003)	(0.002)	(0.002)	(0.003)	(0.002)	(0.000)
Observations	35 912	8 415	7 310	17 675	8 415	7 310	6 050
Regions (NUTS 3/TL3)	1 332	1 318	1 314	1 311	1 318	1 314	1 276
R^2	0.190	0.203	0.312	0.224	0.203	0.312	0.310
Years	1983-2014	2000-2006	2009-2014	1983-1999	2000-2006	2009-2014	2009-2015
Fixed Effects	country; year	country; year	country; year	country; year	country; year	country; year	country; year
Area	EU	EU	EU	EU	EU	EU	OECD

Note: Population refers to the total resident population in the region, employment to total employment at place of work, the employment rate is the ratio of the two variables and (labour) productivity is the ratio of total GDP in EUR at constant 2005 prices. Growth rates are calculated as the difference in the natural logarithm between the indicated year and the year prior (e.g. employment growth in t for t= 2010 is calculated as ln(employment in 2010) – ln(employment in year 2009). In specifications IV-VII, productivity growth is separated into positive (growth) and negative (decline) values allowing for a different impact of prior productivity growth and decline on employment growth. The data covers small regions (TL3 in the OECD classification, NUTS3 in the EU classification). Countries included in the EU sample are BE, BG, CZ, DE, DK, EE, EL, ES, FI, FR, HR, HU, IE, IT, LT, LU, LV, MT, NL, PL, PT, RO, SE, SI, SK, UK, The OECD sample excludes BG, NO, RO and includes CH, LU, KR, NZ in that list.

Source: Calculations based on OECD Regional Statistics [Database] and Cambridge Econometrics (2017) European Regional Database [Database].

Regional productivity growth in OECD countries mainly follows two models: catching up or concentration

The impact of regional productivity catching-up on the aggregate productivity of countries can be illustrated by the contribution of each region to the aggregate GDP growth rate, as well as the regional contribution to the growth rate of national productivity. The regional contribution to GDP growth is straightforward; it is simply the growth rate between *t* and *t-1* of each region multiplied by the share of that region in the national GDP in the period *t-1*. The contribution to aggregate productivity is more complicated because labour productivity is a ratio. In this study, a counterfactual calculation has been used instead. It corresponds to the theoretical aggregate productivity without a given region. If, under this counterfactual, the aggregate productivity is higher than national average that means that a given region contributes negatively to the aggregate growth rate, and vice-versa.[50]

From this perspective, two types of countries emerge (Bachtler et al., 2017[10]). The first category (Type-I) comprises countries such as Austria, Germany, Czech Republic, Spain, Italy, Poland, Portugal or Romania.[51] Frontier regions have typically big contributions to GDP growth because they are large, but in these countries they have much smaller or even negative contributions to aggregate productivity growth. Most of the productivity performance of these countries is therefore the result of lagging regions' efforts to catch up to the frontier regions. Put differently, the frontier regions sustain high productivity levels, but productivity growth dynamics occur elsewhere in the country. Regional policy favouring the productivity performance of lagging regions acts as an important driver of a country-wide growth strategy. Interestingly, the convergence of lagging regions in a country may also depend on the interaction with frontier regions. For example, the growth of rural regions close to cities tends to be much higher than the growth of remote rural regions (OECD, 2016[1]).

The second category (Type-II) includes countries such as Bulgaria, Denmark, France, United Kingdom, Greece, Hungary, Netherlands, Slovak Republic or Sweden. In these countries, both GDP growth and aggregate productivity growth are dominated by the frontier regions. This means that most of the growth dynamics are concentrated at the frontier, with limited effects from the catching-up process. Often, these frontier regions correspond to the largest city in the country, where agglomeration effects are maximised. Such a strong territorial asymmetry may signal a potential for productivity catching-up at the regional level that has not yet materialised or could be further mobilised.

The composition of each group accounts for the diversity of countries in Europe: developed economies, low-income and low-growth countries. These two patterns of regional dynamics are strikingly contrasted in the EU (Figure 1.15). There seems to be little middle ground as most countries see their growth either driven by their frontier or by a catching up of less productive regions.

In the Type-I countries, there are several regions converging to the country frontier, which contribute significantly to the aggregate productivity (e.g. Germany or Poland). In the Type-II countries, most of regions are diverging or maintaining large gaps vis-à-vis the frontier (e.g. France or the United Kingdom). Therefore, the aggregate productivity is mainly determined by the performance of the frontier (Figure 1.15).[52]

Figure 1.15. Productivity dynamics at the regional level in the EU

Classification of TL2 regions, 2000-14

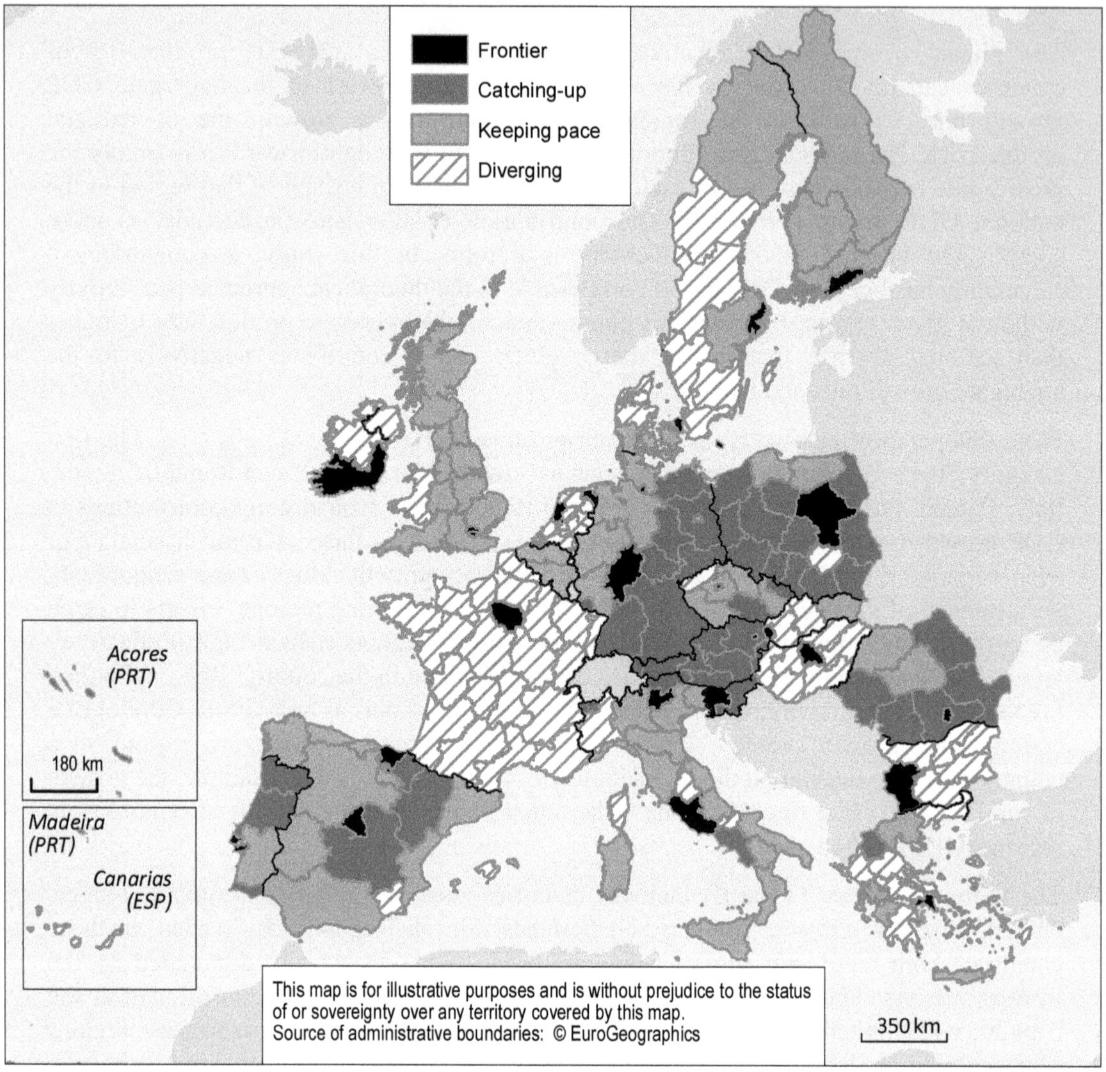

Note: Catching-up/diverging regions grew by at least 5 percentage points in 14 years more/less than their national frontier over the 2000-14 period. The frontier is defined as the aggregation of regions with the highest GDP per worker and representing 10% of national employment.
Source: Calculations based on OECD Regional Statistics [Database].

StatLink http://dx.doi.org/10.1787/888933707779

There may be certain trade-offs between being concentrated or more dispersed when it comes to generating aggregate productivity. As shown in Figure 1.16, the regional frontier in Type-I countries is less dynamic than in Type-II. The former grew, on average, at a rate of 1% per year during the period 2000-14, while the latter increased at an annual growth rate of 1.6%. As the lagging regions in type-I countries grew on average at a rate of 1.1% per year, this implies a slow convergence process. In Type-II, the lagging regions have grown only at 0.9% per year, implying that most regions are diverging.

All of the above suggests that there may be untapped potential to increase country-wide productivity by improving the performance of regions. This is the main argument underpinning the case for regional policy. Indeed, governments should not only address regional disparities on the basis of territorial equity objectives alone, but also as a way of increasing aggregate productivity growth. In this way, regional policy can be considered an integral part of the structural policy package targeted to enhance growth potential of countries as a whole.

Figure 1.16. The challenge of combining dynamic growth and catching up

Annual average labour productivity (per worker GDP in USD at constant prices and PPPs of 2010) in small (TL3) regions

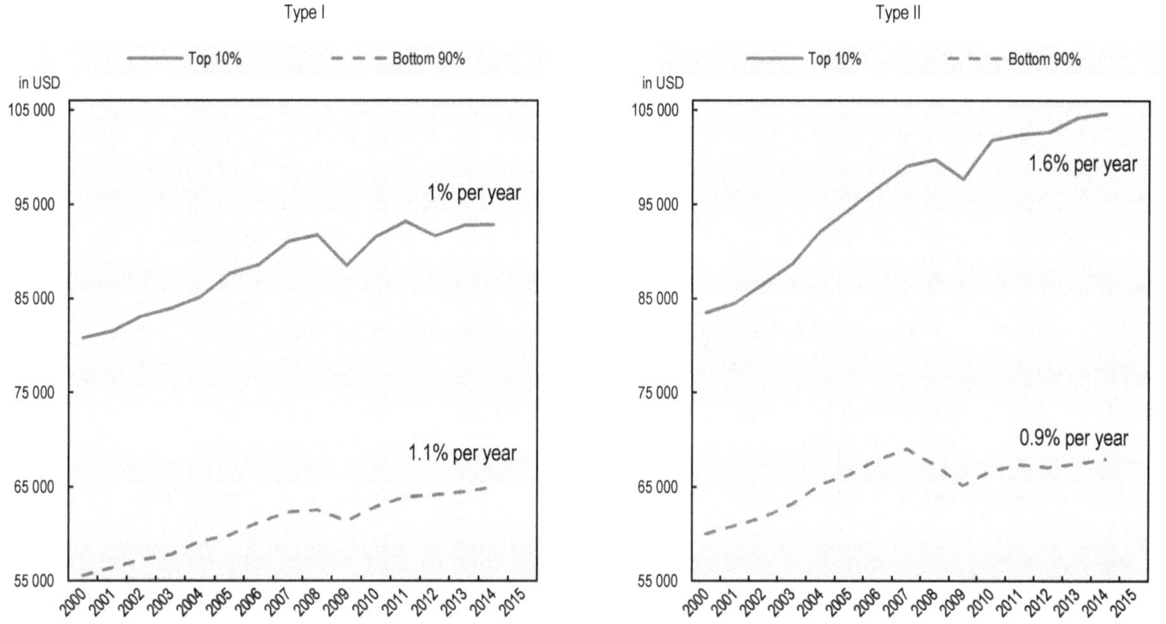

Note: Type I countries are those with strong regional catching-up dynamics in terms of labour productivity across regions, while Type II countries experienced divergence of most regions and the productivity advantage in the most productive "frontier" regions increased. Type I countries are AUT, CZE, DEU, ESP, ITA, POL, PRT, and ROU; Type II countries are BGR, DNK, FIN, FRA, GBR, GRC, HUN, NLD, SVK, and SWE.
Source: Calculations based on OECD Regional Statistics [Database].

StatLink http://dx.doi.org/10.1787/888933707798

Inaction comes at the price of growing inequality and a "geography of discontent"

The repercussions of letting regions fall behind can be severe. Inequality is rising and transfers cannot substitute for true opportunities. Across the OECD, a "geography of discontent" has been emerging, expressing itself in dissatisfaction with global trends, diversity and established policies. General discontent with the status quo, particularly the downsides of open and globalised economies are dominating the public discussion and people's perceptions, rather than the tremendous benefits they create. When people feel they are being left behind, these open and globalised economies become difficult to sustain.

Many dividing lines can be drawn with respect to discontent in OECD countries. Commentators highlight different attitudes and ways to express discontent for the young and the old, those with high or low levels of education, the employed and the unemployed or the well-off and the poor. What is striking is that there is usually a clear spatial dimension to the discontent. This "geography of discontent" highlights that building resilient regions that can adapt to the challenges and opportunities created by globalisation and industrial transition is not only an economic prerogative, but necessary to ensure social cohesion.

A growing divide in countries that seize opportunities is no foregone conclusion, historically catching-up in both fast- and slow-growing countries has kept inter-regional inequalities in check. In contrast, countries where the economy became increasingly concentrated over the 2000-14 period also saw inequality rise (Figure 1.17). Per capita GDP inequality, measured by the Gini coefficient remained stable across regions in countries where regions managed to "catch up" to their country's frontier in terms of labour productivity. In contrast, inequality increased in countries where the frontier regions kept pulling away from other regions. Inequality between more and less populous TL3 regions amplifies the overall trend. Weighted inequality grew continuously and faster than unweighted inequality indicating an increasing gap between more populous TL3 regions and smaller ones throughout the 2000-14 period. This implies that more populous regions were more likely to have either relatively high or relatively low levels of income.

Figure 1.17. Inequalities grow when regions fail to catch up

Per capita GDP inequality (Gini coefficient) in TL3 regions, 2000-14

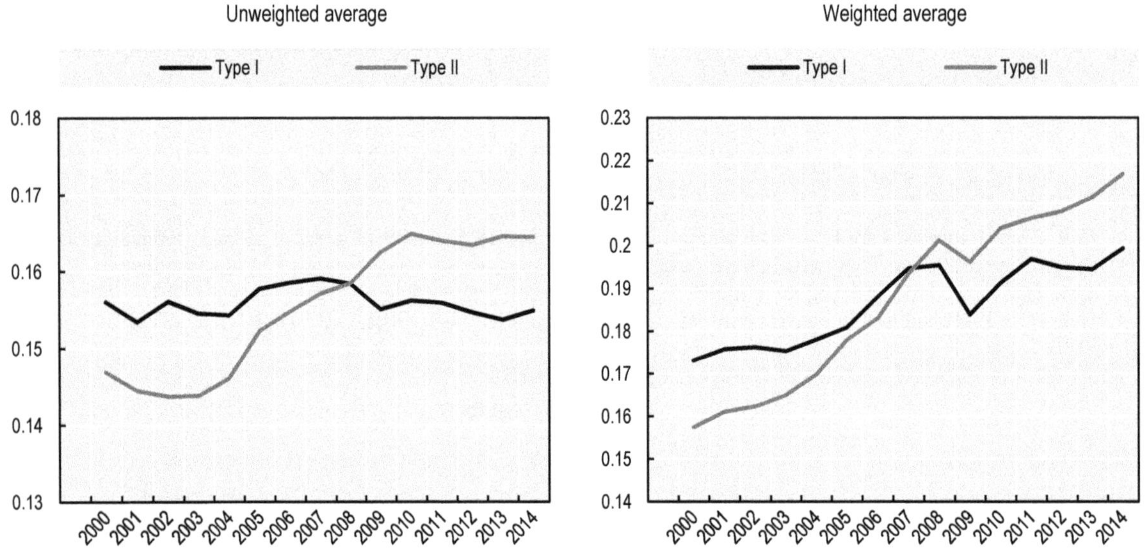

Note: Type I countries are those with strong regional catching-up dynamics in terms of labour productivity across regions, while Type II countries experienced divergence of most regions and the productivity advantage in the most productive "frontier" regions increased. Type I countries are AUT, CZE, DEU, ESP, ITA, POL, PRT, and ROU; Type II countries are BGR, DNK, FIN, FRA, GBR, GRC, HUN, NLD, SVK, and SWE. Per capita GDP inequality with GDP measured in USD at constant 2010 prices and purchasing power parities. The simple average assigns the same weight to each region; the weighted average gives more weight to more populous regions.
Source: Calculations based on OECD Regional Statistics [Database].

StatLink http://dx.doi.org/10.1787/888933707817

There are no quick fixes to a growing geography of discontent. But raising the productivity of the workforce is a crucial long-term goal. It is necessary to ensure that living standards can be maintained given that in an ageing society dependency rates are likely to further increase in the future. A focus on individual regions might have growth benefits in some countries, but it risks missing growth opportunities that arise in all types of regions. Leveraging this potential is often more difficult, there is no "one-size-fits-all" strategy for regional development. Policies should not aim to retain people in certain regions, sectors or firms if there is no growth potential and might even support them to move to seek better opportunities. But there should also not be the conception of a "flat world", where all regions are equal. The difficult balance is to not lock people in places through continuous subsidies, but rather give them a chance to grow where they are.

Leveraging growth potential requires constant efforts, e.g. through continuous investment in worker skills. Globalisation and technological progress require new and evolving skill sets and ensuring that workers are ready for future jobs is essential. Productivity is directly linked to material living conditions as it raises workers' wages and ensures that their jobs are not only here today, but remain tomorrow.

Notes

1. Borrowing from William Easterly's (2001[29]) famous "The Elusive Quest for Growth".
2. Moretti (Moretti, 2012[18]) documents the "great divide".
3. In the short term, boom periods are often followed by slow growth or even recession. The euro area has gone through five cycles in which high growth was followed by periods of low growth since the 1970s. Recessions, i.e. periods of economic decline, were part of all five cycles. Centre for Economic Policy Research: Euro Area Business Cycle Dating Committee, available at http://cepr.org/content/euro-area-business-cycle-dating-committee (accessed 19 June 2017).
4. See e.g. McCann (2016[2]) for a UK-centric discussion.
5. E.g. the OECD Regional Outlook 2014 (OECD, 2014[45]) argues that complementary investment is required to leverage the growth potential of infrastructure investments. Duranton (2011[30]) warns against an excessive focus on policies that aim to affect productivity directly and suggests to focus on reducing costs of agglomeration and attracting workers.
6. In Paul Krugman's words: "[p]roductivity isn't everything, but in the long run it is almost everything. A country's ability to improve its standard of living over time depends almost entirely on its ability to raise its output per worker" (Krugman, 1995, p. 11[21]).
7. See the OECD Regional Outlook country pages (OECD, 2016[1]) for Korea and Turkey and http://ec.europa.eu/regional_policy/en/policy/what/territorial-cohesion/ (accessed 18 October 2017).
8. The five targets are focused on employment, research and development, climate change and energy sustainability, education and fighting poverty and exclusion. http://ec.europa.eu/regional_policy/en/policy/what/investment-policy/ (accessed 14 November 2017).
9. See OECD (2014[47]) on how to integrate well-being indicators in policy making, including additional examples and OECD (2016[42]) for a focus on the Danish example.

10. See also European Commission (2017[27]) for evidence of declining disparities along different dimensions.

11. In addition to growing economic gaps, the disparity in the social fabric has widened in many countries as well. The gap between the region with the highest percentage of post-secondary education and the region with the lowest percentage increased in most OECD countries between 2000 and 2014 (OECD, 2016[46]).

12. "Low-income" regions in Europe are defined as part of the EU Lagging Regions Initiative as those with less than 50% of EU-average per capita GDP in 2000 (European Commission, 2017[11]).

13. See e.g. Gill and Kharas (2015[24]) for a critical discussion.

14. "Low-growth" regions in Europe are defined by the EU Lagging Regions Initiative as those regions with less than 90% of EU-average per capita GDP in 2000 and less than EU-average per capita GDP growth over the 2000-13 period (European Commission, 2017[11]).

15. Calculations based on Cambridge Econometrics (2017) European Regional Database [Database]. Countries where the most productive region did not change are Austria, Bulgaria, Czech Republic, Germany, Denmark, Finland, France, Hungary, Norway, Poland, Portugal, Romania, Sweden and the United Kingdom. Change occurred in Belgium, Greece, Spain, Italy and the Netherlands.

16. The great divide documented by (Moretti, 2012[18])

17. See OECD (2016[1]) and Lembcke and Maguire (2017[19]).

18. Calculations based on OECD Regional Statistics [Database]. Bavaria's labour productivity (measured in gross value added per capita) grew by 0.84% annually over the 2000-14 period, Hamburg and Hesse combined grew at 0.28%. In 2014, labour productivity was USD 77 000 at constant 2010 prices and purchasing power parities for Bavaria and USD 83 700 for Hamburg and Hesse (combined).

19. See Storper et al. (2015[14]) for a comparison of the development since the 1970s in the two combined metropolitan statistical areas.

20. Following Cronon (1991[32]), see the foreword of Combes, Mayer and Thisse (2008[33]) for further delineation between "first nature" and "second nature" in Economic Geography.

21. As an example, see Angerer et al. (2009[38]) for a projection of demand for raw materials that is expected to arise from future innovations.

22. The trade-off between economies of scale and transport costs is at the core of models that follow "New Economic Geography" theory (Fujita, Krugman and Venables, 1999[25]). When scale economies are not limited, "natural" monopolies emerge and single producers dominate the market.

23. Examples are CRH PLC, which employs 87 000 people in about 3 800 locations www.crh.com/our-group (accessed 15 November 2017) and HeidelbergCement, which employs around 60 000 people in more than 3 000 locations www.heidelbergcement.com/en/company (accessed 15 November 2017).

24. The most productive "frontier" regions are those regions with the highest values of per worker GDP in a country that account for at least 10% of total employment (OECD, 2016[1]).

25. See Ahrend et al. (2017[39]) for evidence for five OECD countries.

26. Predominantly rural areas are those with at least 50% of the population living in low-density areas (grid cells in Europe, local units, e.g. municipalities in non-European OECD countries), intermediate areas have 20-50% of their population in low-density grid cells in Europe and 15-50% in local units in non-European OECD countries (OECD, 2016[49]).

27. See Lee (2016[20]) for a macroeconomic view on the economics of ageing societies.

28. Excludes countries without predominantly rural TL3 regions.

29. See OECD (2015[48]) and The State of European Cities 2016 (European Commission and UN-HABITAT, 2016[43]) for recent estimates on global urbanisation trends.

30. For Europe, total urbanisation actually declined between 1990 and 2015 (European Commission, 2016[28]). The flow into metropolitan areas is therefore not only a shift from rural to urban areas, but also from smaller to larger urban agglomerations.

31. The onset of the crisis occurred at different points in time in different countries and regions. Consequently, the analysis considers the larger of the two values for per capita GDP in 2007 and 2008 as the peak of the growth period and the lower of the two values as the starting point for its development since the crisis.

32. See also Annex Figure 1.A.1, which zooms into the left panel of the figure and shows the regions' TL2 codes.

33. North Dakota is the notable exception, with per capita GDP growth of more than 45% both before and since the crisis, most likely driven by the natural resource boom in the state.

34. NUTS 1 regions where data for NUTS 2 regions was not available.

35. This argument is echoed by OECD (2016[1]) and European Commission (2017[27]). The absence of EU cohesion policy during the 2007-08 crisis in particular might have created even bigger investment shortfalls in many parts of Europe.

36. See e.g. Young (1995[12]), who highlights the key role of factor accumulation (labour participation, skills and capital) in explaining successful growth in East Asian countries.

37. See (OECD, 2015[44]) for details.

38. Basic economic models of wage setting find that firms pay wages equal to the value marginal product of a worker, i.e. the value of the additional output produced by the worker's efforts. In more elaborate models (e.g. Equilibrium Search and Matching Framework) productivity still determines part of the wage, but another part depends on the shared benefit (the economic rent) that is created for the firm as a job is filled. See Mortensen and Pissarides (1994[17]) and Burdett and Mortensen (1998[35]) for the seminal models in this literature.

39. See e.g. OECD (2016[16]) for a discussion on how to boost productivity and simultaneously reduce inequalities.

40. An extreme view was propagated by Jack Welch (2005[13]), dubbed "manager of the century" by Fortune Magazine (1999[34]), who famously promoted a "differentiation" strategy that ranked employee performance and argued that termination of the bottom-10% performers was the only way for companies to go forward.

41. Baily, Bartelsman and Haltiwanger (1996[37]) document a similar variation in US manufacturing firms that managed to combine productivity and employment growth and those that did not. They find that manufacturing plants that increased both employment and productivity contributed almost as much to overall productivity growth in the 1980s as those that increased productivity while reducing employment.

42. Adalet McGowan, Andrews and Millot (Adalet McGowan, Andrews and Millot, 2017[40]) document a large and rising percentage of firms that struggle to meet their interest payments, which is partly linked to prevailing insolvency regimes that limit restructuring and reallocation of capital and labour towards more productive firms (Adalet McGowan, Andrews and Millot, 2017[41]).

43. See e.g. Boulhol and Turner (2009[36]) for a model that also considers heterogeneous labour and that shows the importance of taking the local demographic structure into account when assessing the productivity-employment relationship.

44. Gordon (1997[22]) outlines the argument that capital investment and divestment create a dynamic path that leads to unemployment reduction after an initial structural shock to the economy…a shock that results in higher growth in productivity and unemployment.

45. Cross-country evidence for OECD countries based on a policy indicators on insolvency regimes constructed based on a recent OECD questionnaire to member countries (Adalet McGowan, Andrews and Millot, 2017[41]).

46. See Dew-Becker and Gordon (2012[31]), who discuss why the impetus from deregulation and improved labour market flexibility in Europe seems to not have led to productivity and employment growth between the mid-1990s and the onset of the global crisis.

47. Misallocation seems to be prevalent in parts of Europe and likely contributed to low growth before the crisis. Researchers have proposed several explanations for the increase in misallocation. Gopinath et al. (2017[23]) suggest that the trends towards capital misallocation in Europe's south arise from financial friction. As interest rates were declining and investment opportunities were opening up, firms that had higher net worth – and therefore collateral – were able to invest more than firms with low net worth. But firms with high net worth were not necessarily more productive, which led to an imbalance in investment and lower returns. For Portugal, Reis (2013[15]) stresses the role of an underdeveloped domestic credit market that favoured lending in less-productive non-tradable sectors.

48. Whether this has fully materialised is not clear. At least one study fails to find evidence for improved allocation of capital in Spain (Gopinath et al., 2017[23]). Taking the dispersion of return on capital as a measure of misallocation – the idea being that the wider the spread in returns the more room exists for better allocation of capital – the authors find that misallocation accelerated in Spain between 2008 and 2012.

49. See Foster, Grim and Haltiwanger (2016[26]) for details.

50. For more details see OECD (2016[1]).

51. For the individual country productivity profiles, the reader can refer to the country pages of the OECD regional Outlook 2016 (OECD, 2016[1]).

52. See Bachtler et al. (2017[10]) for more detail.

References

Adalet McGowan, M., D. Andrews and V. Millot (2017), "The Walking Dead?: Zombie Firms and Productivity Performance in OECD Countries", *OECD Economics Department Working Papers*, No. 1372, OECD Publishing, Paris, http://dx.doi.org/10.1787/180d80ad-en. [40]

Adalet McGowan, M., D. Andrews and V. Millot (2017), "Insolvency regimes, zombie firms and capital reallocation", *OECD Economics Department Working Papers*, No. 1399, OECD Publishing, Paris, http://dx.doi.org/10.1787/5a16beda-en. [41]

Ahrend, R. et al. (2017), "What Makes Cities More Productive?: Agglomeration Economies and the Role of Urban Governance: Evidence from 5 OECD Countries", *OECD Productivity Working Papers*, No. 6, OECD Publishing, Paris, http://dx.doi.org/10.1787/2ce4b893-en. [39]

Angerer, G. et al. (2009), "Rohstoffe für Zukunftstechnologien: Einfluss des branchenspezifischen Rohstoffbedarfs in rohstoffintensiven Zukunftstechnologien auf die zukünftige Rohstoffnachfrage", *Schlussbericht*, Fraunhofer Institut für System- und Innovationsforschung and Institut für Zukunftsstudien und Technologiebewertung. [38]

Bachtler, J. et al. (2017), *Towards Cohesion Policy 4.0: Structural Transformation and Inclusive Growth*, Regional Studies Association (RSA Europe). [10]

Baily, M., E. Bartelsman and J. Haltiwanger (1996), "Downsizing and Productivity Growth: Myth or Reality?", *Small Business Economics*, Vol. 8/4, pp. 259-278. [37]

BMF (2012), *Ausgleichsbeträge (-) und Ausgleichszuweisungen im Länderfinanzausgleich in den Jahren 1950 bis 1994*, http://www.bundesfinanzministerium.de/Content/DE/Standardartikel/Themen/Oeffentliche_Finanzen/Foederale_Finanzbeziehungen/Laenderfinanzausgleich/Ausgleichsbetrage-und-Ausgleichszuweisungen-im-Laenderfinanzausgleich.pdf (accessed on 14 November 2017). [3]

Boulhol, H. and L. Turner (2009), "Employment-Productivity Trade-off and Labour Composition", *OECD Economics Department Working Papers*, No. 698, OECD Publishing, Paris, http://dx.doi.org/10.1787/224146182015. [36]

Burdett, K. and D. Mortensen (1998), "Wage Differentials, Employer Size, and Unemployment", *International Economic Review*, Vol. 39/2, pp. 257-273. [35]

Calvino, F., C. Criscuolo and C. Menon (2015), "Cross-country evidence on start-up dynamics", *OECD Science, Technology and Industry Working Papers*, No. 2015/6, OECD Publishing, Paris, http://dx.doi.org/10.1787/5jrxtkb9mxtb-en. [8]

Colvin, G. (1999), "The Ultimate Manager: In a Time of Hidebound, Formulaic Thinking, General Electric's Jack Welch Gave Power to the Worker and the Shareholder", *Fortune Magazine*. [34]

Combes, P., T. Mayer and J. Thisse (2008), *Economic Geography: The Integration of Regions and Nations*, Princeton University Press, Princeton and Oxford. [33]

Criscuolo, C., P. Gal and C. Menon (2014), "The Dynamics of Employment Growth: New Evidence from 18 Countries", *OECD Science, Technology and Industry Policy Papers*, No. 14, OECD Publishing, Paris, http://dx.doi.org/10.1787/5jz417hj6hg6-en. [7]

Cronon, W. (1991), *Nature's Metropolis: Chicago and the Great West*, W.W. Norton, London. [32]

Dew-Becker, I. and R. Gordon (2012), "The Role of Labor-Market Changes in the Slowdown of European Productivity Growth", *Review of Economics and Institutions*, Vol. 3/2, pp. 1-45. [31]

Donaldson, D. and R. Hornbeck (2016), "Railroads and American Economic Growth: A "Market Access" Approach", *The Quarterly Journal of Economics*, Vol. 131/2, pp. 799-858. [4]

Duranton, G. (2011), "California Dreamin': The Feeble Case for Cluster Policies", *Review of Economic Analysis*, Vol. 3/1, pp. 3-45. [30]

Easterly, W. (2001), *The Elusive Quest for Growth : Economists' Adventures and Misadventures in the Tropics*, MIT Press. [29]

European Commission and UN-HABITAT (2016), *The State of European Cities 2016: Cities leading the way to a better future*, European Commission, Publications Office of the European Union. [43]

Pesaresi, M. et al. (eds.) (2016), *Atlas of the Human Planet 2016: Mapping Human Presence on Earth with the Global Human Settlement Layer*, EUROPA. [28]

European Commission (2017), *Seventh Report on Economic, Social and Territorial Cohesion: My Region, My Europe, Our Future*, European Commission. [27]

European Commission (2017), "Competitiveness in Low-Income and Low-Growth Regions: The Lagging Regions Report", *European Commission Staff Working Document*, European Commission. [11]

Foster, L., C. Grim and J. Haltiwanger (2016), "Reallocation in the Great Recession: Cleansing or Not?", *Journal of Labor Economics*, Vol. 34/S1, pp. S293-S331. [26]

Fujita, M., P. Krugman and A. Venables (1999), *The Spatial Economy: Cities, Regions and International Trade*, MIT Press, Cambridge. [25]

Gill, I. and H. Kharas (2015), "The Middle-Income Trap Turns Ten", *World Bank Group Policy Research Working Paper*, No. 7403, The World Bank Group. [24]

Gopinath, G. et al. (2017), "Capital Allocation and Productivity in South Europe", *The Quarterly Journal of Economics*, Vol. 132/4, pp. 1915-1967. [23]

Gordon, R. (1997), "Is There a Tradeoff between Unemployment and Productivity Growth?", in Snower, D. and G. de la Dehesa (eds.), *Unemployment Policy: Government Options for the Labour Market*, Cambridge University Press. [22]

Haltiwanger, J. et al. (2017), "High-Growth Young Firms: Contribution to Job, Output, and Productivity Growth", in Haltiwanger, J. et al. (eds.), *NBER Studies in Income and Wealth: Measuring Entrepreneurial Businesses - Current Knowledge and Challenges*, National Bureau of Economic Research, The University of Chicago Press. [9]

Kerr, W. and S. Kominers (2015), "Agglomerative Forces and Cluster Shapes", *Review of Economics and Statistics*, Vol. 97/4, pp. 877–899. [5]

Krugman, P. (1995), *The Age of Diminished Expectations*, MIT Press. [21]

Lee, R. (2016), "Macroeconomics, Aging and Growth", in Piggott, J. and A. Woodland (eds.), *Handbook of the Economics of Population Aging*, North Holland. [20]

Lembcke, A. and K. Maguire (2017), "Arbeitsproduktivität: Eine Herausforderung für alle RegionenHighlights des OECD Regional Outlook 2016: Productive Regions for Inclusive Societies", *Wirtschaftspolitische Blätter* 1/2017, pp. 7-19. [19]

Matray, A. (2014), "The Local Innovation Spillovers of Listed Firms", *Unpublished manuscript*, HEC Paris. [6]

McCann, P. (2016), *The UK Regional-National Economic Problem: Geography, Globalisation and Governance*, Regional Studies Association, Regions and Cities, Routledge. [2]

Moretti, E. (2012), *The New Geography of Jobs*, Houghton Mifflin Harcourt. [18]

Mortensen, D. and C. Pissarides (1994), "Job Creation and Job Destruction in the Theory of Unemployment", *The Review of Economic Studies*, Vol. 61/3, pp. 397-415. [17]

OECD (2014), *OECD Regional Outlook 2014: Regions and Cities: Where Policies and People Meet*, OECD Publishing, Paris, http://dx.doi.org/10.1787/9789264201415-en. [45]

OECD (2014), *How's Life in Your Region?: Measuring Regional and Local Well-being for Policy Making*, OECD Publishing, Paris, http://dx.doi.org/10.1787/9789264217416-en. [47]

OECD (2015), *The Future of Productivity*, OECD Publishing, Paris, http://dx.doi.org/10.1787/9789264248533-en. [44]

OECD (2015), *The Metropolitan Century: Understanding Urbanisation and its Consequences*, OECD Publishing, Paris, http://dx.doi.org/10.1787/9789264228733-en. [48]

OECD (2016), *The Productivity-Inclusiveness Nexus: Preliminary version*, OECD Publishing, Paris. [16]

OECD (2016), *Well-being in Danish Cities*, OECD Publishing, Paris, http://dx.doi.org/10.1787/9789264265240-en. [42]

OECD (2016), *OECD Regional Outlook 2016: Productive Regions for Inclusive Societies*, OECD Publishing, Paris, http://dx.doi.org/10.1787/9789264260245-en. [1]

OECD (2016), *Job Creation and Local Economic Development 2016*, OECD Publishing, Paris, http://dx.doi.org/10.1787/9789264261976-en. [46]

OECD (2016), *OECD Regional Outlook 2016: Productive Regions for Inclusive Societies*, OECD Publishing, Paris, http://dx.doi.org/10.1787/9789264260245-en. [49]

Reis, R. (2013), "The Portuguese Slump and Crash and the Euro Crisis", *Brookings Papers on Economic Activity*, Vol. 46/1, pp. 143-210. [15]

Storper, M. et al. (2015), *The Rise and Fall of Urban Economies: Lessons from San Francisco and Los Angeles*, Stanford University Press. [14]

Welch, J. (2005), *Winning*, with S. Welch, HarperBusiness. [13]

Young, A. (1995), "The Tyranny of Numbers: Confronting the Statistical Realities of the East Asian Growth Experience", *The Quarterly Journal of Economics*, Vol. 110/3, pp. 641-680. [12]

Annex 1.A. Low-growth and low-income regions in Europe

Annex Table 1.A.1. Classification of European low-growth and low-income regions

Low-growth regions		Low-income regions	
NUTS 3	Name	NUTS 3	Name
ES42	Castilla-La Mancha	BG31	Severozapaden
ES61	Andalucía	BG32	Severen tsentralen
ES62	Región de Murcia	BG33	Severoiztochen
ES64	Ciudad Autónoma de Melilla	BG34	Yugoiztochen
ES70	Canarias	BG42	Yuzhen tsentralen
GR11	Anatoliki Makedonia, Thraki	HU23	Dél-Dunántúl
GR12	Kentriki Makedonia	HU31	Észak-Magyarország
GR13	Dytiki Makedonia	HU32	Észak-Alföld
GR14	Thessalia	HU33	Dél-Alföld
GR21	Ipeiros	PL31	Lubelskie
GR22	Ionia Nisia	PL32	Podkarpackie
GR23	Dytiki Ellada	PL33	Świętokrzyskie
GR24	Sterea Ellada	PL34	Podlaskie
GR25	Peloponnisos	PL62	Warmińsko-Mazurskie
GR41	Voreio Aigaio	RO11	Nord-Vest
GR43	Kriti	RO21	Nord-Est
ITF1	Abruzzo	RO22	Sud-Est
ITF2	Molise	RO31	Sud - Muntenia
ITF3	Campania	RO41	Sud-Vest Oltenia
ITF4	Puglia		
ITF5	Basilicata		
ITF6	Calabria		
ITG1	Sicilia		
ITG2	Sardegna		
PT11	Norte		
PT15	Algarve		
PT16	Centro (PT)		
PT18	Alentejo		

Source: European Commision (2017[11]).

Annex Figure 1.A.1. For some regions the 2007-08 crisis halted growth only briefly, others entered prolonged decline

Per capita GDP growth before/since the 2007 08 crisis in regions with above median growth before the crisis

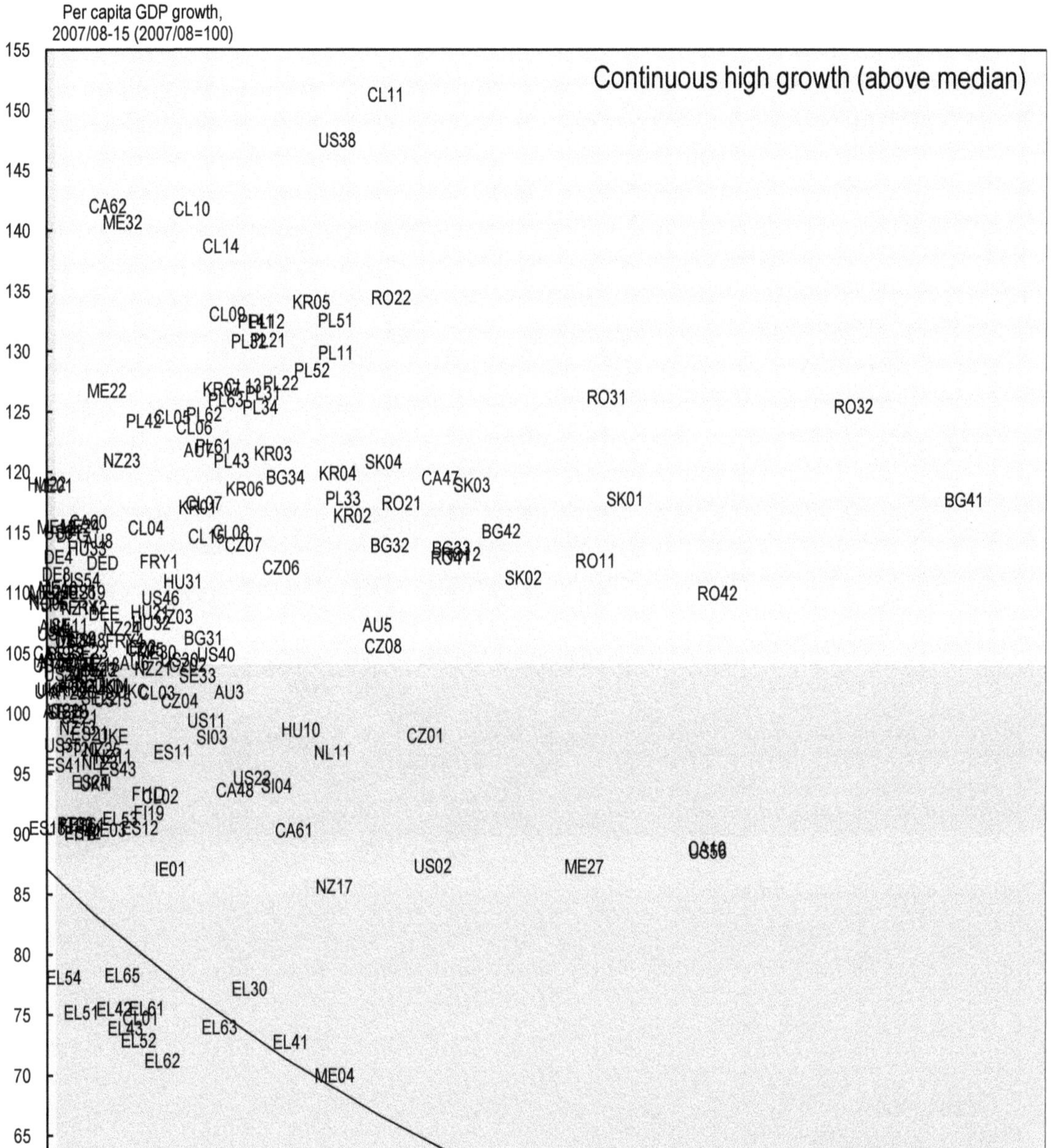

Note: Real per capita GDP growth in large (TL2) regions from 2000 (or closest year available) to 2007-08 (lower value) and from 2007-08 (higher value) to 2015 or closest year available. Shaded quadrants depict the above/below median value growth (median for 2000-07/08: 115.9; 2007/08-15: 104.1). The solid black line indicates the growth rates that lead to stagnation between 2000 and 2015, i.e. the decline after the 2007-08 crisis offsets the growth from before the crisis.
Source: Calculations based on OECD Regional Statistics [Database]

Annex Figure 1.A.2. Growth in many regions stagnated even before the 2007-08 crisis

Per capita GDP growth before/since the 2007-08 crisis in regions with below median growth before the crisis

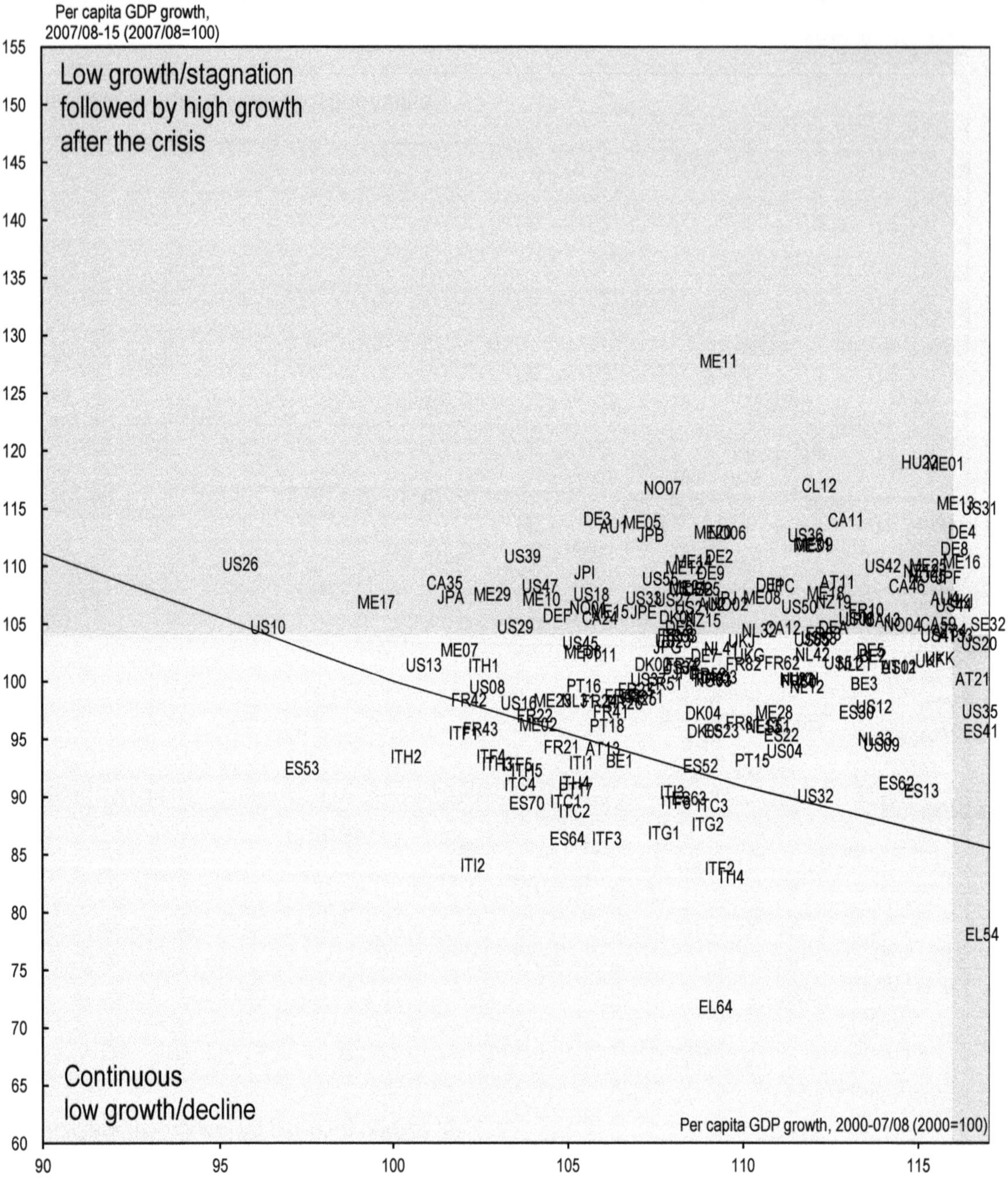

Note: Real per capita GDP growth in large (TL2) regions from 2000 (or closest year available) to 2007-08 (lower value) and from 2007-08 (higher value) to 2015 or closest year available. Shaded quadrants depict the above/below median value growth (median for 2000-07/08: 115.9; 2007/08-15: 104.1). The solid black line indicates the growth rates that lead to stagnation between 2000 and 2015, i.e. the decline after the 2007-08 crisis offsets the growth from before the crisis.
Source: Calculations based on OECD Regional Statistics [Database]

Chapter 2. Thinking global, developing local: Tradable sectors, cities and their role for catching up

The key challenge for policy is how to sustain aggregate growth while promoting catching up of lagging regions and job creation at the same time. This is a daunting challenge as there are some clear trade-offs outlined in Chapter 1. This chapter considers two important characteristics of regions that support catching up in terms of labour productivity.

Chapter synopsis

Regions that were able to narrow the productivity gap with their country's most productive "frontier" region distinguish themselves from regions that were further diverging from the frontier in two important characteristics. These characteristics are a strong and growing tradable sector and the presence of well-functioning cities.

In European regions that were catching up, tradable sectors contributed, on average, about 37% of the total output in the region in 2000 and this percentage increased even further to nearly 40% in 2014. In contrast, diverging regions started with a lower percentage of gross value added (GVA) in tradable sectors in 2000 than catching-up regions and the contribution of tradable sectors had not increased by 2014. In tradable sectors – those that could be traded – growth and success of the firm is not limited by the size of the local market, at the same time firms in tradable sectors are exposed to international competition and need to be dynamic and innovative to succeed.

A breakdown of the productivity dynamics in regions shows that in the tradable sector, increasing productivity was based on improvements by firms within the sector and region over the 2000-13 period. For non-tradable sectors this within-sector and region improvement accounts for only half the growth, the other half was due to shifts of employment from less to more productive non-tradable economic activities.

Manufacturing is still a key element of the tradable sector, but tradable activities are not limited to manufacturing. Tradable services accounted for 15% of total regional output in 2013 and they had the highest growth rates – more than 2.5% per year between 2000 and 2013 in most European regions. Yet, many regions are not taking advantage of this potential. In European regions with the lowest per capita GDP levels and growth rates, tradable services grew by a mere 1% annually between 2000 and 2013.

A focus on tradable sectors might be seen to increase the exposure to global shocks and risks the jobs and livelihoods of people in a region. The experience of European regions before and since the 2007-08 crisis shows that the opposite is the case. On average, employment grew by about 0.7% annually between 2008 and 2014 in regions that experienced only small shifts in employment to the non-tradable sector before the crisis. In contrast, regions that experienced strong shifts experienced an average decline in employment of nearly 1% and the 10% of regions with the largest pre crisis shifts also experienced the strongest post crisis employment losses (2.9% annually).

Well-functioning cities contribute to productivity dynamics through different channels. They attract more tradable services and high-tech manufacturing activities, whereas rural areas tend to specialise in mature manufacturing sectors and resource extraction. Business creation tends to be most dynamic in a country's region that includes the largest or capital city. An important reason for these patterns and for productivity differences within a country are so-called "agglomeration economies".

The positive economic impact of a city does not need to be constrained by its limits but is often measureable well into a city's surroundings. By linking rural regions and cities, policies can make an important difference in the degree to which they can harness the benefits of agglomeration economies. These links include physical transport connections but are not limited to them. Large cities also come with pecuniary and non-pecuniary "agglomeration costs". Congestion, environmental degradation, high housing prices and other downsides from agglomeration partially offset the productivity gains from agglomeration and reduce the well-being of urban residents.

Two key factors in narrow the regional productivity gap within countries

Tradable sectors are associated with successful catching up

The first factor is tradable activities' relatively large contribution to the regional economy. Tradable sectors are those that produce goods or services that can be traded across regions and international borders. The analysis in this chapter does not focus on actual trade, which will be covered in Chapter 3. Instead, the following sections consider economic activities that could be traded irrespective of whether such trade actually takes place.

At the regional level this distinction between traded and tradable is often academic. Those sectors that are tradable typically engage in some trade. But it acknowledges that firms can operate in sectors that are tradable without actually engaging in trade themselves. Even without selling their goods and services abroad, firms in tradable sectors are exposed to competition from abroad. Farmers selling their produce on local markets compete with the supply from other regions or countries, a programmer working for a local company needs to provide a better service than those that can be purchased cheaply on global platforms, or a carpenter needs to offer furniture that meets local needs better than the furniture available at global furniture chains.

What unifies trade and tradability is hence the need to be competitive in a global environment. Competitiveness is a diffuse term that is often solely focused on "cost competitiveness", i.e. producing a given amount of output at costs that are on par with those in other regions or countries. This view can easily lead to an excessive focus on cost savings, e.g. by limiting wage growth. But this is a view that is too narrow. Competitiveness can also be enhanced by using technology to improve production, developing new markets and products, and rethinking the way goods are produced.

Well-functioning cities support productivity within their limits and beyond

The second characteristic associated with catching up is a well-functioning link between cities and regions. Through "agglomeration benefits", firms and workers are more productive in larger (and denser) cities than they would be in smaller cities or rural areas. Agglomeration benefits arise, in part, when firms gain access to a larger market for their goods and services. Firms can increasingly specialise as the size of the local market increases, which raises their productivity.[1] It also allows workers to find jobs that better match their skills, and firms to fill vacancies with better suited candidates, i.e. those that will be the most productive in the job. A third channel relates to the potential for more frequent interaction between people and firms. The knowledge gained and shared in talking to other people or in discovering other firms' innovations and techniques can help companies generate new ideas, products or processes, which they can leverage to become more productive.

"Agglomeration benefits" are not necessarily limited to the borders of a city. Firms in the surrounding rural areas can access lawyers, marketing specialists or logistics services in larger cities. Rural areas, within easy commuting distance from large cities, provide an alternative to dense urban living and can attract firms through lower land prices while providing access to the large pool of workers the nearby city provides. The strength of these links depends on local infrastructure and integration of the main city with its surrounding area.

Tradable sectors are associated with successful catching up

Many regions that were lagging behind the most productive "frontier" regions in their country were able to narrow the gap between 2000 and 2014. The OECD Regional Outlook 2016 considers a range of possible characteristics that support this "catching-up" process (OECD, 2016[1]). Few characteristics distinguish regions that were narrowing the gap from those that fell further behind their country's frontier region(s),[2] but one important feature appears to be the contribution of tradable sectors to overall economic production (Figure 2.1). In European regions that were catching up, tradable sectors accounted for, on average, about 37% of the total output in their respective region in 2000 and this percentage increased even further to nearly 40% in 2014. In contrast, diverging regions started with a lower percentage of gross value added (GVA) in tradable sectors in 2000 than catching-up regions and the contribution of tradables had not increased by 2014.

The growth in contribution to total output is, however, not accompanied by an increase in the contribution to total employment. In fact, in both types of regions, i.e. those catching up to and those diverging from the frontier, the number of employees in tradable sectors has declined as a percentage of overall employment, on average (OECD, 2016[1]). The share of tradable sectors in employment is initially smaller than its contribution to GVA and did not follow the increase (or stagnation) of the contribution to total output. This implies that tradable sectors were not only more productive than non-tradable sectors in 2000, their productivity advantage increased further.[3] This increasing gap between tradable sectors that raise productivity (and thereby wages) and non-tradable sectors that create jobs poses a challenge for sustained growth in the region (as outlined later in this chapter, in the section entitled, "Is a large tradable sector more risky for a region?"). It also raises the concern that income inequality will (further) increase.[4] As sustainable wage growth is tied to productivity growth, the divergence in productivity will also be reflected in income divergence.

In some cases, the decline in employment is concentrated in particular sectors or regions. In Korea, for instance, employment in agriculture across all regions fell by 26% between 2008 and 2014, while output remained constant, reducing the number of jobs in the sector by more than half a million.[5] The total output in the sector slightly increased, but job losses were only partially compensated by an increase in other tradable sectors (e.g. manufacturing). The largest increases in employment in Korean regions were in public services (public administration, health, social affairs and education) and retail, transport and hospitality services, but skills required for agricultural work are not necessarily transferable to activities in these sectors and workers might find the shift towards new opportunities difficult or even impossible, especially while retaining a decent wage (also see the section below, "Successful sectoral transitions require skills, ideas and stamina").

Figure 2.1. Economies in "catching-up" regions are more focused on tradable sectors

Contribution of tradable sectors to gross value added and employment in TL3 regions

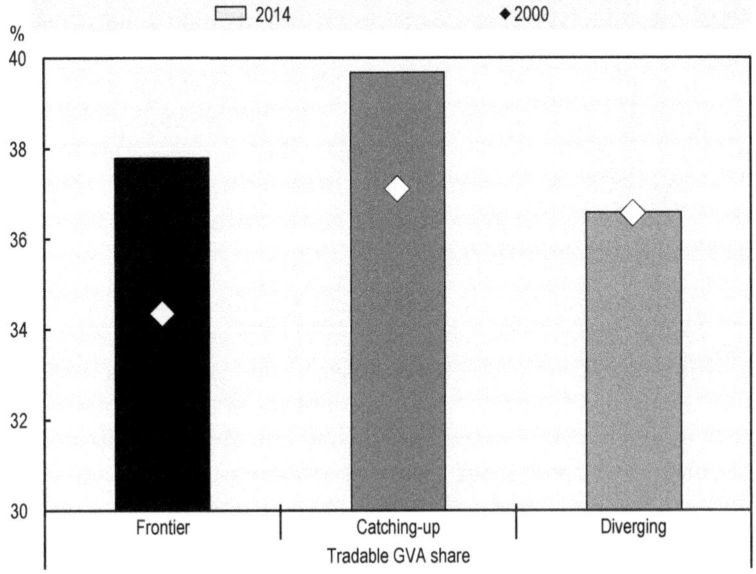

Note: Catching-up/diverging regions grew by at least 5 percentage points in 14 years more/less than their national frontier over the 2000-14 period. The frontier is defined as the aggregation of regions with the highest GDP per worker and representing 10% of national employment. Due to lack of regional data over the period, only 22 countries are included in the averages. Tradable sectors are defined by a selection of the 10 industries defined in the SNA 2008. They include: agriculture (A), industry (BCDE), information and communication (J), financial and insurance activities (K), and other services (RSTU). Non-tradable sectors include construction, distributive trade, repairs, transport, accommodation, food services activities (GHI), real estate activities (L), business services (MN), and public administration (OPQ).
Source: OECD (2016[1]) and OECD Regional Statistics [Database].

StatLink http://dx.doi.org/10.1787/888933707836

Tradables are not just manufactured goods and natural resources

What constitutes a tradable good or service is difficult to delineate. Ranging from goods and services to the industries in which they are produced amplifies the challenge. Innovation in communication, transport and other sectors also changes which goods and services can be traded and the extent to which they can be traded. Data-driven delineations often rely on actual trade volumes to assess whether an industry is "tradable" (De Gregorio, Giovannini and Wolf, 1994[2]). Another avenue is the localisation of industries, in particular of services. Non-tradable services are those that are distributed widely across a given territory, while those that are geographically concentrated are considered tradable (Jensen et al., 2005[3]). Despite being data-driven, both methodologies retain a degree of arbitrariness as both require the choice of thresholds, either for the degree of trade exposure or the degree of concentration.

As most physical goods can be shipped fairly easily, manufacturing, agricultural production and resource extraction are considered tradable sectors. Conversely, non-tradable services typically include governmental services, education, health care, the construction sector and retail. A growing range of business and technical services is becoming increasingly tradable, but a large percentage remains local. Marketing or public relations agencies have a global reach, lawyers much less so and cleaning services are clearly a locally provided and non-tradable service. Another challenge arises in when it comes to hotels and restaurants. While tourism is an important contributor to the trade balance in some regions, they provide mainly domestic or even only local services.

Since industry-level data for OECD regions is only available for a maximum of 10 industry groups, the classification of tradable and non-tradable sectors will inadvertently require some compromise. Following the OECD Regional Outlook 2016, tradable sectors are defined as agriculture (A), industry (BCDE), information and communication services (J), financial and insurance activities (K), and other services (RSTU). Non-tradable sectors are composed of construction, distributive trade, repairs, transport, accommodation, food services activities (GHI), real estate activities (L), business services (MN), and public administration (OPQ).

All types of tradable sectors can create productivity growth. It is not "just" the goods manufacturing sector; indeed, resource extraction and tradable services can also be drivers of growth. Increasingly, tradable services are gaining in importance among tradable sectors. In the United States, they account for about half of the value added in tradable sectors (Gervais and Jensen, 2013[4]). In Europe, the relative size of tradable service sectors and goods producing sectors is similar across regions (see the section, "Sustaining growth requires sectoral transition"). There is, however, an important difference between manufacturing and tradable services. Manufacturing has traditionally employed not only the highly skilled, but also a large number of medium- and low-skilled workers at relatively high wages, which sets it apart from other high-productivity sectors such as mining or finance (Rodrik, 2016[5]).

What makes tradable sectors different?

Tradable sectors are more exposed to international competition than non-tradable sectors. While this might seem obvious, it has a direct impact on the economic mechanisms that affect firms in tradable sectors. For firms, it means that growth and success are not limited to the size of the local market. A company might start out serving the local community, but tradable sectors can extend their reach beyond their local borders. This decouples the growth of tradables, to a certain degree, from the rest of the economy. The flipside of wider reach is that competition is also fiercer. This includes not only actual competition as firms start exporting, but also potential competition as companies from other regions or countries could enter a firm's local market. For tradable goods and services this limits the flexibility firms have in setting prices.

To remain profitable, firms active in tradable sectors need to be dynamic and innovate, either to align costs of production with the prices that they can reasonably charge for their products, or by creating new products and carving out niches that allow them to gain some pricing power. This process can create significant positive effects for other firms in the area. A study on the impact of the opening of large scale manufacturing plants in counties in the United States between 1980 and the early 1990s finds that the productivity of other existing firms in the county increased by an additional 12% over 5 years compared to productivity in firms in comparable counties where the large manufacturing plant did not locate.[6] Moretti (2010[6]) finds substantial job creation multipliers associated with the tradable (manufacturing) sector in the United States. For each job created in manufacturing, the number of local jobs in non-tradable goods and services increases by 1.6. In Sweden, Moretti and Thulin (2013[7]) find a smaller multiplier, with estimates ranging from 0.4 to 0.8 jobs.

The drivers of productivity growth differ in tradable and non-tradable sectors

Productivity in a country or a region can increase as the economic sectors become more productive, e.g. because firms invest in new machinery, create new products or implement more efficient processes of creating their goods or services. At the sectoral level, this growth can be driven by incumbent firms or when new, more productive and dynamic firms enter the market and force out older, less productive firms. This source of productivity growth is the "within" component in a three-way decomposition of productivity growth (Box 2.1).

Box 2.1. Breaking down labour productivity growth

Sectoral and regional contributions to labour productivity growth

Labour productivity growth can be broken down by sector or region in a multitude of ways including one useful method that divides labour productivity into three components: the productivity growth of the units (within), the reallocation of employment towards the initially more productive units (reallocation level) and the reallocation of employment towards units with faster labour productivity growth (reallocation growth).

With GDP measured at constant prices, labour productivity (LP) measured as real GDP per worker in a country (i) and year (t), i.e. $\frac{GDP_{it}}{EMP_{it}}$, can be expressed as the sum of sectoral/regional labour productivity weighted by the employment share (ES) of the sector/region with j indexing sectors/regions.

$$LP_{it} = \sum_{\forall j} LP_{ijt} * ES_{ijt}$$

The growth rate in labour productivity can be separated into two components, one that depends on the change in sectoral/regional labour productivity and a second component that captures the change in employment in more or less productive sectors and regions. The result indicates that both relative shifts in employment across sectors or regions – as well as productivity growth within sectors/regions – contribute to productivity growth. However, the initial formula does not have a straightforward interpretation. Moreover, the combination of beginning- and end-period as "weights" for the changes is not very intuitive either.

$$\dot{LP}_{it} = \frac{LP_{it} - LP_{it-1}}{LP_{it-1}}$$

$$= \frac{\sum_{\forall j}\left(LP_{ijt} - LP_{ijt-1}\right) * ES_{ijt} + LP_{ijt-1} * \left(ES_{ijt} - ES_{ijt-1}\right)}{LP_{it-1}}$$

Different options exist to change the breakdown into a more easily interpretable formula. The drawback of having several options is that there is no unique decomposition of labour productivity growth. The traditional choice is to add and subtract $\frac{LP_{ijt-1}}{LP_{it-1}} ES_{ijt-1} \dot{LP}_{ijt}$ to/from the above formula, which yields a formula with three distinct terms.

$$\dot{LP}_{it} = \sum_{\forall j} \frac{GDP_{ijt-1}}{GDP_{it-1}} \dot{LP}_{ijt} + \frac{LP_{ijt-1}}{LP_{it-1}} \Delta ES_{ijt} + \dot{LP}_{ijt} \frac{LP_{ijt-1}}{LP_{it-1}} \Delta ES_{ijt}$$

The first term captures the direct contribution of sectoral/regional labour productivity growth to total productivity growth. The direct contribution of a sector/region is larger than its initial contribution to the economy (GDP share). The second and third term capture the reallocation of employment towards sectors/regions that were more (or less) productive in the base period (second term) and those where labour productivity grew or declined (third term).

Source: Based on de Avillez (2012[8]).

Another source of productivity growth is the shift of employment from less to more productive sectors or from less to more productive regions. Here "less" or "more" is relative to the country's average productivity. Historically, productivity growth is increased by workers transitioning from agricultural production with low productivity to employment in manufacturing with significantly higher productivity. Relatedly, overtime productivity growth is also positively affected if employment shifts from sectors with low productivity growth to sectors with higher productivity growth. The shift of workers in a sector or region can be employment neutral, as workers move from one sector to another, but can also coincide with either employment growth or decline. Over the 2000-13 period, growth in tradable sectors was driven by within-sector productivity growth, i.e. the tradable sector became more productive. In contrast, productivity in non-tradable sectors grew mostly through employment shifts.[7]

Figure 2.2. Productivity growth in tradable sectors has been driven by improvements within these sectors

Drivers of labour productivity growth in tradable and non-tradable sectors, 2000-13

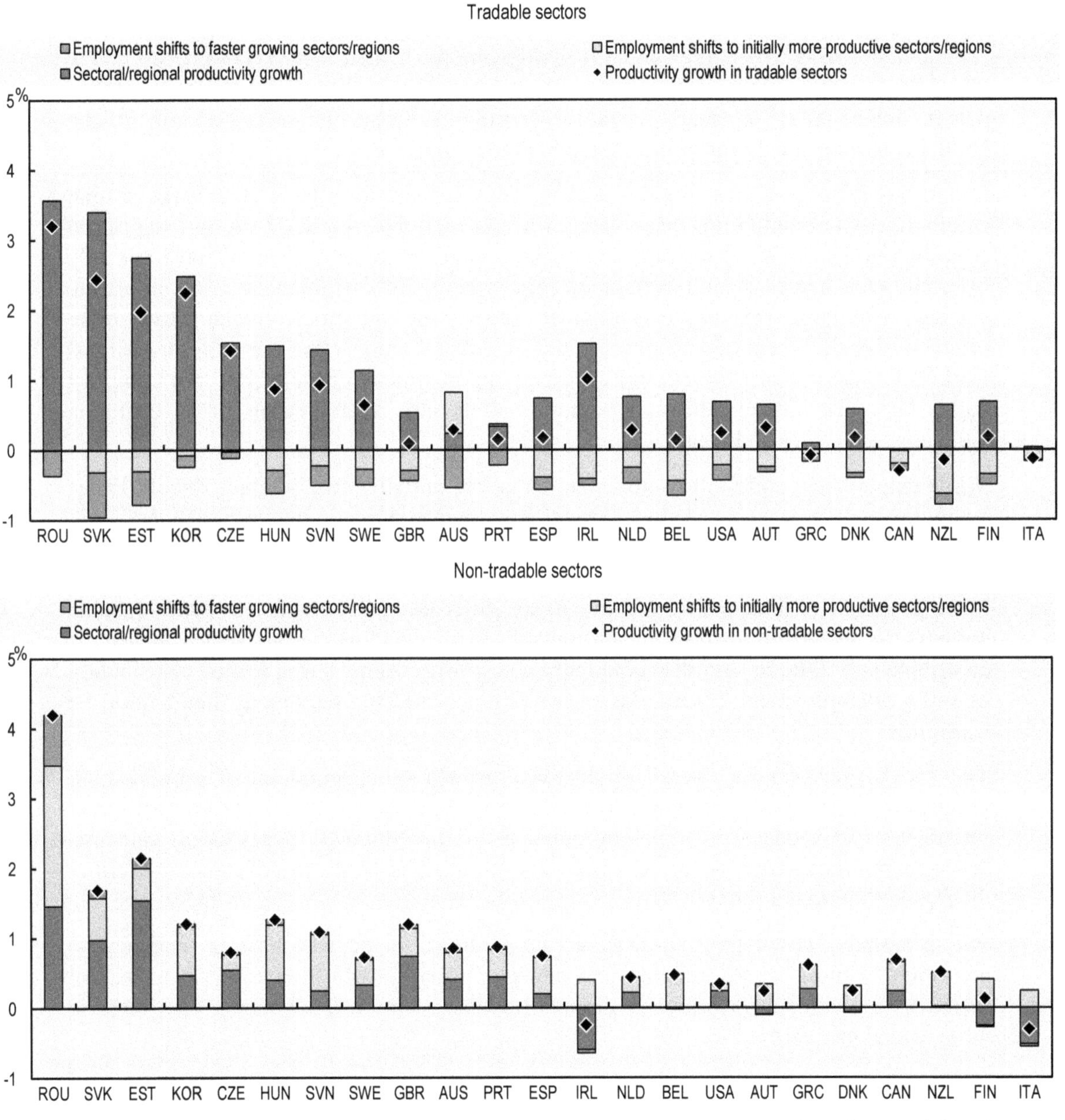

Note: Countries ordered by total productivity growth (highest to lowest). Labour productivity growth based on per worker GVA within tradable and non-tradable sectors. See Box 2.1 for details on the breakdown. Tradable sectors are defined by a selection of the 10 industries defined in the SNA 2008. They include: agriculture (A), industry (BCDE), information and communication (J), financial and insurance activities (K), and other services (RSTU). Non-tradable sectors are composed of construction, distributive trade, repairs, transport, accommodation, food services activities (GHI), real estate activities (L), business services (MN), and public administration (OPQ).

Source: Calculations based on OECD Regional Statistics [Database].

StatLink http://dx.doi.org/10.1787/888933707855

Employment shares shifting to more productive regions contributes to productivity growth in large (capital) city regions

A further breakdown of the productivity growth shows that the non-tradable transition of employment towards more productive non-tradable activities is mostly due to increased concentration in regions with large cities, typically regions that include the country's capital city. Taking Spain, the United Kingdom and the United States as examples, nearly all of the impact of jobs shifting towards more productive sectors or more productive places comes from a single region, Madrid in Spain, Greater London in the United Kingdom and Texas in the United States (Figure 2.3).

In part this is because these regions are big. They account for a large percentage of total employment and shifts in these large regions will be amplified in the aggregate contribution. But it is not just the size of the regions. Most other regions have not only little but even negative contributions of employment shifts to total growth. One of the reasons why large regions, in particular those with big cities, might create more productive employment opportunities in non-tradable sectors is that they offer the largest markets for services and therefore the greatest opportunities to benefit from economies of scale. They also attract more competitors and thereby create returns on investing in innovative processes and ideas.

While employment shifting towards sectors that are initially more productive contributes a significant percentage in Madrid, Greater London and Texas – between 40% and 50% of the regions' productivity growth contribution –the employment shift's overall contribution to national growth is actually very small (country aggregate in Figure 2.3). Since positive contributions from employment shifts are nearly exclusive to non-tradable sectors, the sectoral transition in non-tradable sectors within regions seems, hence, to contribute very little to overall productivity growth. The same is true for the contribution of shifts of employment towards faster growing non-tradable sectors, as they tend to be negligible.

The two key drivers for overall productivity growth – concentration of jobs in more productive regions and within-sector productivity improvements – have very different implications for inequality. While improving sectoral productivity raises living standards and opportunities everywhere, increased concentration is likely to contribute to further divergence within countries.

Put differently, productivity growth in the tradable sector will have a tendency to contribute to more spatial equality in a country, possibly with the exception of natural resources. In contrast, increases in the non-tradable sector will ultimately contribute to more spatial inequality.

Figure 2.3. Employment shifting towards more productive sectors and regions is concentrated in a few regions

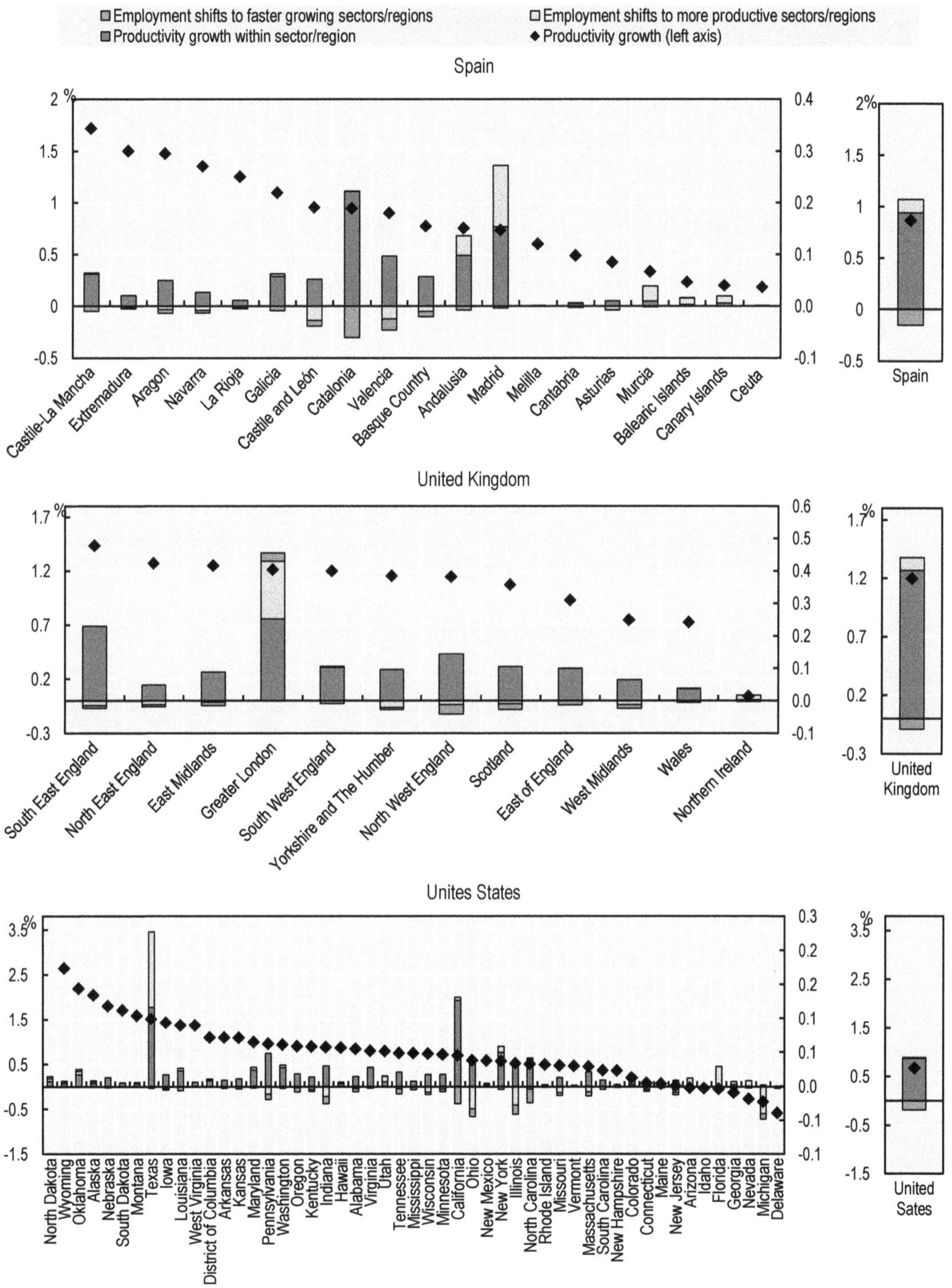

Note: The breakdown in national productivity growth equals the sum of the regional contributions. Regions are ordered by total labour productivity growth over the 2000-13 period. See also Figure 2.2.
Source: Calculations based on OECD Regional Statistics [Database]

StatLink http://dx.doi.org/10.1787/888933707874

Sustaining growth requires sectoral transition

The dynamism of tradable sectors is an essential feature of their success. Without constant innovation and progress, firms in tradable sectors risk falling behind competitors or being replaced by new entrants. The introduction of the assembly line by Henry Ford in 1913 and 1914 revolutionised the production of automobiles. Standardisation and separation of tasks increased efficiency and left the more flexible, but less efficient, craftsmen-based production model behind. In the 1950s, the Toyota Motor Company pioneered an adapted version of the mass production system that increased flexibility in the use of key machinery through the standardisation of components and replaced large inventories with "just-in-time" production chains.[8] The result was a rapid expansion in Toyota's production from less than 50 000 vehicles in 1955 to more than 400 000 in 1965 and 1.1 million in 1970, based on tremendous efficiency gains compared to their competitors.[9]

The innovation on the production side changed the way automobiles were assembled, quality was ensured and inventories were handled. But the product itself changed continuously as well. Today's cars still run on four wheels and have a steering wheel (at least for now), but little else remains of the 1914 Model T. This progress can change the face of an industry. Until 2003, apprentices in Germany were trained as car mechanics. Since 2003, the changing nature of cars and the car mechanic's job has been acknowledged and the prior separate tracks of car mechanic and car electrician have been merged into a joint vocational track in car mechatronics.[10]

Tradable services are becoming increasingly important

Despite all progress, car manufacturers still produce "just" cars. But the components that make up a car are dramatically changing. Beyond mechanical engineering, the need for new materials, chemicals and electrical components is matched by an increasing reliance on software to monitor and control the car. This transition means that services that support the production are becoming increasingly important. But the change is not limited to the product itself. Services are becoming increasingly attached to products. Car manufacturers operate their own banks to provide loans or manage leasing, and they run large budgets on marketing, spending more than the total gross domestic product of Slovenia or Lithuania.[11]

Car manufacturing is cited here just as an example, but the pattern is replicated in other industries, e.g. in footwear manufacturing (Box 2.2). The examples combine two important insights into industrial transition. The first is the constant change in the nature of products, new materials, new processes and new ways of using products, which requires industry to adapt constantly. The second is that services, especially those that are tradable, are becoming more prevalent and more prominent in production, opening up new opportunities.

Box 2.2. Transition towards services in the footwear sector

Rivera del Brenta, Italy

In the Riviera del Brenta industrial district in northern Italy, firms in the footwear sector have collaborated to pool investment in training while also collectively upgrading product market strategies in order to engage in high quality international markets. Not far from Venice, the region traditionally hosted cottage industries that mainly employed low-skilled blue collar workers. However, the area has now become a global centre for the production of high quality ladies footwear (supplying Giorgio Armani, Louis Vuitton, Chanel, Prada, Christian Dior among others). This was achieved when the local employers association, known as ACRIB, developed an international brand. High-skilled jobs in design, R&D, management and marketing have increased as a percentage of overall employment in the region. Before the 1993-94 repositioning, almost all workers in shoe manufacturing were blue collar workers; nowadays this proportion is around 40%, with the remaining 60% comprised roughly of 50% designers and 10% sales and marketing staff). Close co-operation with local unions ensured that improvements in productivity led to wage gains and better working conditions, particularly in terms of health and safety.

The economic development of the district has been driven by the privately-run local polytechnic, Politecnico Calzaturiero, which employs managers from surrounding companies to train local workers and job seekers after hours, while also offering management training, and investment in research, innovation and technology transfer. The organisation therefore invests in skills supply while also optimising skills utilisation through new product development and improved human resource management. The fact that firms are members of ACRIB means that they are less concerned about pooling training, technology and new innovations. Indeed, investment in local human capital will not only improve prospects for individual firms but also for the global brand as a whole.

Source: OECD (2014[9]) based on Froy, Giguère and Meghnagi (2012[10]).

Parts of Europe transition towards tradable services

Across Europe, a sectoral shift is underway in the core EU regions. Services account for more than 80% of the total output produced in 2014, with less than 20% of services were in the tradable sector. But tradable sectors are expanding rapidly with growth of more than 2.5% per year, while non-tradable services grew less than 1.4% per year over the 2000-14 period (Figure 2.4). Although industry, which includes manufacturing, is still larger than tradable services, at least in terms of total output produced, its slow growth means that tradable services are likely to overtake industrial production in the coming years.

Growth in low-income regions is led by industrial production

Tradable services do not play the same key role in all parts of Europe. In Europe's least-developed ("low-income") regions (i.e. those with less than 50% of the EU average per capita GDP) industrial production accounts for one-third of total output. In these regions, located in Bulgaria, Hungary, Poland and Romania, industry is also the fastest growing sector. Non-tradable services in these regions account for smaller shares of the regional economies than in other parts of Europe, but these sectors are growing at nearly the same pace as the industrial sector. But when it comes to tradable services, "low-income regions" are at the very early stages of development. Tradable services account for less than 6% of their economies and only grew at a rate of about 1.2% per year over the 2000-14 period (Figure 2.4). While that might be a relatively high growth rate in the overall EU context, among low-income regions the expansion of tradable services was slow, and even slower than growth in agriculture (1.5%).

Low-growth regions are struggling to diversify into tradable services

The picture is very different for struggling regions in Europe's south. Industrial production accounts for less than 14% of total output in these "low-growth" regions, which were lagging behind the EU average in terms of per capita GDP in the 2000s and grew below the EU average between 2000 and 2013.[12] In addition to already being a small sector, industry declined by 0.7% per year between 2000 and 2013 (Figure 2.4).

What is missing in "low-growth" regions is a transition towards new tradable opportunities. Non-tradable services account for more than 70% of total economic activity, with tradable services contributing less than 10% – one-third less than in other parts of Europe. In addition, tradable services only expanded by 0.8% per year, more than other sectors in low-growth regions, but below the growth rates of tradable services in other parts of Europe.

In addition to a lack of transition towards tradable services, the goods-producing sector appears to be stagnating. Manufacturing remains an important contributor to regional economies in many regions. Production of goods, however, is now more than the manufacturing and assembly of parts. In an increasingly globalised world, the main source of value added is often found in up- or downstream steps in the production process. Research and development (R&D) and design of new products, as well as marketing and aftersales services often carry higher value added than the assembly of the product itself.[13]

Figure 2.4. Low-growth regions in Europe struggle to transition towards high-growth sectors

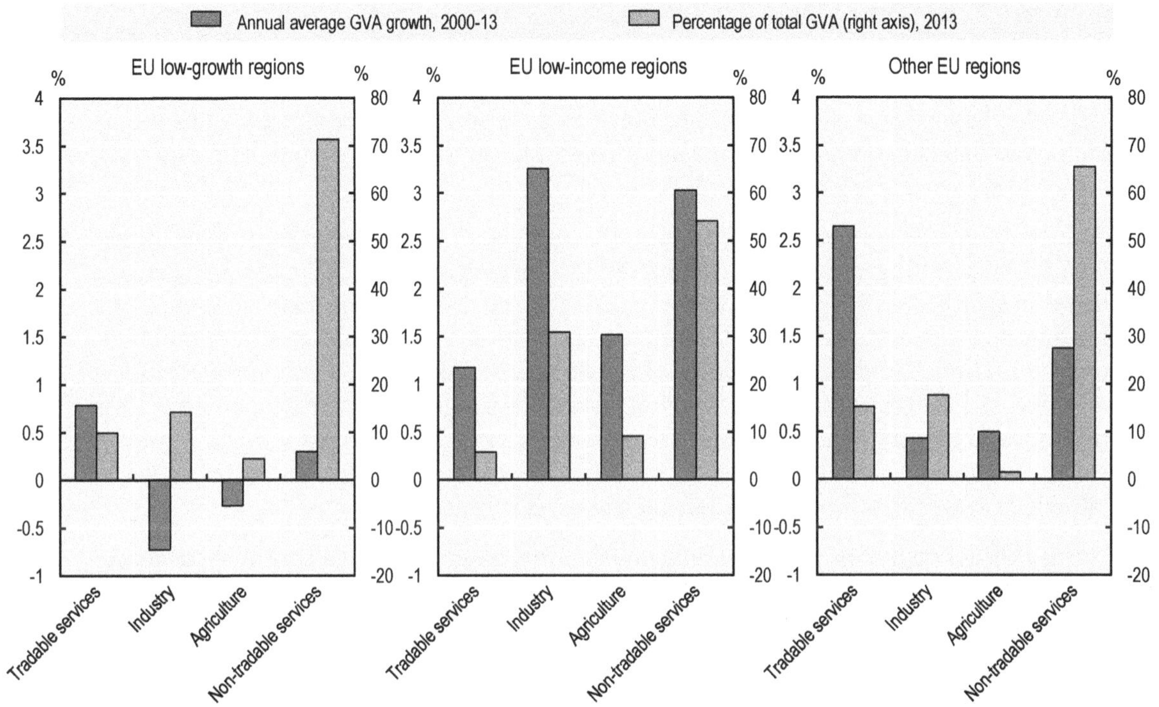

Note: GVA level and growth (2000-13) in 2010 USD at constant prices and PPPs. Data for 17 EU countries. Low-income regions are EU regions with less than 50% of EU-average per capita GDP in 2000; low-growth regions are EU regions with less than 90% of the EU-average per capita GDP in 2000 (less-developed and transition regions) that grew less than the EU average over the 2000-13 period (full list in Annex Table 1.A.1) Tradable services include information and communication (J), financial and insurance activities (K), and other services (RSTU). Non-tradable services are composed of construction, distributive trade, repairs, transport, accommodation, food services activities (GHI), real estate activities (L), business services (MN), and public administration (OPQ).
Source: Calculations based on OECD Regional Statistics [Database].

StatLink http://dx.doi.org/10.1787/888933707893

Successful sectoral transitions require skills, ideas and stamina

Sectoral transition is a difficult task. The legacy of the decline in mining in England's north or Germany's Ruhr area is still evident today. Cities like Gelsenkirchen or Duisburg in Germany's Ruhr area, which were once thriving economic centres in coal mining and steal production, struggle with unemployment rates that are more than twice the country average even decades after the major decline in Germany's extractive industries.[14] The closure of heavy industries in the "Rust Belt" in the United States did not result in such a spike in unemployment rates, but instead led to large net migration flows and thereby an erosion of the local economic base.[15]

Technological progress has always changed the nature of jobs and rendered some obsolete. The move from artisanal to factory production in textiles reduced the need for shop-floor workers, but created new jobs for engineers and technicians, as well as demand for supervisory workers, bookkeepers and other administrative staff. Therefore the disruptions caused by major technological shifts have been temporary, at least in aggregate. But "temporary" does not mean short-lived nor are the disruptions evenly distributed across workers or regions in a country.[16]

Loss of job-specific skills can make transitions costly for workers

For displaced workers, finding new jobs, especially those with equivalent income is difficult. As the nature of jobs changes, the knowledge and skills specific to their jobs and tasks that they have built up over time becomes obsolete. In economic terms, this means that their "human capital", i.e. the sum of their knowledge and personal attributes that allow them to create economic value, depreciates.

A manufacturing worker with 20 years of experience in metalworking, using heavy welding and cutting equipment, cannot easily transition into service jobs. Some of the habits might be useful in other jobs, e.g. as a truck driver, given that supporting the loading and unloading of materials might come natural to someone used to working in teams on physically demanding tasks. However, transitioning into a chemical technician working in a laboratory, a cargo and freight agent in logistics or a manager in retail is difficult and usually impossible. But these are the service jobs that pay a similar average salary as those of a metal worker.[17] Jobs that are more easily accessible, e.g. janitor, bartender or taxi driver, pay much less than manufacturing jobs.

Across OECD countries, a decline in manufacturing employment in a region is associated with a decline in total employment (Figure 2.5). This might be due to lower re-employment prospects of displaced manufacturing workers, but could also be due to the positive multipliers of employment in tradable sectors. As expanding tradable sectors create demand for jobs in local services, so could a decline in tradable sectors, here in manufacturing, lead to further contraction.

Figure 2.5. Income inequality across regions rose more in countries with larger losses in manufacturing employment

Percentage point change in the ratio of 90th and 50th percentile primary income, 2000-14

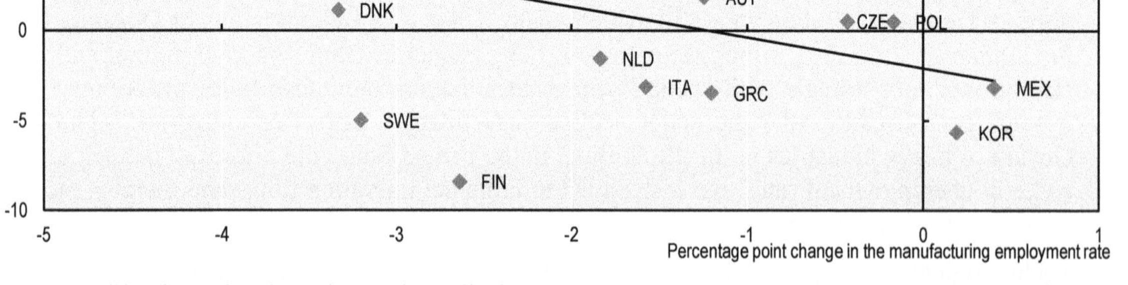

Note: The change in primary income inequality is measured as the change in the ratio of the TL2 region with average primary income at the 90th percentile to the TL2 region with average income at the 50th percentile average income. Data for 2000-14 or closest years available.
Source: OECD (2017[11]) based on OECD Regional Statistics [Database].

StatLink http://dx.doi.org/10.1787/888933707912

Gains from industrial transition are not evenly distributed

Since at least the 1990s, jobs in OECD countries have increasingly polarised with gains in "lousy and lovely jobs" (Goos and Manning, 2007[12]). Employment increased in both occupations paying high wages and in those paying low wages.[18] The polarisation of jobs has been linked to the degree of routinisation of tasks required for the job. The more standardised a task, the more easily it is replaced. This is the case for both cognitive and manual routine tasks. Some administrative jobs, such as record keeping, or those including repetitive services, e.g. bank tellers, are examples of jobs with a high degree of routine tasks that can be relatively easily replaced through computerisation. Industrial robots can replace routine manual tasks, such as sorting or repetitive assembly. Conversely, creative writing or cleaning services are harder to replace as they are highly non-routine.[19] There is also evidence from the United States that suggests that social skills and tasks that focus on interaction play an important role in driving relative employment growth (Deming, 2017[13]).

Industrial change and technological progress does not destroy all jobs, but those that remain often change significantly. A factory worker producing machine parts might have manually filed, wielded and assembled pieces in the past, tasks that were then increasingly supported by specialised tools, which finally become ICT supported. This means that production moved from using predominantly blue collar workers in manual roles to using robots and engineers that monitor and program these tools. Occupational changes in the United States since the 1980s seem mainly driven by these within-industry shifts, whereas prior to the 1980s the driving force behind the changing structure in jobs was the shift between different types of industry (Acemoglu and Autor, 2011[14]).

The gains from new opportunities have mainly accrued to those with higher levels of education and, more generally, those individuals who are more "skilled". This "skill-biased technological change" has been linked to rising income inequality. Despite a growing supply in highly educated workers, wages relative to those of workers without a university degree have increased steadily since the 1980s. This implies that demand rose even faster than supply.[20] Both the growing integration of information and communication technologies (ICT) and the attendant increase in the value of non-routine tasks in production, as well as incentives to focus on skill- and knowledge-intensive sectors and parts of value chains have been linked to skill-biased technological change.[21] Importantly, it appears to be the combination of computerisation and the increase in non-routine tasks – rather than computerisation on its own – that is driving demand for skilled workers.[22] The concept of "skills" in this context refers to workers that are more adept at a variety of (non-routine) tasks. Non-routine tasks and offshoring both play a role in explaining growing polarisation as both lower the demand for middle-wage jobs. However, evidence from 16 Western European countries suggest that it has been the change in the nature of tasks rather than offshoring that has driven polarisation (Goos, Manning and Salomons, 2014[15]).

High levels of education and skill benefit the individual who possesses them, but such qualities can also create positive spillover effects on other workers. An advanced degree can create significant personal benefits for workers. Personal incomes rise with the level of education, but also other aspects improve, e.g. health outcomes.[23] But working in an environment where the educational attainment of others is higher can also raise the productivity and wages of workers without increased education. The presence of such social (as opposed to private) returns to education often justifies subsidising education and training.

Structural change is more challenging for low-density economies

The impact of industrial transition in the local labour market is particularly severe when the local economy is not diversified. The more heavily an area depends on specific sectors, the larger the potential shock to its economic structure. Diversification is particularly problematic for low-density – rural – economies where labour markets are too "thin" to allow for a large variety of firms to be established. These places need to specialise to achieve critical mass and economies of scale (OECD, 2016[16]). But the need to specialise implies that when the local industry is adversely affected by competition or declining demand, a mass of newly unemployed workers swells the supply of labour while demand shrinks. In larger markets, e.g. large cities, the increased number of job seekers can be absorbed by other sectors more easily.

In some cases the transition is created by a sudden shock. This was the case when the People's Republic of China ("China" hereafter) joined the World Trade Organisation (WTO) and competition increased for some manufacturing companies around the world. Particularly hard hit were certain companies manufacturing ICT equipment and textiles, China's first and second largest group of exports in 2001, the year when the country joined the WTO.[24] More generally, labour-intensive manufacturing was facing strong competition from China.[25] A study for the United States estimates that local labour markets that were more exposed to the growth in imports from China experienced, on average, a 4.5% fall in manufacturing employment and a decline in the employment rate by 0.8 percentage points, relative to a local labour market that was less exposed.[26] In other cases, the change has been gradual. For instance, in Italy's north, the Province of Bergamo is gradually shifting away from traditional medium- and low-tech activities towards medium-high tech activities with higher productivity and value-added potential (OECD, 2016[17]).

Buffering shocks requires supply and demand side measures

The central challenge in adapting to industrial transition is that obsolete skills need to be replaced. At the regional level the next generation of workers might provide those skills. An inflow of workers from other places, both within the same country but even from other countries, can provide firms in regions with the capacity to utilise opportunities arising from industrial and technological change. But displaced workers might find it more difficult to adapt. The personal cost they incur can be quite significant with the less-educated often more affected than others. They are less mobile and therefore less able to find alternative opportunities in other regions. In addition, their skills are often more specific to the tasks they used to perform, and therefore no longer in demand.[27]

This challenge is amplified by the increasing digitisation of jobs and an increasing pace of industrial transition. Workers need to combine specific skills to be competitive in their industries, with general skills that allow them to adapt to upcoming challenges. Successful moves towards high-value added activities require general skills, tacit, non-codified knowledge in areas such as original design, the creation and management of cutting-edge technology and complex systems, as well as management or organisational know-how (OECD, WTO and World Bank Group, 2014[18]). Regions with traditional strengths in manufacturing used to make school-to-work transitions relatively easy. As a result, young people often joined the labour market as soon as they had completed compulsory schooling, without finishing secondary education or obtaining a post-secondary degree. They found work and acquired job-specific skills in the workplace. The result is a large percentage of employees who are highly skilled in job- or firm-specific tasks but who lack the general skills required to adapt to modern production techniques and to implement innovative practices.

Adapting to sectoral transition therefore requires measures that target the next generation of workers, as well as those individuals who already work. Lifelong learning is not a new concept, but it requires further differentiation. Training to prepare for sectoral transition is not just specific to the task at hand, but has a general component that can be useful in other occupations or help upgrade the workers' profile. When it comes to computerisation and digitisation this remains an uphill battle. On average, over 40% of those using software at work every day do not have the skills required to use digital technologies effectively (OECD, 2016[19]). But the changing nature of jobs makes digital skills increasingly important. A recent study estimates that 9% of jobs in OECD countries are at high risk of being automated (Arntz, Gregory and Zierahn, 2016[20]).

Supply-side measures focused on workers need to be coherent with demand-side developments if they are expected to succeed, in particular in low-density economies. Retraining and new skills are only valuable if there are employment opportunities in which they can be used. In areas with large and dynamic labour markets and high rates of new firm creations these opportunities might arise naturally. In other areas there might be room for targeted policy interventions that create incentives for investment and the creation of new firms.

Is a large tradable sector more risky for a region?

The exposure of tradable sectors to international fluctuations in demand and to global shocks might make them seem less resilient than non-tradable sectors that depend on the local economy. This raises the question of whether a strong focus on tradable sectors is creating risks that could be avoided by instead focusing on sectors that only serve their local economy. The 2007-08 crisis can provide some insights into the resilience of tradable sectors.

Many regions experienced employment decline after the 2007-08 crisis

Employment declined in many regions following the 2007-08 crisis, with unemployment rates surging and remaining high for years after the initial shock. In the Norte region in Portugal, for example, 150 000 fewer people were employed in 2015 than in 2008, a nearly 9% drop in employment. Low productivity growth in non-tradable sectors is likely to contribute to the pattern. In Norte, manufacturing firms increased labour productivity at the cost of declining employment, whereas tradable services grew both in terms of productivity and employment (Figure 2.6). New jobs were mainly created in non-tradable services, but these jobs were less productive than the existing ones, which led to a decline in average labour productivity in the sectors. With the shock of the 2007-08 crisis, these jobs were not sustained and non-tradable services reduced employment by 77 000 jobs, more than were created before the crisis. Manufacturing, instead, underwent continuous restructuring as productivity increased; although many jobs were lost – more than 150 000 over the 2000-15 period. Norte is not alone in this experience. Central Macedonia in Greece had 170 000 fewer people employed, nearly 22% less than in 2008, and more than half a million fewer people worked in Andalusia (Spain) in 2014 than in 2008, a drop of 17%.

Regions with the largest non-tradable sector expansions suffered the strongest employment losses

Employment post-2008 declined (more) in regions that expanded their non-tradable sectors relative to tradable activities in the pre-crisis period (2000-07). Employment in regions where non-tradable employment increased by less than 2.5 percentage points between 2000 and 2007 grew, on average, by nearly 0.7% per year between 2008 and 2014. Employment growth was, on average, about 0.4% in regions with moderate increases in non-tradable employment and negative for regions with large expansions of non-tradable employment. Since the crisis, employment has declined, on average, by nearly 1% for regions where employment shifted by 5-7.5 percentage points from tradable to non-tradable sectors and by 2.9% for regions with more than 7.5 percentage point shifts (Figure 2.6).

This might seem surprising, but non-tradable activities are not truly insulated from global trends. Local links tie tradable and non-tradable sectors together. Demand factors play a role as well. As global economic conditions suffer, non-tradable sectors have to rely on local demand to pick up again, while firms in tradable sectors have the opportunity to develop new and alternative markets (or even start trading if they had not done so before).

Figure 2.6. Regions with strong pre-crisis increases in non-tradable sectors lost more jobs

Annual average employment growth (2008-13) and change in the share of non-tradable workers in total employment in 2007 compared to 2000

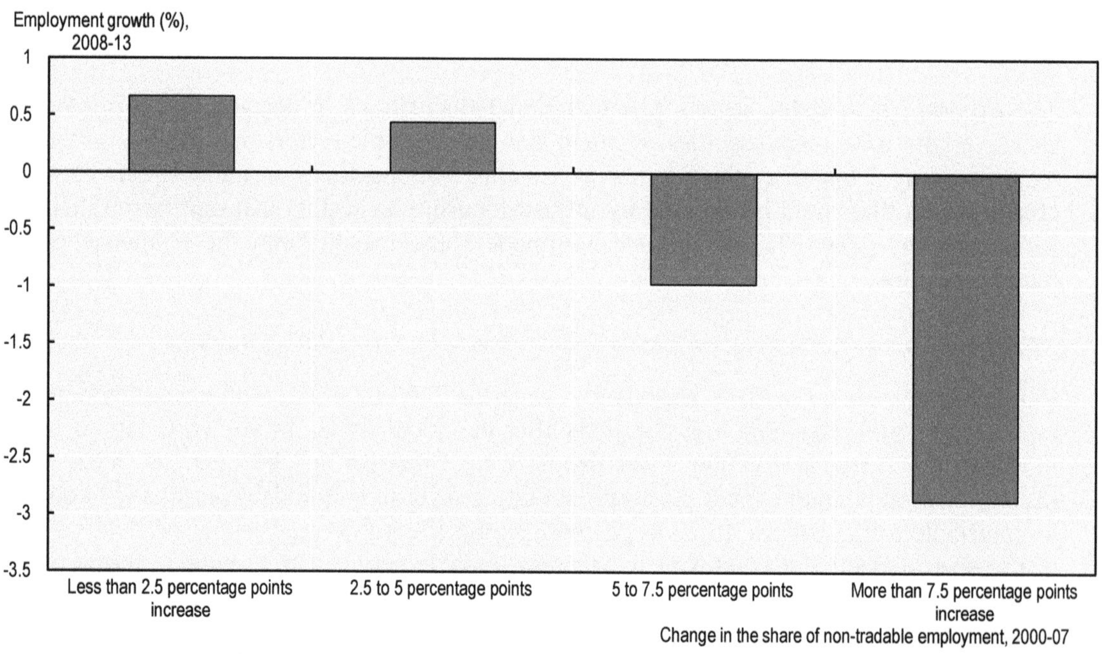

Note: Data for 203 territorial level 2 (TL2) regions in 19 OECD countries: Austria, Australia, Belgium, Bulgaria, Czech Republic, Denmark, Finland, Greece, Ireland, Italy, the Netherlands, Portugal, Romania, Slovenia, Slovak Republic, Spain, Sweden, the United Kingdom and the United States. Categories from left to right include 81, 84, 19 and 19 regions.
Source: Calculations based on OECD Regional Statistics [Database].

StatLink http://dx.doi.org/10.1787/888933707931

Figure 2.7. New non-tradable jobs were less productive and quickly lost after the 2007-08 crisis in Norte, Portugal

Employment and labour productivity growth in Norte (Portugal) by sector

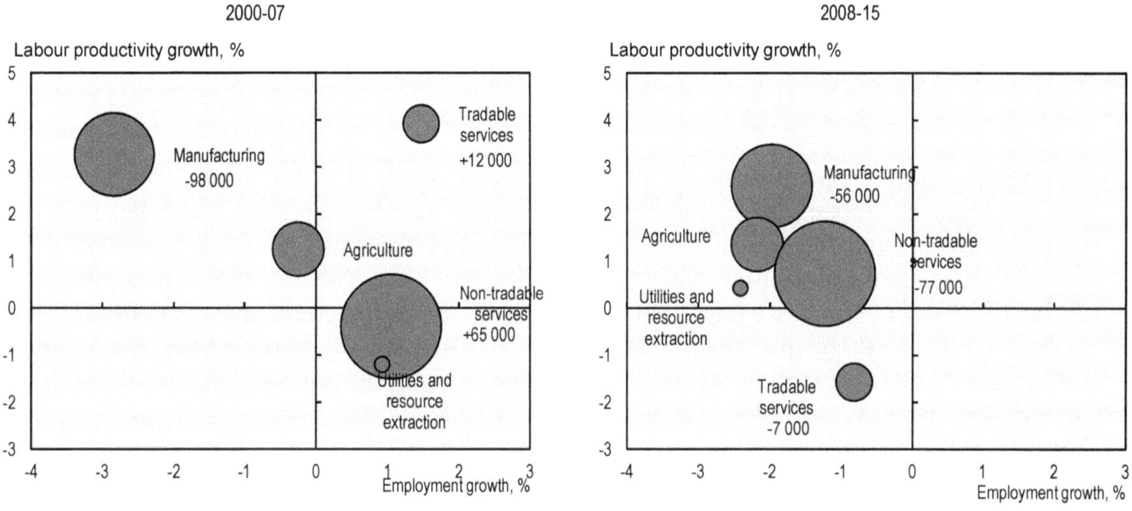

Note: Labour productivity is real gross value added in USD in constant 2010 prices and PPPs per worker. Numbers indicate employment change over the period, bubble size indicates the size of the sector in terms of employment in 2000. Tradable services are taken as information and communication (J), financial and insurance activities (K), and other services (RSTU). Non-tradable services are composed of construction, distributive trade, repairs, transport, accommodation, food services activities (GHI), real estate activities (L), business services (MN), and public administration (OPQ). Real estate activities are excluded in this chart.
Source: Calculations based on OECD Regional Statistics [Database].

StatLink http://dx.doi.org/10.1787/888933707950

Economic imbalances accrued before the 2007-08 crisis

During the 2007-08 crisis the expansion of non-tradable sectors led to significant adjustments of imbalances that accrued in the pre-crisis period. Economies that focused on non-tradable sectors were quick to rise and equally quick to fall in the wake of the 2007-08 crisis. An important reason is that countries sustained consumption through mounting current account deficits and increasing debt. As countries import more than they export they build up liabilities towards their export partners. With flexible exchange rates, current account imbalances can be addressed by allowing the currency to devalue, thereby increasing the cost of imports and lowering the cost of exports. But the fixed exchange rate regime among euro area members means that external imbalances need to be addressed through other channels. Construction- and consumption-fuelled growth turned out to be unsustainable.

Imbalances within countries can be sustained, but require constant transfers. Public agencies, for example, that are located in regions whose economies are lagging behind the country average can be financed through central funds. With implicit or even explicit transfers, regions can support a strong non-tradable sector. But this strategy comes at a price. It typically requires increasing transfers from other regions to support the regions that are lagging behind, as wages tend to rise relative to productivity in non-tradable sectors (see Chapter 4.).

Moreover, it tends to lock regions in as it lowers the momentum for local growth and the creation of new sectors. Fledgling firms in the tradable sector have to compete with the opportunities offered by the subsidised sectors. In addition to the challenges of setting up and running a new firm, they have to offer wages that attract talent and secure financing at premium rates to compensate investors for foregoing less risky investments in subsidised sectors or in other parts of the country.

Well-functioning cities are supporting successful catching up

The discussion to this point focused on tradable sectors as a catalyst for catching up. The OECD Regional Outlook 2016 highlights a second source of successful convergence: well-functioning and integrated cities (OECD, 2016[16]). Proximity to large cities can support growth and catching up. Divergence in productivity is, however, not necessarily driven by distance from those cities. Different channels create the productivity benefits of cities. In part, they are due to the difference in the sectoral structure, in part due to differences in the characteristics of the workforce, but they are also the result of productivity benefits found in larger and denser cities – so called "agglomeration benefits" (OECD, 2015[21]).

Cities play an important role for growth within and outside their region

Workers in larger cities are more productive than those in smaller cities or in rural areas. The gap arises, in part, due to differences in the characteristics of the local workforce. Workers in larger cities are, on average, more educated and have skills that would make them more productive no matter where they live or work (OECD, 2015[21]). But other factors, such as sectoral composition, play an important role as well. This benefits the city, but also the region where it is located.

For rural areas, stronger linkages between urban and rural places are increasingly emphasised as possible drivers for differences in growth performance. Flows between rural and urban areas are facilitated when the two are in close proximity (OECD, 2013[22]). Rural amenities, such as green space, are easy to reach, while rural residents can make use of specialised public and private services that are often only found in cities. In remote and rural places, by contrast, there are fewer direct connections with cities, and local residents and firms must rely almost exclusively on local providers of goods and services.

Characteristics of the workforce, firms and "agglomeration benefits" make larger cities more productive

Among the most productive "frontier" regions, 80% are "predominantly urban", i.e. more than 80% of their population lives in densely populated areas.[28] The higher productivity in cities is linked to their size. For OECD metropolitan areas with at least 500 000 inhabitants, every 10% increase in population is associated with 1% higher productivity in terms of gross domestic product (GDP) per worker. Going back to the example of Paris, this implies that the output per worker in the metro area of the French capital – with its 12 million inhabitants – is expected to be more than 18% higher than in the second largest metro area Lyon with close to 2 million inhabitants.[29]

About half of the success of (larger) cities comes from their ability to attract highly educated and highly skilled workers. These workers would be more productive in any place that they work, but they choose to work in larger cities. The other half of the effect comes through "agglomeration economies", economic benefits that arise from working in larger and denser places. Taking the characteristics of workers into account, the productivity benefits provided by the city in which they live are estimated between 0.2% and 0.5% for each 10% increase in city size.[30] This means that the same person working in Madrid with its more than 6 million inhabitants is nearly 15% more productive than he or she would have been working in Toledo with its 120 000 inhabitants.[31]

Cities attract more tradable services, while resource extraction and mature industries are more prevalent in rural regions

Most non-tradable services need to be provided locally and are therefore present in all types of regions. Manufacturing or tradable services, on the other hand, tend to be concentrated in one area. In manufacturing, this concentration arises as suppliers and producers locate close to each other or companies working on similar products or with similar technologies work in the same place. But the variety of needs and niches in manufacturing results in a relatively wide distribution of industrial jobs. Modern tradable services are, however, significantly more concentrated than manufacturing or local services.

Large metropolitan areas, like London, New York or Tokyo, are home to some of the most productive and innovative firms. They are mainly focused on services, often business services, but also health care, higher education and information and communications technologies (OECD, 2014[23]). Manufacturing firms located in large cities are typically focused on innovation and skill intensive production and often only parts of the company (e.g. the headquarters) remain in the city. Unsurprisingly, wages paid by firms in tradable clusters that are more likely to be located in urban areas are, on average, higher than in clusters in less-densely populated areas. However, the average can hide some significant outliers, especially among resource-rich rural regions. In many OECD countries, resource-rich regions are among the most productive regions, if not the most productive themselves, as they are drawing on "resource rents".[32] The benefits from most resource extraction activities are, however, temporary as extraction depletes the local reserves, which is typically not captured in national accounts and therefore productivity calculations.

Figure 2.8. Traded clusters in cities are higher paying

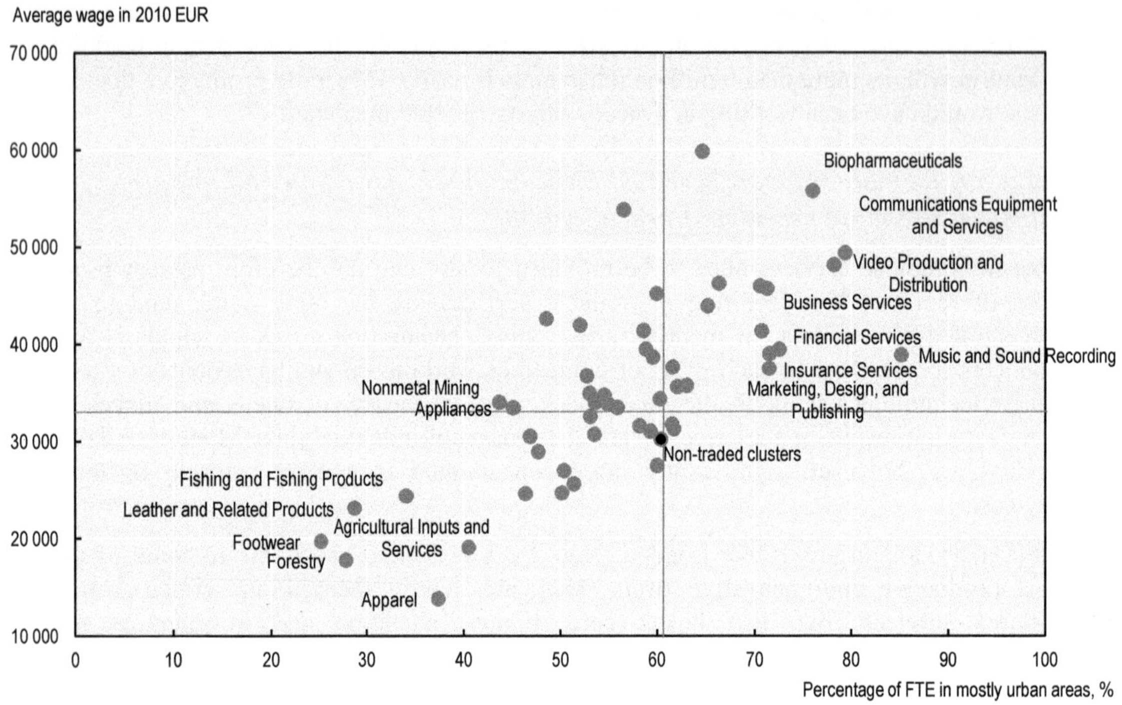

Note: Full-time equivalent employment (FTE) and average wages in firms operating in traded clusters in NUTS 2 regions. Percentage of FTE in mostly urban areas is defined as the total FTE in the traded cluster in NUTS 2 regions with at least 70% of their population living in an FUA (or some percentage of their population living in a large metropolitan area with more than 1.5 million inhabitants) as a percentage of total FTE in the traded cluster.
Source: Calculations based on Ketels and Protsiv (2016[24]) with data provided by the authors and OECD Regional Statistics [Database].

StatLink http://dx.doi.org/10.1787/888933707969

Economies in rural areas

Rural economies are often heavily reliant on agricultural production or natural resource exploitation (OECD, 2016[1]). Manufacturing in these areas tends to be in "mature" parts of the product cycle using established technologies and processes. The small size of the labour market in rural, i.e. low-density, areas also leads to less diversification than can be achieved in large cities. The reality of rural areas is, however, quite diverse and most regions mix rural and urban elements in their economies.

Links between rural and urban regions can be a key asset to overcome disadvantages associated with low-density economies. The OECD Regional Outlook 2016 (2016[1]) finds that rural areas close to cities have been more dynamic and resilient since the 2007-08 crisis as compared to rural remote regions and even predominantly urban regions.[33]

Business creation is most dynamic in the largest or capital cities

Predominantly urban regions have higher firm entry, but also higher firm exit rates than predominantly rural regions

Business creations differ across OECD countries between urban and rural areas. Average business creation rates are 13% (of the total number of existing firms) in predominantly urban regions, but 10.9% in predominantly rural ones. For the remote rural regions, those not in the vicinity of an urban agglomeration with at least 50 000 inhabitants, the percentage of business births is 9.3%, i.e. even lower than in other rural regions.

This distinction is particularly relevant for the sectoral composition of new firms, as urban regions attract relatively more knowledge-intensive firms. More than 60% of firms created in knowledge-intensive sectors take place in predominantly urban regions. In comparison, predominantly urban regions account for 52% of all new firms and 50% of existing firms (OECD, $2017_{[25]}$). These higher rates in predominantly urban regions do not necessarily translate into higher firm survival rates, measured by survival for at least three years after creation. Instead, the higher churn might indicate a stronger tendency towards creative destruction as more innovative businesses more rapidly replace old businesses.[34]

Figure 2.9. The most dynamic business environment is typically the capital city region

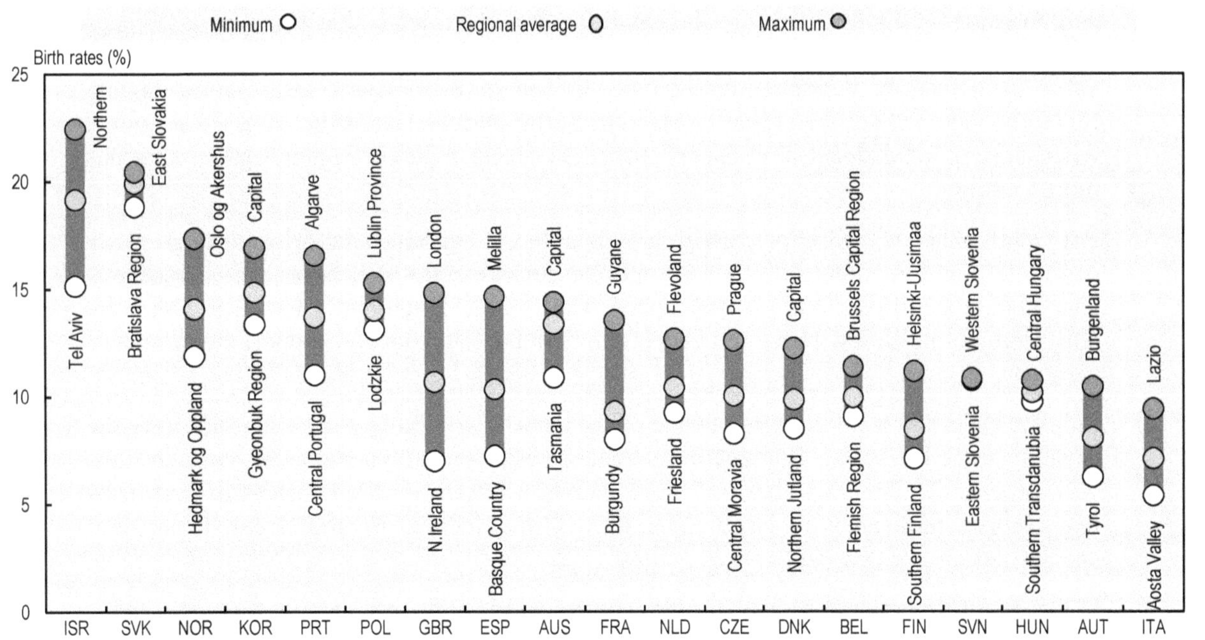

Note: The figure refers to the total number of new businesses being created as a proportion of total active firms in the region (TL2) in the year 2014 (or last available). All firms are included (total across sectors and size classes).

Source: Calculations based on data collected in OECD ($2017_{[25]}$).

StatLink http://dx.doi.org/10.1787/888933707988

Smaller firms, slower growth and less entrepreneurship limit Europe's lagging regions

Europe's low-growth and low-income regions tend to have more small firms and often lack larger ones. They also tend to see fewer new firms created and when new firms enter the market their average size tends to be smaller than in other parts of the country (European Commission, 2017[26]).[35] Small size and low churn can limit the flow of innovation and be a sign of a lack of efficient reallocation of capital and workers towards more productive activity.

Firm size in itself does not imply success, but in many instances it is associated with it. Agricultural labour productivity in Poland is higher in regions with more large farms and lower in regions dominated by small farms.[36] In some countries, firm size can explain a significant part of the gap between national champions and global champions in terms of productivity. For example, one estimate suggests that two-thirds of the productivity gap between Italy's most productive manufacturing firms and those operating at the global frontier is due to Italy's most productive manufacturers being relatively small compared to those at the frontier (Andrews, Criscuolo and Gal, 2015[27]).

The positive impact of a city is not constrained by its geographical limits

Large cities can support growth and catching-up momentum in smaller cities and rural areas. Firm growth in rural areas tends to be driven by urban demand for resources, goods and amenities (OECD, 2016[16]). The small local market means that firms have to focus outward, providing goods and services to nearby cities or even abroad. But beyond the value as a market, nearby cities can be service hubs for rural areas, consolidating functions that lack sufficient market size in smaller places. This is the case, for example, when several weak local newspapers merge to create a single regional paper that has more viability.

For rural areas in close proximity to cities these benefits can arise through daily commuting and economic flows. Metropolitan areas extend well beyond their core city and include significant parts of the surrounding, rural "hinterland", which is linked by daily commuting flows. These rural areas can both benefit from and support the growth of their core cities.

Smaller cities and rural villages outside of the direct commuting zone might not have the capacity to create strong agglomeration economies in their own right, but through links with other cities they can "borrow" agglomeration benefits.[37] Short drives or train trips that connect rural areas to large cities allow firms, located in rural areas, to tap into specialised services available only in cities.

In Germany, the town of Montabaur was connected via high-speed rail in the early 2000s. At the time, the town had less than 15 000 inhabitants. After the train line was opened in 2002, Montabaur could be reached from Frankfurt and Cologne within 40 minutes of travel and the international airports of the two cities could be accessed within 20 minutes. Since then, the industrial park located next to the train station has attracted more than 50 firms. Estimates for Montabaur and two further counties that became connected suggest that between 2002 and 2006 the new connection led to an increase of about 8.5% in GDP and an increase in labour productivity of about 3.8%. Productivity increased through the creation of new firms and jobs, rather than improvements in productivity in those firms already located in the area (Ahlfeldt and Feddersen, 2015[28]).

However, for agglomeration benefits in metro areas and "borrowed" agglomeration benefits to fully materialise, governance problems need to be addressed such as a lack of local co-ordination in transport or land-use planning, low levels of institutional capacity, and the lack of an integrated metropolitan strategy. Without a well-functioning governance framework, the potential benefits of metropolitan areas is underutilised and "catching up" limited (OECD, 2012[29]).

Borrowed agglomeration benefits raise productivity close to large cities

Urban centres play an important role not only through their contribution but also as markets, links and service centres for rural areas. They can create positive effects, as larger cities provide specialised services and serve as hubs for trade and transport. By providing these services, they are essential for well-functioning rural parts of the economy. As proximity to cities facilitates businesses' and rural residents' access to these functions, it also makes it easier to "borrow" agglomeration economies from the city. This effect can be substantial. Estimates of agglomeration benefits for the Netherlands show little gain from larger size. But a closer look shows that the lack of an average effect is driven by small cities that border the country's large, highly-productive metropolitan areas (OECD, 2016[30]).

Along the western Scandinavia coast, the regions around Oslo, Gothenburg and Malmö are highly integrated. Jobs and homes are spread across the whole region with more than 10% of the local workforce routinely commuting from the less-densely populated parts of the region into the city, and vice-versa (Figure 2.10). There are potential drawbacks from being located close to a large metro area as well. Concentration of activity in metropolitan centres might cast an "agglomeration shadow" on smaller cities and surrounding areas as the core benefits from productivity and population growth focus on cities at the expense of surrounding areas (Fujita, Krugman and Venables, 1999[31]). The migration flows and increasing population concentration in large cities documented in Chapter 1 are indicative of such shadows for population flows; but for productivity, the ability to borrow agglomeration benefits seems to prevail.

The benefits of cities for their surrounding regions are linked to the ease with which they can be accessed. Regions closer to cities, and especially those in proximity to larger cities, have grown faster in terms of per capita GDP than regions that are more remote (Figure 2.11). The positive spillovers decline with distance, but are measurable up to 200-300 kilometres away. The actual travel time from a region to the nearest metropolitan area is the key factor that needs to be considered. Cutting travel time by half is associated with an increase of 0.2-0.4 percentage points in annual per capita GDP growth.[38]

Figure 2.10. Strong rural-urban linkages within Western Scandinavia

Commuting flows in Western Scandinavia (percentage of working population and absolute numbers), 2014

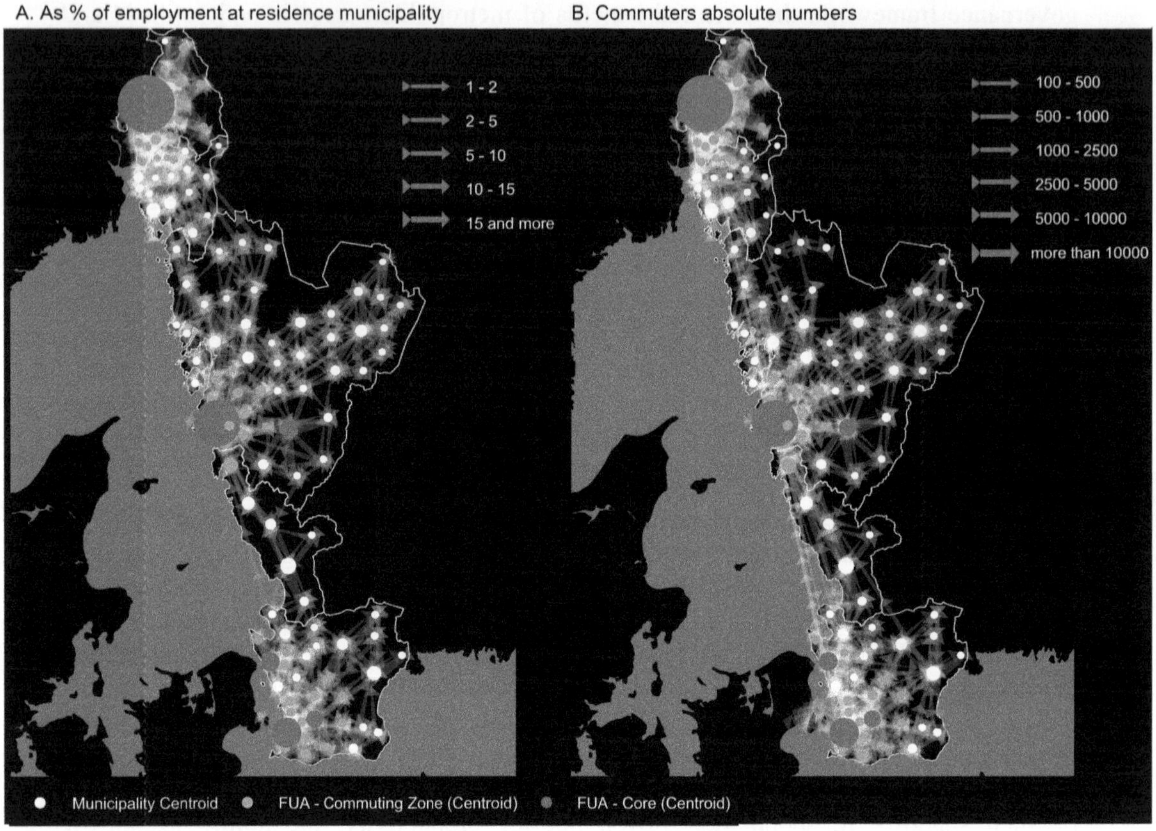

Note: Borders delineate the regions of Oslo, Akershus and Ostfold in Norway and Västra Götalands Län, Hallands Län and Skane Län in Sweden. The sizes of the circles indicate the working population in a given municipality. The larger the circle is, the bigger the working population. The three Functional Urban Areas are Oslo, Gothenburg and Malmö (from north to south).

Source: OECD (2018[32]) based on data from Örestat; Statistics Norway; Statistics Sweden; and Västra Götalandsregionen.

StatLink http://dx.doi.org/10.1787/888933708007

Figure 2.11. Per capita GDP growth is higher in regions that are close to large metro areas

Annual average per capita GDP growth controlling for country effects and initial per capita GDP levels, 1995-2010

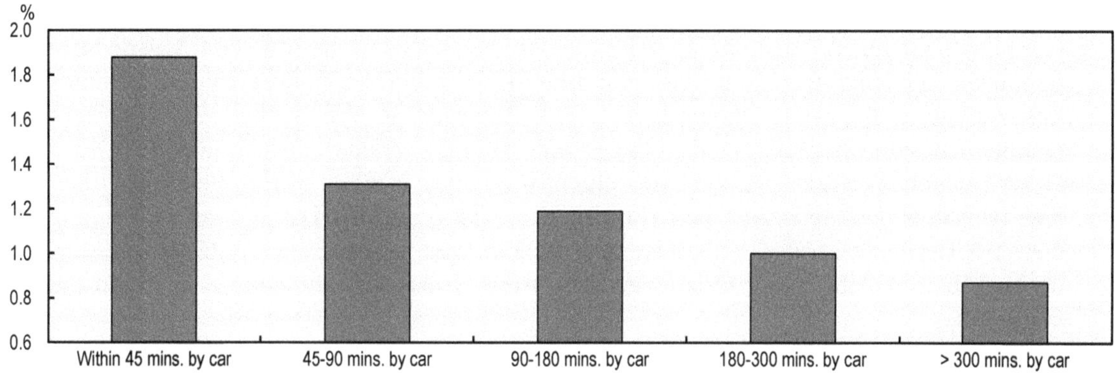

Source: OECD (2015[21]) and Ahrend and Schumann (2014[33]).

StatLink http://dx.doi.org/10.1787/888933708026

Agglomeration costs balance agglomeration benefits, creating space for second tier cities and city networks

Larger cities create benefits, but as benefits grow, so do "agglomeration costs". These costs can be pecuniary (e.g. higher housing costs and higher costs for goods or services) but also non-pecuniary (e.g. pollution or congestion). That benefits are balanced by increasing costs is perhaps unsurprising. If there were no drawbacks to locating in an ever-growing megacity, people should keep flocking towards the largest metro areas and smaller cities and rural would depopulate. But costs and benefits increase in parallel, reducing the pull of larger cities.

Empirical estimates for Germany find that the cost-of-living in urban areas increases, on average, at the same rate as agglomeration benefits raise productivity and wages.[39] Similarly, the expenditure for housing in France increases with city size (and population density) at roughly the same rate as the city creates agglomeration benefits. The increase comes as housing and land prices increase disproportionately as cities become denser. If growth can be managed and the available land area adapted to population growth, the returns in the long run are positive and appear to be linearly increasing with city size (Combes, Duranton and Gobillon, 2016[34]).

Increasing concentration of economic activity in few or individual "megacities" is also associated with increasing inequality within countries (see also "Inaction comes at the price of growing inequality and a "geography of discontent"). This growing imbalance can limit growth potential outside of the main cities and threaten social coherence within countries. The aim to "balance" economic development is therefore common across many regional development strategies. Korea, for example, has enshrined balanced development in law since 2004. The National Balanced Development Act has been maintained, pursued and amended by all subsequent administrations. Among the efforts to distribute economic and political activity across Korea was the creation of an inter-ministerial Presidential Committee on Balanced National Development, renamed Presidential Committee on Regional Development in 2009, which consisted of 12 ministers and 19 experts in 2015. Efforts also included the development of the Sejong

Special Autonomous City in July 2012, the country's new "administrative capital", where 36 national government agencies and 9 ministries were located as of 2014.[40]

As costs increase with the size of a city, a well-connected "megaregion" with rural areas and a network of smaller, but well-connected cities, could provide agglomeration benefits while limiting the costs from congestion and densification. The fastest growing firms in Germany's famous *Mittelstand* are more likely to be located in the small and less-densely populated municipalities along the main arterial highways that connect the major cities rather than in the cities themselves.[41] The Randstad in the Netherlands leverages complementarities between the four largest cities and the smaller cities around the "Green Heart", which it covers.[42] It combines one of the largest airports in Europe (Amsterdam Airport Schiphol), the largest port (Port of Rotterdam) and the Dutch centre for public administration and services (The Hague). The links are supported by a strong transport network between the major cities with train trips of less than 40 minutes between the major cities.[43]

Whether the costs and benefits of a megaregion or a connected "system of cities" outweigh those associated with concentration in large metropolitan areas is an open question. Borrowed agglomeration benefits are unlikely to match actual agglomeration benefits and connecting cities with high-frequency, reliable and uncongested transport facilities is costly. It also increases the flow of traffic and related environmental costs. Conversely, the provision of housing, the density in which people live and the dispersion of pollution likely benefit residents of a megaregion. Though over time, there might be an uneven development within the megaregion that leads to concentration in the area. Likewise, a study on five megaregions in China finds that between 1990 and 2010 the population concentrated increasingly in the larger cities of the megaregions (Tan, 2017[35]).

Notes

1. Already famously pointed out in 1776 by Adam Smith in his "Wealth of Nations" (Smith, 1776[37]).

2. Frontier regions are the most productive regions (here TL3 regions) in a country and account for at least 10% of total national employment. The frontier is selected based on the whole sample period and includes all regions that were among the most productive regions in their country in at least half of the years during the first half of the growth period.

3. If the share of tradable sectors in total GVA is greater than the share of tradable employment, tradable sectors are more productive than non-tradable sectors.

4. See Hlatshwayo and Spence (2014[42]) for a discussion of the impact of relative tradable productivity growth and non-tradable employment growth in the United States. Note that the definition of tradables in this report covers the same sectors but has to rely on a coarser industrial classification and is therefore not directly comparable.

5. During this period Korea became increasingly open to agricultural trade as a result of the EU-South Korea free trade agreement, which went into effect provisionally in July 2011, and the U.S.-Korea Trade Agreement (KORUS), which entered into force in 2012. This has raised concerns about the repercussions on internal food security and social

coherence. Sources for dates on trade agreements: http://ec.europa.eu/trade/policy/countries-and-regions/countries/south-korea/ (accessed 22 December 2017) and www.fas.usda.gov/data/us-agriculture-reaps-benefits-free-trade-agreement-korea (accessed 22 December 2017), Employment data: OECD Regional Statistics [Database].

6. Productivity refers to total factor productivity, i.e. the combined productivity of capital and labour. See Greenstone, Moretti and Hornbeck (2010[44]) for details.

7. Non-tradable sectors and firms can, of course, also increase their productivity. The contribution of productivity improvements in retail trade in the United States contributed nearly as much as the IT-producing industries to productivity growth in the country between the late-1980s and 2004 (Byrne, Fernald and Reinsdorf, 2016[51]). This development was driven by large national retail chains entering local markets and by the new, high-productivity establishments replacing existing lower productivity ones (Foster, Haltiwanger and Krizan, 2006[45]).

8. This idea of "lean" manufacturing and the relative advantages of different modes of production are discussed by Krafcik (1988[41]) and created a whole literature on the management of lean production systems.

9. See Cusumano (1988[47]) for a brief summary of the changes introduced by Toyota and the channels through which they had an impact on productivity, as well as relative productivity estimates: Throughout the 1970s and 1980s Toyota's vehicle productivity was more than twice the average across US producers (taking vertical integration, capacity utilisation and labour hour differences into account).

10. See www.biat.uni-flensburg.de/kfz-neuordnung/default.htm (accessed 06 November 2017)

11. The 16 automotive companies in the World's top-100 largest advertisers spend USD 47 billion in 2015 (http://adage.com/article/advertising/world-s-largest-advertisers/306983/, accessed 06 November 2017). The GDP in USD at current prices and exchange rates was USD 41.4 billion in Lithuania and USD 43.1 billion in Slovenia.

12. Both low-income and low-growth regions have been defined as part of the EU Lagging Regions Initiative (European Commission, 2017[26]). Low-growth regions are identified among the less-developed and transition regions (i.e. those with 75% or less/90% or less than average per capita GDP in the EU).

13. See Ye, Meng and Wei (2015[36]) for empirical evidence on the "smile curve" that shows higher value added in upstream and downstream parts of the production.

14. The unemployment rate for Germany was 5.4% in October 2017; 11.7% in Gelsenkirchen and 11.8% in Duisburg. https://statistik.arbeitsagentur.de/Navigation/Statistik/Statistik-nach-Regionen/Politische-Gebietsstruktur-Nav.html and https://statistik.arbeitsagentur.de/Navigation/Statistik/Statistik-nach-Regionen/BA-Gebietsstruktur/Nordrhein-Westfalen/bis-09-2012/Nordrhein-Westfalen-bis-09-2012-Nav.html (accessed 09 November 2017).

15. The "Rust Belt" is the area from the Great Lakes to the Upper Midwest States, albeit analysis uses varying delineations. Alder, Lagakos and Ohanian (2014[58]) consider Illlinois, Indiana, Michigan, New York, Ohio, Pennsylvania, West Virginia and Wisconsin part of the "Rust Belt", while Blanchard and Katz (1992[52]) focus on Illinois, Indiana, Ohio and Michigan.

16. Mokyr, Vickers and Ziebarth (2015[38]) discuss the development of employment and incomes in the wake of the industrial revolution.

17. Data for US salaries from www.sokanu.com/careers/ (accessed 10 November 2017).

18. See Acemoglu and Autor (2011[14]) for detailed trends for the United States and other OECD countries.

19. See Autor, Levy and Murnane (2003[56]) for a classification of routine jobs and its relation to technological change. Examples are provided by the authors. Being "Routine" does not necessarily mean the job is devoid of technological progress. The authors give "truck driving" as a non-routine manual task, but advances in autonomous driving are rapidly shifting this view.

20. See Autor, Katz and Kearney (2008[54]) for a discussion of skill-biased technological change, inequality and polarisation in the United States.

21. Acemoglu, Gancia and Zilibotti (2015[61]) study how technological progress is linked to offshoring from more to less-advanced economies and what effect this link has on wages. Offshoring makes less skill-intensive products cheaper, which increases investment in (innovation in) skill-intensive products, at least at low levels of offshoring.

22. Early research found that computerisation played an important role in explaining growing wage differentials (Krueger, 1993[40]), but similar results can be found when considering the impact of pencil use (DiNardo and Pischke, 1997[46]), which points to unobserved underlying drivers of both computerisation and returns to skills.

23. Empirical research on the returns to education since the seminal contribution by Mincer (1974[39]) finds positive returns to education, but the true extent is difficult to ascertain as educational choices depend on innate and acquired skills (Card, 2001[49]). For a recent contribution that aims to combine structural modelling and robust estimation of treatment effects for schooling see Heckman, Humphries and Veramendi (2016[43]).

24. Based on the Observatory of Economic Complexity, available at https://atlas.media.mit.edu/en/visualize/tree_map/hs92/export/chn/all/show/2001/ (accessed 13 November 2017).

25. "By 2007, China accounted for over 40 percent of US imports in four four-digit SIC industries (luggage, rubber and plastic footwear, games and toys, and die-cut paperboard) and over 30 percent in 28 other industries, including apparel, textiles, furniture, leather goods, electrical appliances, and jewellery." (Autor, Dorn and Hanson, 2013, p. 2123[57]).

26. Comparison of commuting zones defined as agglomerations of US counties. More/less exposed commuting zones are those at the 75th/25th percentile of the exposure distribution to Chinese import growth between 2000 and 2007. Exposure is defined as the change in per worker imports in the industries weighted by the share of total employment in the industries located in the region (Autor, Dorn and Hanson, 2013[57]).

27. See Autor et al. (Autor et al., 2014[55]) for evidence on manufacturing workers in the United States.

28. Population at the grid cell level for Europe in municipalities (or other local units) outside of Europe. The threshold is 80% of the population in grid cells with at least 300 inhabitants per km^2 for Europe and 85% of population in local units with similar density levels in other countries. See Bachtler et al. (2017[53]) for productivity frontier regions in Europe. Among larger (TL2) OECD countries, the percentage of "mostly urban" regions among the most productive regions is 75% as resource rich rural regions are highly productive in several non-European OECD countries (OECD, 2016[1]).

29. The actual difference in 2014 was 30%. See Ahrend, Lembcke and Schumann (2017[59]).

30. See the overview article by Combes, Duranton and Gobillon (2011[48]).

31. There is also evidence that cities can become victims of their own success. As the urban agglomeration expands and incorporates an increasing number of local administrations (e.g. municipalities), the complexity of co-ordination increases, which appears to accrue a productivity penalty roughly in the same order of magnitude as agglomeration economies (c.f. Chapter 1).

32. For example, Alberta in Canada, Antofagasta in Chile or Groningen in the Netherlands were their countries' regions with the highest labour productivity (gross value added per worker) in 2014 (OECD Regional Statistics [Database]).

33. Predominantly rural areas close to cities are small (territorial level 3, TL3) rural regions in which at least 50% of the population lives within a 60-minute drive of an urban centre with at least 50 000 inhabitants (OECD, 2016[67]).

34. See the results and discussions in OECD (2017[25])for details.

35. Italian low-growth regions are an exception for new firm creations as the southern regions have higher birth rates than the north, but the average size remains smaller than in the new firms created in the north. For Portugal there are less firm creations in the lagging parts of the country, but their size is, on average, larger than in Lisbon and on the Portuguese archipelagos.

36. See OECD (2018[68]) for details.

37. See Ahrend et al. (2017[60]) for evidence on borrowed agglomeration benefits for five OECD countries, Camagni, Capello and Caragliu (2015[50]) for evidence for Europe and OECD (2015[63]) for a general discussion.

38. See OECD (2015[21]) and Ahrend and Schumann (2014[33]) for details.

39. Microdata estimates for Germany for 1999-2007 (Ahrend and Lembcke, 2016[66]).

40. See OECD (2016[64]) and OECD (2017[62]) for details.

41. The top-100 companies in the German *Mittelstand* are selected from a sample of about 3 500 companies based on growth in turnover and profits. The *Mittelstand* classification is not based on an official categorisation. It broadly aims to capture medium-sized companies, but many firms in the sample exceed thresholds typically used in terms of size or turnover. www.munich-strategy.com/de/publikationen/branchenstudien/management-reader/top-100-ranking-des-mittelstands-2016.html (accessed 09 November 2017).

42. See OECD (2007[65]) for a delineation of the Randstad.

43. See OECD (2016[30]) for details on the metro areas of Rotterdam-The Hague and connections to Amsterdam (the longest link between major cities in the Randstad).

References

Acemoglu, D. and D. Autor (2011), "Skills, Tasks and Technologies: Implications for Employment and Earnings", in Card, D. and O. Ashenfelter (eds.), *Handbook of Labor Economics*, Elsevier. [14]

Acemoglu, D., G. Gancia and F. Zilibotti (2015), "Offshoring and Directed Technical Change", *American Economic Journal: Macroeconomics*, Vol. 7/3, pp. 84-122. [61]

Ahlfeldt, G. and A. Feddersen (2015), "From Periphery to Core: Measuring Agglomeration Effects Using High-Speed Rail", *SERC Discussion Paper*, No. 172, Spatial Economics Research Centre. [28]

Ahrend, R. and A. Schumann (2014), "Does Regional Economic Growth Depend on Proximity to Urban Centres?", *OECD Regional Development Working Papers*, No. 2014/7, OECD Publishing, Paris, http://dx.doi.org/10.1787/5jz0t7fxh7wc-en. [33]

Ahrend, R. and A. Lembcke (2016), "Does It Pay to Live in Big(ger) Cities? : The Role of Agglomeration Benefits, Local Amenities, and Costs of Living", *OECD Regional Development Working Papers*, No. 2016/9, OECD Publishing, Paris, http://dx.doi.org/10.1787/e0490ba8-en. [66]

Ahrend, R., A. Lembcke and A. Schumann (2017), "The Role of Urban Agglomerations for Economic and Productivity Growth", *International Productivity Monitor, CSLS-OECD Special Issue from the First OECD Global Forum on Productivity*, Vol. 32, pp. 161-179. [59]

Ahrend, R. et al. (2017), "What Makes Cities More Productive? Evidence From Five OECD Countries on the Role of Urban Governance", *Journal of Regional Science*, Vol. 57/3, pp. 385-410. [60]

Alder, S., D. Lagakos and L. Ohanian (2014), "Competitive Pressure and the Decline of the Rust Belt: A Macroeconomic Analysis", *NBER Working Paper*, No. 20538, National Bureau of Economic Research. [58]

Andrews, D., C. Criscuolo and P. Gal (2015), "Frontier Firms, Technology Diffusion and Public Policy: Micro Evidence from OECD Countries", *OECD Productivity Working Papers*, No. 2, OECD Publishing, Paris, http://dx.doi.org/10.1787/5jrql2q2jj7b-en. [27]

Arntz, M., T. Gregory and U. Zierahn (2016), "The Risk of Automation for Jobs in OECD Countries: A Comparative Analysis", *OECD Social, Employment and Migration Working Papers*, No. 189, OECD Publishing, Paris, http://dx.doi.org/10.1787/5jlz9h56dvq7-en. [20]

Autor, D., F. Levy and R. Murnane (2003), "The Skill Content of Recent Technological Change: An Empirical Exploration", *The Quarterly Journal of Economics*, Vol. 118/4, pp. 1279-1333. [56]

Autor, D., L. Katz and M. Kearney (2008), "Trends in U.S. Wage Inequality: Revising the Revisionists", *The Review of Economics and Statistics*, Vol. 90/2, pp. 300-323. [54]

Autor, D., D. Dorn and G. Hanson (2013), "The China Syndrome: Local Labor Market Effects of Import Competition in the United States", *American Economic Review*, Vol. 103/6, pp. 2121-2168. [57]

Autor, D. et al. (2014), "Trade Adjustment: Worker-Level Evidence", *The Quarterly Journal of Economics*, Vol. 129/4, pp. 1799-1860. [55]

Bachtler, J. et al. (2017), *Towards Cohesion Policy 4.0: Structural Transformation and Inclusive Growth*, Regional Studies Association (RSA Europe). [53]

Blanchard, O. and L. Katz (1992), "Regional Evolutions", *Brookings Papers on Economic Activity*, Vol. 1. [52]

Byrne, D., J. Fernald and M. Reinsdorf (2016), "Does the United States Have a Productivity Slowdown or a Measurement Problem?", *Brookings Papers on Economic Activity*, pp. 109-157. [51]

Camagni, R., R. Capello and A. Caragliu (2015), "The Rise of Second-Rank Cities: What Role for Agglomeration Economies?", *European Planning Studies*, Vol. 23/6, pp. 1069-1089. [50]

Card, D. (2001), "Estimating the Return to Schooling: Progress on Some Persistent Econometric Problems", *Econometrica*, Vol. 69/5, pp. 1127-1160. [49]

Combes, P., G. Duranton and L. Gobillon (2011), "The Identification of Agglomeration Economies", *Journal of Economic Geography*, Vol. 11, pp. 253-266. [48]

Combes, P., G. Duranton and L. Gobillon (2016), "The Costs of Agglomeration: House and Land Prices in French Cities", *CEPR Working Paper* 9240 (revised version). [34]

Cusumano, M. (1988), "Manufacturing Innovation: Lessons from the Japanese Auto Industry", *MIT Sloan Management Review*, Vol. 30/1. [47]

de Avillez, R. (2012), "Sectoral Contributions to Labour Productivity Growth in Canada: Does the Choice of Decomposition Formula Matter?", *International Productivity Monitor*, Vol. 24, pp. 97-117. [8]

De Gregorio, J., A. Giovannini and H. Wolf (1994), "International evidence on tradables and nontradables inflation", *European Economic Review*, Vol. 38/6, pp. 1225-1244. [2]

Deming, D. (2017), "The Growing Importance of Social Skills in the Labor Market*", *The Quarterly Journal of Economics*, Vol. 132/4, pp. 1593-1640. [13]

DiNardo, J. and J. Pischke (1997), "The Returns to Computer Use Revisited: Have Pencils Changed the Wage Structure Too?", *The Quarterly Journal of Economics*, Vol. 112/1, pp. 291-303. [46]

European Commission (2017), "Competitiveness in Low-Income and Low-Growth Regions: The Lagging Regions Report", *European Commission Staff Working Document*, European Commission. [26]

Foster, L., J. Haltiwanger and C. Krizan (2006), "Market Selection, Reallocation, and Restructuring in the U.S. Retail Trade Sector in the 1990s", *The Review of Economics and Statistics*, Vol. 88/4, pp. 748-758. [45]

Froy, F., S. Giguère and M. Meghnagi (2012), "Skills for Competitiveness: A Synthesis Report", *OECD Local Economic and Employment Development (LEED) Working Papers*, No. 2012/9, OECD Publishing, Paris, http://dx.doi.org/10.1787/5k98xwskmvr6-en. [10]

Fujita, M., P. Krugman and A. Venables (1999), *The Spatial Economy: Cities, Regions and International Trade*, MIT Press, Cambridge. [31]

Gervais, A. and J. Jensen (2013), "The Tradability of Services: Geographic Concentration and Trade Costs", *National Bureau of Economic Research*, No. 19759. [4]

Goos, M. and A. Manning (2007), "Lousy and Lovely Jobs: The Rising Polarization of Work in Britain", *The Review of Economics and Statistics*, Vol. 89/1, pp. 118-133. [12]

Goos, M., A. Manning and A. Salomons (2014), "Explaining Job Polarization: Routine-Biased Technological Change and Offshoring", *American Economic Review*, Vol. 104/8, pp. 2509-2526. [15]

Greenstone, M., R. Hornbeck and E. Moretti (2010), "Identifying Agglomeration Spillovers: Evidence from Winners and Losers of Large Plant Openings", *Journal of Political Economy*, Vol. 118/3, pp. 536-598. [44]

Heckman, J., J. Humphries and G. Veramendi (2016), "Returns to Education: The Causal Effects of Education on Earnings, Health and Smoking", *NBER Working Papers*, No. 22291, National Bureau of Economic Research, Cambridge, MA, http://dx.doi.org/10.3386/w22291. [43]

Hlatshwayo, S. and M. Spence (2014), "Demand and Defective Growth Patterns: The Role of The Tradable and Non-Tradable Sectors in an Open Economy", *American Economic Review: Papers & Proceedings*, Vol. 104/5, pp. 272-277. [42]

Jensen, J. et al. (2005), "Tradable Services: Understanding the Scope and Impact of Services Offshoring [with Comments and Discussion]", *Brookings Trade Forum*, pp. 75-133. [3]

Ketels, C. and S. Protsiv (2016), "European Cluster Panorama 2016", *European Cluster Observatory*. [24]

Krafcik, J. (1988), "Triumph of the Lean Production System", *MIT Sloan Management Review*, Vol. 30/1. [41]

Krueger, A. (1993), "How Computers Have Changed the Wage Structure: Evidence from Microdata, 1984-1989", *The Quarterly Journal of Economics*, Vol. 108/1, pp. 33-60. [40]

Mincer, J. (1974), *Schooling, Experience, and Earnings*, National Bureau of Economic Research, Columbia University Press. [39]

Mokyr, J., C. Vickers and N. Ziebarth (2015), "The History of Technological Anxiety and the Future of Economic Growth: Is This Time Different?", *The Journal of Economic Perspectives*, Vol. 29/3, pp. 31-50. [38]

Moretti, E. (2010), "Local Multipliers", *American Economic Review*, Vol. 100/2, pp. 373-377. [6]

Moretti, E. and P. Thulin (2013), "Local multipliers and human capital in the United States and Sweden", *Industrial and Corporate Change*, Vol. 22/1, pp. 339-362. [7]

OECD (2007), *OECD Territorial Reviews: Randstad Holland, Netherlands 2007*, OECD Territorial Reviews, OECD Publishing, Paris, http://dx.doi.org/10.1787/9789264007932-en. [65]

OECD (2012), *Promoting Growth in All Regions*, OECD Publishing, Paris, http://dx.doi.org/10.1787/9789264174634-en. [29]

OECD (2013), *Rural-Urban Partnerships: An Integrated Approach to Economic Development*, OECD Rural Policy Reviews, OECD Publishing, Paris, http://dx.doi.org/10.1787/9789264204812-en. [22]

OECD, WTO and World Bank Group (2014), *Global Value Chains: Challenges, Opportunities and Implications for Policy*, Report prepared for submission to the G20 Trade Ministers Meeting, OECD Publishing, https://www.oecd.org/tad/gvc_report_g20_july_2014.pdf. [18]

OECD (2014), *Employment and Skills Strategies in the United States*, OECD Reviews on Local Job Creation, OECD Publishing, Paris, http://dx.doi.org/10.1787/9789264209398-en. [9]

OECD (2014), *Innovation and Modernising the Rural Economy*, OECD Rural Policy Reviews, OECD Publishing, Paris, http://dx.doi.org/10.1787/9789264205390-en. [23]

OECD (2015), *The Metropolitan Century: Understanding Urbanisation and its Consequences*, OECD Publishing, Paris, http://dx.doi.org/10.1787/9789264228733-en. [63]

OECD (2015), *The Metropolitan Century: Understanding Urbanisation and its Consequences*, OECD Publishing, Paris, http://dx.doi.org/10.1787/9789264228733-en. [21]

OECD (2016), "Skills for a Digital World: 2016 Ministerial Meeting on the Digital Economy Background Report", *OECD Digital Economy Papers*, No. 250, OECD Publishing, Paris, http://dx.doi.org/10.1787/5jlwz83z3wnw-en. [19]

OECD (2016), *Road Infrastructure, Inclusive Development and Traffic Safety in Korea*, OECD Publishing, Paris, http://dx.doi.org/10.1787/9789264255517-en. [64]

OECD (2016), *OECD Territorial Reviews: The Metropolitan Region of Rotterdam-The Hague, Netherlands*, OECD Territorial Reviews, OECD Publishing, Paris, http://dx.doi.org/10.1787/9789264249387-en. [30]

OECD (2016), *OECD Territorial Reviews: Bergamo, Italy*, OECD Territorial Reviews, OECD Publishing, Paris, http://dx.doi.org/10.1787/9789264251984-en. [17]

OECD (2016), *OECD Regional Outlook 2016: Productive Regions for Inclusive Societies*, OECD Publishing, Paris, http://dx.doi.org/10.1787/9789264260245-en. [16]

OECD (2016), *OECD Regional Outlook 2016: Productive Regions for Inclusive Societies*, OECD Publishing, Paris, http://dx.doi.org/10.1787/9789264260245-en. [1]

OECD (2016), *OECD Regions at a Glance 2016*, OECD Publishing, Paris, http://dx.doi.org/10.1787/reg_glance-2016-en. [67]

OECD (2017), *Urban Transport Governance and Inclusive Development in Korea*, OECD Publishing, Paris, http://dx.doi.org/10.1787/9789264272637-en. [62]

OECD (2017), *The Geography of Firm Dynamics: Measuring Business Demography for Regional Development: Demography for Regional Development*, OECD Publishing, Paris, http://dx.doi.org/10.1787/9789264286764-en. [25]

OECD (2017), *OECD Economic Outlook, Volume 2017 Issue 1*, OECD Publishing, Paris, http://dx.doi.org/10.1787/eco_outlook-v2017-1-en. [11]

OECD (2018), *OECD Territorial Reviews: The Megaregion of Western Scandinavia*, OECD Publishing, Paris, http://dx.doi.org/10.1787/9789264290679-en. [32]

OECD (2018), *OECD Rural Policy Reviews: Poland 2018*, OECD Publishing, Paris, http://dx.doi.org/10.1787/9789264289925-en. [68]

Rodrik, D. (2016), "Premature deindustrialization", *Journal of Economic Growth*, Vol. 21/1, pp. 1-33. [5]

Smith, A. (1776), *An Inquiry into the Nature and Causes of the Wealth of Nations*, Project Gutenberg. [37]

Tan, M. (2017), "Uneven growth of urban clusters in megaregions and its policy implications for new urbanization in China", *Land Use Policy*, Vol. 66/Supplement C, pp. 72-79. [35]

Ye, M., B. Meng and S. Wei (2015), "Measuring Smile Curves in Global Value Chains", *IDE Discussion Paper* 530. [36]

Chapter 3. Global trends and regional links: Jobs, clusters and global value chains

The previous chapters outlined the role of tradable sectors and of cities as sources and catalysts of productivity growth. This chapter considers two concrete aspects of global trade. The first aspect is the clustering of related traded activities within regions and the role of concentration and diversification in productivity growth. The second is the integration of regions in global trade relationships. Rather than exports themselves, "global value chains" measure the overall contribution of a region's economy to products that are comprised of parts made in different countries and regions before being assembled into a final good.

Chapter synopsis

Clusters of economic activity are important sources of innovations and productivity growth. Yet, the importance of individual clusters for regional economies varies strongly. In some European regions, the largest cluster employs less than 5% of the workforce, whereas in others it employs more than 40% of the workforce. At the same time, there appears to be no statistical link between the size of the largest cluster in a region and the total share of regional economic activity that occurs within clusters. This indicates that greater specialisation in a few clusters does not lead to a greater overall importance of clusters and raises the question to what degree regions should try to specialise in just a few, potentially very large clusters, or diversify across many smaller clusters.

While highly specialised regions tend to have higher levels of per capita gross domestic product (GDP) than regions whose economy is more evenly distributed across many clusters, their per capita GDP growth rate is lower than in more diversified regions. This implies that specialisation is increasing when regions become richer, but this effect can limit their future growth potential.

Policy makers should therefore consider counteracting excessive specialisation by encouraging diversification of the regional economy. In this context, optimal degrees of diversification differ from region to region. Dense urban economies can generate greater economic diversity than economies in sparsely-populated, rural areas. Not all forms of diversification are likely to have the same positive effects. Evidence suggests that diversification into so-called “related varieties” (economic activities that are characterised by similar, but not identical processes) is most beneficial. Through such diversification, innovations can spread from one cluster to another without restricting opportunities for future growth through excessive concentration in a single economic activity.

The integration of regions in global production process as part of a “global value chain” (GVC) can also create benefits in terms of innovation and productivity. Global value chains is a term used to describe supply chains that divide production processes into different stages distributed across several countries. After growing rapidly in importance throughout the 1990s, GVC integration in most regions in Europe remained stable from 2000 to 2010 except for an intense but brief dip in the aftermath of the global financial crisis in 2008. As of 2010, an average of approximately 18% of all value-added in European regions was created within GVCs.

Although GVC integration coincides with higher GDP levels, the effect is not uniform. Regions with either particularly low or particularly high productivity levels have GVC participation rates that are below average. In low productivity regions, this is due to a weak tradable sector. In contrast, the low share of GVC integration in high productivity regions is due to a strong service sector, for which trade might not always be fully captured in the underlying data. Highly productive regions often include large cities, whose economy is dominated by services that are less tradable than manufactured goods.

Moreover, not all types of GVC integration yield the same benefits. The greater the amount of value-added produced in a region, the higher the economic benefits. Labour intensive low-skilled manufacturing that creates little value-added can bring important jobs to regions with high unemployment rates, but it offers little potential to diversify the economy. Furthermore, such production will only stay in a region while wage levels remain low. Instead of focusing on these activities, regions should try to attract production activities at the beginning and at the end of a GVC that are likely to add more value, such as product development, marketing and after-sales services.

Regional clusters

Cluster policies have long been policy instruments in many OECD countries. They have been identified as a well-established mainstay of regional development policy in the OECD (2007[1]) and their on-going importance as a policy instrument has been confirmed in the OECD (2016[2]). In particular, cluster policies are frequently used to promote economic development in lagging regions.

The rationale behind cluster policies is based on agglomeration benefits and economies of scale that are created by clusters. These mechanisms make it beneficial for firms to be located within very close proximity of one another. However, clusters do not always emerge naturally because of friction and co-ordination failures that prevent firms from coordinating with each other about where to locate. In such situations, public intervention can provide the impetus for clusters to emerge and to reap the associated benefits.

Furthermore, cluster policies can also been beneficial if they contribute to a process of learning and self-discovery at the regional level. By bringing together different regional stakeholders, cluster policies and the processes related to their design and implementation can help regional governments to develop a better understanding of the strengths and weaknesses of a region. Through this mechanism, cluster policies can also help to improve other economic policies at the regional level.

Despite these potential advantages, there are risks associated with cluster policies. They can lead to insufficient diversification, lock-in into unsuccessful investment strategies and over-reliance on key firms (OECD, 2007[1]). Furthermore, cluster policies have often been driven by wishful thinking in the sense that policy makers try to promote clusters for which no realistic basis exists in the region. Lastly, cluster policies can also lead to an overreliance on a few or even a single cluster. As discussed in the following, this can stifle innovation and increase susceptibility to economic shocks.

This section does not intend to assess cluster policy in all its dimensions. Instead, it focuses on two angles. First, it analyses how regional specialisation in a few clusters - compared to broad diversification - is related to regional GDP growth and economic convergence. Second, it analyses the growth performance of regions depending on how their clusters are distributed within the tradable and non-tradable sector. Subsequently, it connects the findings to existing literature and develops policy implications.

Cluster data

Traded clusters are defined as groups of firms that are connected through one or more linkages, such as co-location, use of similar skills, and direct input-output relationships. Based on these linkages, the European Cluster Observatory (Ketels and Protsiv, 2016[3]) defines 51 clusters in traded sectors with all remaining firms (and their employment) falling into non-traded "local" clusters (for simplicity this chapter refers to traded clusters as "clusters"). The clusters follow the definition of Delgado, Porter and Stern (2016[4]), but have been adapted to account for differences in the economic structure between Europe and the United States. The focus on the tradable sector is explained by the fact that economic activity in the non-tradable sector is focused on the local market. If goods or services are not traded across regional borders, a region produces by definition the amounts that are demanded within the region. Therefore, the potential for regions to specialise in the non-tradable sector is limited.

Box 3.1. A method for defining traded clusters

The cluster definition developed by Delgado, Porter and Stern (2016[41]) uses data for the United States on co-location patterns of employment and the number of establishments in detailed (3-digit) industry groups, together with national-level information from input-output matrices that calculate flows of products and services across industries and similarity in occupational structure using employment shares in 3-digit occupational categories. These linkages are used to group industries into a set of defined clusters using a hierarchical cluster function for continuous data. The resulting clusters are regionally comparable as the same industries belong to the same cluster in all regions. In that sense the definition is not region-specific, but allows for interregional comparisons.

Source: Delgado, Porter and Stern (2016[4]).

The cluster data of the European Cluster Observatory has several advantages for analysing both the effect of specialisation and the role of the tradable sector on regional economic growth and productivity. Compared to more common data that divides economic activities by sectors, cluster data provides a better representation of the connections between businesses. For example, cluster data would group a service activity and a manufacturing activity within the same cluster if they contribute to the production of the same product. In contrast, such activities would show up in different sectors in sectoral data where the economic links between the two activities are invisible.

While the importance of clusters can be measured in different ways, this report focuses on full-time equivalent employment as the key measure for the size of a cluster. Due to its clarity, this measure provides the best data quality. Other measures, such as gross value-added, depend on accounting methods and are potentially less reliable.

The prevalence of clusters varies significantly across regions

Traded clusters' contribution to employment varies widely across regions. On average, 46% of the total full-time equivalent employment of a region takes place within clusters, with 25% as the lowest share in a region and 86% as the highest share. Figure 3.1 shows the distribution of employment in tradable clusters across all regions. In most regions, between 40% and 60% of the working population works in clusters, but there are several regions where the share is significantly higher or lower.

Figure 3.1. Employment in traded clusters

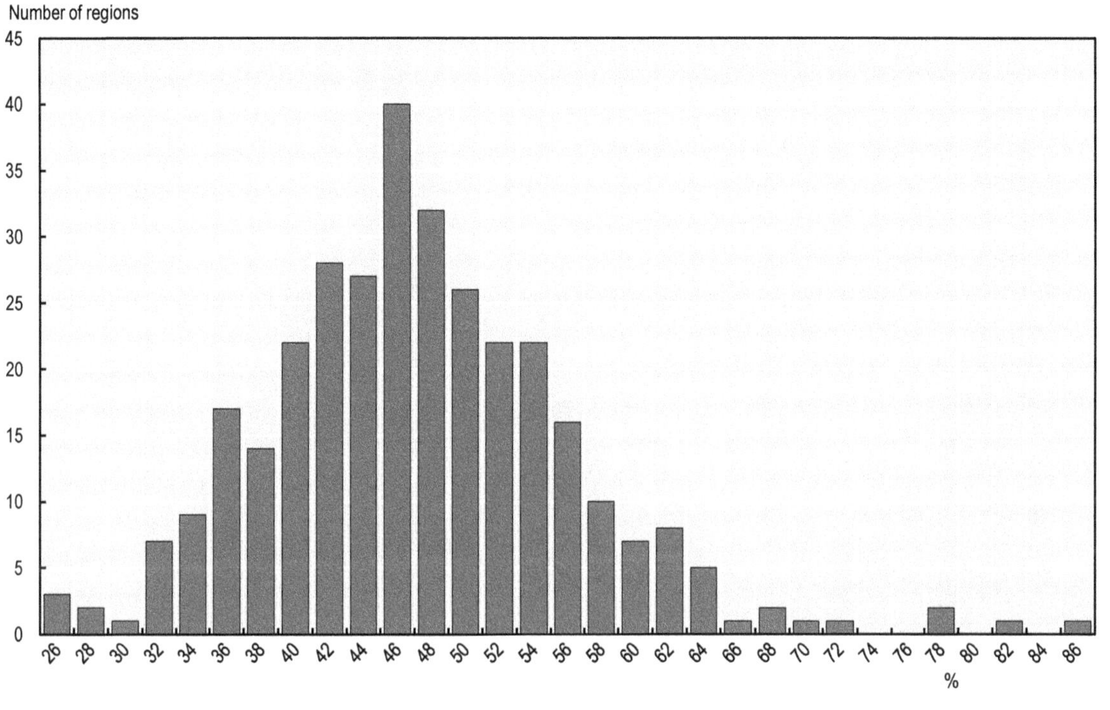

Note: Histogram depicting the number of NUTS 2 regions grouped by FTE employment share in traded clusters.
Source: Calculations based on Ketels and Protsiv (2016[3])with data provided by the authors.

StatLink http://dx.doi.org/10.1787/888933708045

Across all regions, 8.5%, on average, of full-time equivalent employment is provided by the largest cluster. The importance of individual clusters varies substantially. In most regions, the largest cluster in terms of jobs provides between 5% and 15% of all full time employment. But Figure 3.2 shows that in some regions the most dominant cluster accounts for a much higher percentage of employment. In 12 regions, the largest cluster provides more than 20%of all jobs. In eight out of those 12 regions, *Transport and Logistics* is the dominant cluster, providing up to 40% of all employment.

Figure 3.2. Share of employment provided by largest cluster

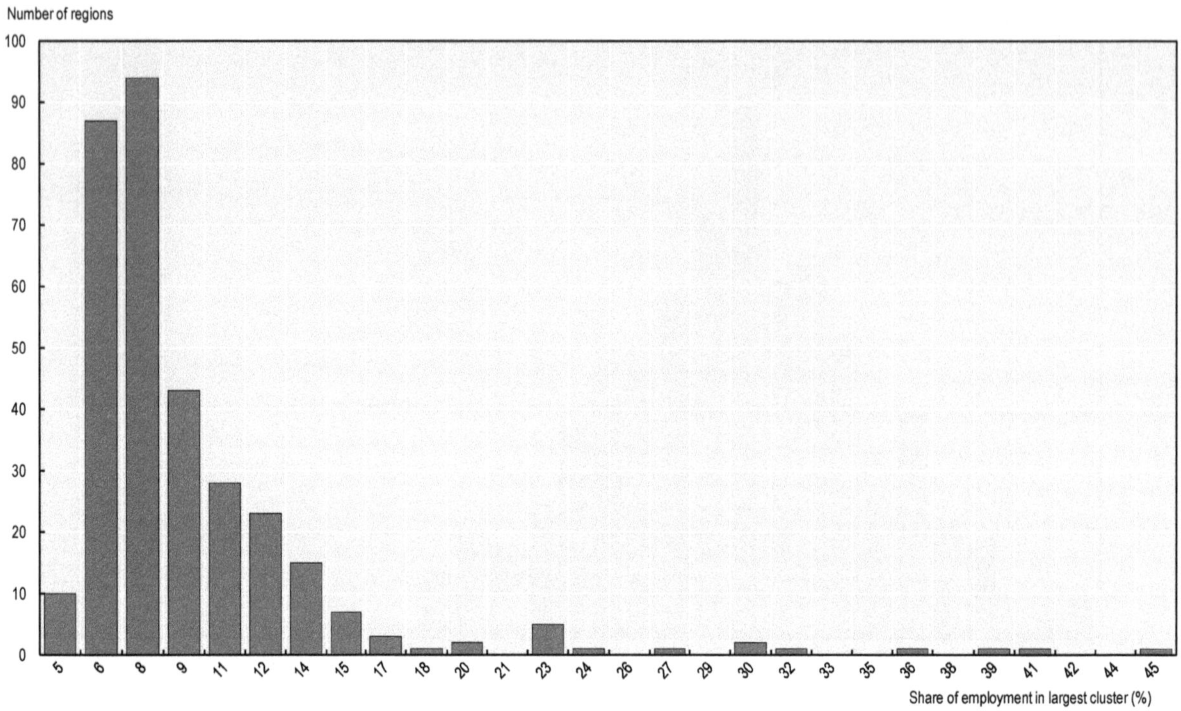

Note: Histogram depicting the number of NUTS 2 regions grouped by the share of total FTE employment in the largest traded cluster.
Source: Calculations based on Ketels and Protsiv (2016[3]) with data provided by the authors.

StatLink http://dx.doi.org/10.1787/888933708064

The degree of specialisation in a single cluster is unrelated to the overall share of jobs provided by clusters. However, some regions stand out because of particularly strong specialisation in single clusters. In particular, regions in Greece show an exceptional reliance on their largest cluster. On average, a Greek region relies on the largest cluster for 17% f all employment, approximately twice the average of all European regions.

More generally, low-growth regions differ from other regions due to a low prevalence of economic activity in traded clusters in combination with a strong reliance on their largest cluster.[1] As can be seen in Figure 3.3, low-growth regions tend, on average, to have a much smaller share of jobs in clusters. Given that clusters are only defined for traded activities, this confirms the finding that low-growth regions tend to have underdeveloped tradable sectors.

Even though low-growth regions have comparatively few jobs in clusters, the relative size of their largest cluster compared to all other clusters is significantly bigger than average. The largest cluster employs approximately 2 percentage points more people than the average largest cluster in all NUTS2 regions. As a result, most lagging regions fall into the upper left quadrant of Figure 3.3.

Figure 3.3. Specialisation and employment in regional clusters

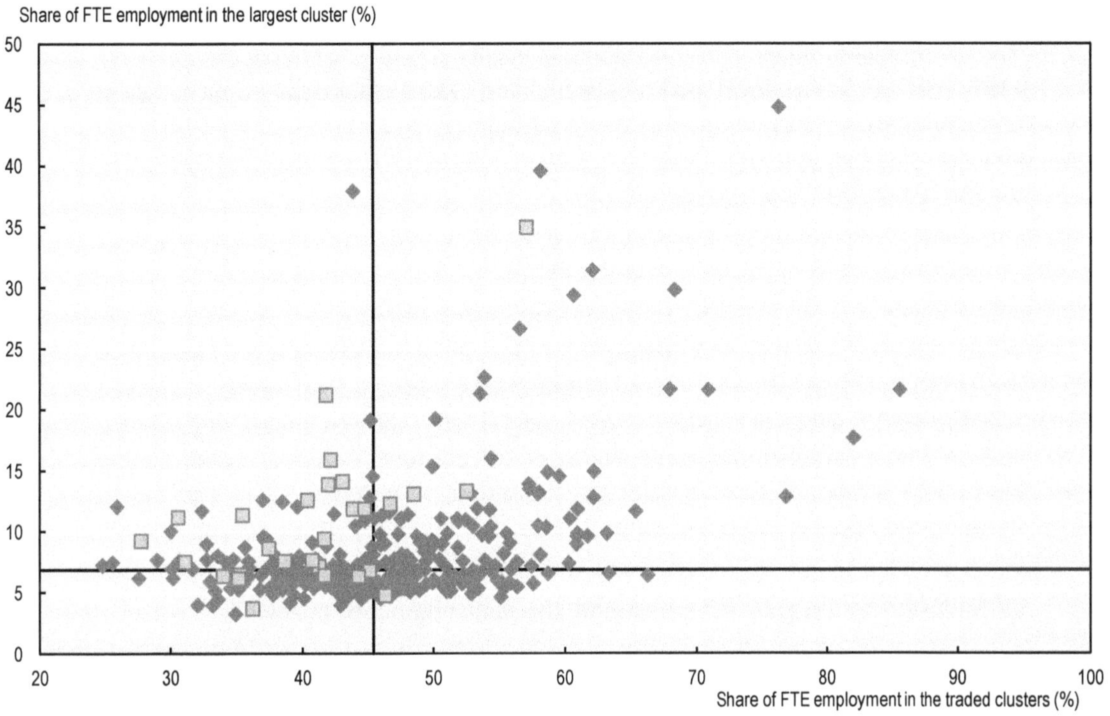

Note: The vertical and horizontal lines indicate the median share of jobs in traded clusters and the median share of FTE employment in the largest cluster, respectively. Diamonds indicate European NUTS2 regions, squares indicate low-growth and low-income regions as defined by the EU Lagging Regions Initiative (European Commission, 2017[5]).

Source: Calculations based on Ketels and Protsiv (2016[3]) with data provided by the authors.

StatLink http://dx.doi.org/10.1787/888933708083

Highly specialised regions – high per capita GDP but low growth rates

The question of whether regions benefit from being specialised or diversified has been discussed in a seminal article by Glaeser et al. (1992[6]). Studying different cities in the United States, the authors find that cities with a diversified industrial structure have higher employment growth rates than cities with a high degree of industrial specialisation.

The data on regional clusters can be used to test this hypothesis at the regional level. In order to measure the degree to which a region is specialised into selected clusters, a Herfindahl-type index can be computed. The Herfindahl index is a well-established measure that can be used to describe concentration or specialisation in a variety of settings (see Box 3.2). It takes a value of close to 0 if all clusters contribute equally to employment and a value of 1 if all employment is concentrated in a single cluster. In other words, a higher value of the Herfindahl index is associated with greater specialisation.

Box 3.2. The Herfindahl index

The Herfindahl index is a commonly used measure of concentration or specialisation. It was developed by Herfindahl (1950[71]) to measure concentration and market power of individual firms in an industry and has since been used as a measure of concentration in a variety of other settings. It is computed according to the following formula:

$$H = \sum_{i=1}^{N} c_i^2 .$$

When used to calculate the degree of regional specialisation into clusters c_i represents the share of employment within cluster i among total employment and N is the total number of clusters. Expressed verbally, the Herfindahl index is the sum of the squared employment shares of all clusters. A higher value on the Herfindahl index indicates greater specialisation of a region. The Herfindahl index would take its maximum value of $H = 1$ if all employment within a region were provided by a single cluster and would take its minimum value of $H = \frac{1}{N}$ if all N clusters of a region were to employ the same number of people.

Two patterns appear when analysing the relation between cluster-specialisation and regional economic performance. First, regions where employment is highly concentrated in a few clusters tend to have higher per capita GDP levels than regions where employment is distributed across many clusters. Second, the opposite is true concerning per capita GDP growth. Regions that are diversified in the sense that employment is evenly distributed across many clusters have had, on average, higher growth rates since 2008 than regions where employment is concentrated in a few clusters.

Table 3.1 shows the results of regressions of log per capita GDP levels and average annual per capita GDP growth rates between 2008 and 2014. For ease of interpretation, the Herfindahl index has been normalised by its standard deviation. Thus, the coefficient on the Herfindahl index in Specification 1 implies that regions that have a 1-standard deviation higher Herfindahl index (i.e. are more specialised) and have on average a per capita GDP level that is 7.45% higher. The corresponding coefficient in Specification 2 shows, however, that those regions also had 0.14 percentage points lower annual per capita GDP growth between 2008 and 2014.

Importantly, the relationship between the Herfindahl index of cluster-specialisation and annual per capita GDP growth does not depend on whether a region initially had high or low per capita GDP levels. Specification 3 shows regression results that include log per capita GDP in 2008 as a control variable. The coefficient estimate on the normalised Herfindahl index remains virtually unchanged compared to Specification 2. In other words, a higher specialisation in a few clusters is associated with lower per capita GDP growth between 2008 and 2014, no matter whether the region had high or low per capita GDP levels in 2008.

Table 3.1. The effect of cluster specialisation on per capita GDP and per capita GDP growth

	Log per capita GDP 2014 (1)	Annual per capita GDP growth 2008-14 (2)	Annual per capita GDP growth 2008-14 (3)
Normalised Herfindahl Index	0.0745*** (0.0258)	-0.0014** (0.0006)	-0.0016*** (0.0006)
Log per capita GDP 2008	-	-	0.0031 (0.0030)
Country-fixed effects	Yes	Yes	Yes
Number of regions	279	272	272

Note: ***,**,* indicate statistical significance at the 99%, 95%, and 90% confidence level, respectively. Heteroskedasticity robust standard errors in parenthesis.
Source: Calculations based on Ketels and Protsiv (2016[3]) with data provided by the authors and Eurostat.

The results in Table 3.1 allow for several related explanations. One possible explanation could be that it is not specialisation itself that has positive effects on growth but increasing specialisation that benefits growth. For example, regions that can shift resources from unproductive into productive clusters by specialising in them would see higher levels of per capita growth.

This explanation is consistent with the abovementioned econometric results. Since regions that have low levels of specialisation have greater potential for growing specialisation, it would explain why regions with low levels of specialisation see higher per capita GDP growth. It would also explain why regions with high levels of specialisation have high per capita GDP levels. These regions have gone through the growth-enhancing process of increasing specialisation and have consequently high per capita GDP levels, but due to their already high levels of specialisation they have little scope for further specialisation. The explanation is also in line with findings by Delgado et al. (2012[8]), who show that highly specialised clusters do not contribute to job creation. Instead, the authors find that job creation primarily occurs in related industries where the degree of specialisation is lower.

An alternative explanation that is equally consistent with the pattern above would be a natural trend towards greater specialisation as regions grow richer. More advanced industries tend to require more specialised knowledge and expertise. This may push regional economies towards greater specialisation as they become wealthier. According to this explanation, increasing specialisation does not cause growth. Rather, it would be a side effect of the greater complexity of more advanced economies. If high levels of specialisation prevent future growth, this trend could slow down growth if it is not counteracted by public policies.

Further research is required to determine the underlying causes of the abovementioned empirical regularities. Nevertheless, they have important policy implications even if their causes are not fully understood. They suggest that overly high specialisation can have detrimental effects on growth even though it is associated with high GDP levels. Thus, policy makers should refrain from encouraging excessive specialisation, especially if regions are already heavily reliant on only a few clusters. Instead, they should support continued growth by carefully encouraging diversification.

Box 3.3. Cluster data as a measure of traded activities

As discussed above, the definition of clusters by the European Cluster Observatory covers activities that are primarily or exclusively traded. Thus, the share of employment provided by the 51 defined clusters also provides an alternative measure of the importance of the traded sector in a region.

Specification 1 shows that regions with a larger share of employment in clusters tend to have higher per capita GDP levels than regions with a lower share of employment in clusters. A region with a one percentage point higher share of employment in clusters has a per capita GDP level that is approximately 2.2% higher. In contrast, Specifications 2 and 4 show that no statistically significant relation can be found between employment in tradable clusters and per capita GDP.

Table 3.2. Regional clusters and economic performance

	Log per capita GDP	Per capita GDP growth 2008-14
	(1)	(2)
Employment in tradable clusters in %	0.0219*** (0.0041)	0.0001 (0.0001)
Log per capita GDP in 2008	-	0.0006 (0.0032)
Labour productivity relative to frontier in 2008	-	-
Country fixed-effects	YES	YES
Number of regions	268	272

Note: ***,**,* indicate statistical significance at the 99%, 95%, and 90% confidence level, respectively. Heteroskedasticity robust standard errors in parenthesis.
Source: Calculations based on Ketels and Protsiv (2016[31]) with data provided by the authors and Eurostat.

Diversification and catching-up

Just as specialisation affects per capita GDP levels and per capita GDP growth, it is likely that it has an effect on productivity levels and catching-up dynamics. Nevertheless, the effect might differ from effects on GDP levels, as it is possible that it affects productivity levels differently than employment levels (which determine GDP levels jointly with productivity).

Table 3.3. Specialisation and catch-up productivity growth

	Labour productivity relative to frontier 2014 (1)	Percentage point change in labour productivity frontier gap 2008-14 (2)	Percentage point change in labour productivity frontier gap 2008-14 (3)
Normalised Herfindahl index	0.0458 (0.0287)	-0.0021** (0.0008)	0.0049 (0.0031)
(Normalised Herfindahl index) * (Labour productivity relative to frontier in 2008)	-	-	-0.0084** (0.0033)
Labour productivity relative to frontier in 2008	-	-0.0025 (0.0066)	-0.0016 (0.0065)
Country fixed-effects	YES	YES	YES
Number of regions	239 (excluding frontier regions)	232 (excluding frontier regions)	232 (excluding frontier regions)

Note: ***,**,* indicate statistical significance at the 99%, 95%, and 90% confidence level, respectively. Heteroskedasticity robust standard errors in parenthesis.
Source: Calculations based on Ketels and Protsiv (2016[3]) with data provided by the authors and Eurostat.

In order to calculate catching-up performance, regional productivity is defined relative to productivity levels in frontier regions (i.e. regions that are ranked in the top 10% for productivity in a given country). Specification 1 in Table 3.3 shows that more specialised regions with a one standard-deviation higher Herfindahl index have productivity levels relative to the frontier that are on average 4.5 percentage points higher. The result, albeit not statistically significant, corresponds to the previous finding that more specialised regions have higher per capita GDP levels. Specification 2 confirms that the effect on catching-up performance is equivalent to the effect on per capita GDP growth, too. Highly specialised regions tend to diverge whereas diversified regions catch-up. A one standard deviation higher specialisation leads to a 0.2 percentage point lower catch-up rate in labour productivity.

Specification 3 varies from the previous estimations as it analyses whether specialisation affects lagging regions differently than those close to the frontier. For this purpose, a so-called 'interaction-term' for the Herfindahl index and labour productivity in 2008 is included. This interaction term can show whether regions that had low labour productivity relative to the frontier in 2008 are differently affected by specialisation than regions that had high labour productivity relative to the frontier. The coefficient on the interaction terms is statistically significant and negative. In contrast, the coefficient on the Herfindahl index changes from Specification 2 and becomes positive and statistically insignificant. This implies that the positive effect of low specialisation is strongest for regions that are strongly lagging behind the frontier.

Importantly, the effects of specialisation on catching up are largely driven by very highly-specialised regions. When excluding regions that have a Herfindahl index of more than two standard deviations above the average, coefficients in Specifications 2 and 3 become very small and statistically insignificant. Thus, specialisation appears to be an impediment to catching up in labour productivity mostly when it is very high. In contrast, the coefficient on the Herfindahl index in Specification 1 remains roughly unchanged. This implies that the general pattern (i.e. specialised regions have higher levels of labour productivity despite lower rates of productivity growth) seems to hold more widely across varying levels of specialisation and diversification.

Specialisation and patenting activity

One possible explanation why highly specialised regions have lower per capita GDP and productivity growth could be lower levels of innovation-related activity. This hypothesis is supported by the analysis of patenting activity in regions. Diversification benefits innovation, insofar as it can be measured by patents per capita. More specialised regions tend to have lower patenting activity per capita. Table 3.4 shows that regions with a one standard deviation higher Herfindahl index have approximately 15% fewer patents per capita than other regions.

Table 3.4. Specialisation and patenting activity

	Log patents per capita (1)	Log patents per capita (2)
Normalised Herfindahl index	-0.146*** (0.050)	-0.597*** (0.114)
Labour productivity relative to frontier	-	4.451*** (0.510)
Country fixed-effects	YES	YES
Number of regions	250	220 (excluding frontier regions)

Note: ***,**,* indicate statistical significance at the 99%, 95%, and 90% confidence level, respectively. Heteroskedasticity robust standard errors in parenthesis.
Source: Calculations based on Ketels and Protsiv (2016[3]) with data provided by the authors and Eurostat.

Perhaps surprisingly, the magnitude of the estimated effect increases significantly if the productivity level of a region relative to the frontier is taken into account. After controlling for labour productivity relative to the frontier, the coefficient in Specification 2 indicates that regions with a one standard deviation higher Herfindahl index have almost 60% fewer patents per capita than other regions. This drastic effect on innovative activity provides a potential explanation for why per capita GDP growth rates in regions with higher specialisation tend to be lower.

In contrast to the negative relation between specialisation and productivity levels, the negative relationship between specialisation and patenting activity is not limited to highly specialised regions. In fact, it exists even among regions that are less specialised than average.

"Related varieties"

While the analysis above confirms that diversification can have positive effects on economic growth and innovation, it is likely that not any one type of diversification across clusters has the same positive effect. Frenken, van Oort and Verburg (2007[9]) and Boschma and Iammarino (2009[10]) show that diversification into so-called "related varieties" has positive effects on employment growth whereas unrelated variety across sectors has little or negative effects on employment growth.

Related variety in this context refers to economic activities that require related skills and knowledge. It does not necessarily imply that the activities are related through direct connections of their businesses or that they are located along the same value chains. In practical terms, related variety is often measured by the degree of diversification within very broadly defined economic sectors. For example, a typical economic sector defined at a high-level would be manufacturing. The greater a region's diversification into 'related varieties' the greater the diversification of that region's manufacturing output across different sub-sectors within manufacturing (e.g. manufacturing of vehicles, manufacturing of machinery, manufacturing of textiles, etc.).

The concept of related variety is linked to an academic debate about how knowledge and innovation is diffused throughout the economy. One school of thought emphasises that innovations are spread primarily within industries, whereas another school of thought argues that innovations are spread across industries. The two schools of thought highlight the importance of different types of knowledge-spillovers. So called Marshall-Arrow-Romer-(MAR)-externalities [named after Marshall (1890[11]), Arrow (1962[12]), and Romer (1986[13])] are knowledge-spillovers that occur within the same industry. In contrast, Jacobs-externalities [named after Jacobs (1969[14])] are spillovers that occur across different industries. Jacobs (1969[14]) argued that ideas and innovation in one industry will eventually be picked up by other industries within the same region. However, such knowledge spillovers are unlikely to occur randomly across different industries. Rather, it is more probable that knowledge is diffused across industries if the industries require similar kinds of knowledge.

Depending on which type of knowledge-spillover is more important, the optimal degree of specialisation would differ. If MAR-externalities dominate, regions would benefit from very high specialisation to maximise the probability of innovations and the impact of spillovers within an industry. In contrast, if Jacobs-externalities are more important, regions benefit from diversification across related varieties as described above. The empirical results presented in this report and the related literature appear to support Jacob-externalities.

Box 3.4. Small steps or great leaps – how to best support innovation?

The related varieties argument assumes implicitly that productivity growth is driven by the adoption and combination of ideas and innovations from related sectors. According to this line of reasoning, technological progress and productivity evolve gradually. Any advancement builds on existing capabilities and economic structures that are already in place. Consequently, strategies based on related varieties appear best suited for regions that already have some successful economic clusters already in place. In contrast, lagging regions that are most in need of economic development could struggle to successfully implement development strategies based on related varieties because they lack the economic base from which related varieties could emerge.

Furthermore, it is unclear to what degree public intervention is necessary to promote economic development through related varieties. It is possible that the innovation process based on related varieties occurs naturally without the intervention of public policy. If this is true, policy makers would do better to focus on overcoming coordination failures that prevent the emergence of entirely new clusters instead of supporting the evolution of existing ones. In other words, it could be possible that public policies should focus on promoting great leaps in economic development instead of small steps that would occur anyway.

At this point, too little is known about the nature of knowledge diffusion and spillovers to provide a definitive answer to the question. In any case, it is important to bear in mind that strategies focusing on great leaps to support the emergence of entirely new economic clusters have potentially significant downsides and can easily fail (OECD, 2007[11]). There is no guarantee that public policy will be able to identify coordination failures that prevent the emergence of new clusters or that it has the right tools to overcome such failures. Therefore, public support of evolutionary innovation based on related varieties appears to be more promising and less risky in most cases than big bets on great leaps.

Source: Authors elaboration and OECD (2007[11]), *Competitive Regional Clusters: National Policy Approaches*, OECD Publishing, Paris, http://dx.doi.org/10.1787/9789264031838-en.

The idea of related varieties is also reflected in the concept of smart specialisation, which emphasises public support for economic activities instead of sectors (OECD, 2013[15]). Smart specialisation has been a key element of the European Commission's regional development policy since 2011 and the development of a smart specialisation strategy is a prerequisite to receive funding from the European Regional Development Fund (European Commission, 2017[16]). The focus on activities acknowledges the fact that innovations in an economic activity or process can benefit all sectors that make use of the activity or the process.

Despite the overall evidence pointing towards the importance of Jacobs-externalities and thus the benefits of related variety, important nuances need to be taken into account. Recent work by Caragliu, de Dominicis and de Groot (2016[17]) shows that different regions benefit differently from specialisation. In particular, regions with a high density of economic activity benefit from diversification in related variety as described above. In contrast, in low density regions, specialisation in a single industry can be more beneficial. This can be explained by the fact that many economic sectors require a critical mass to function well. In densely-populated areas with substantial economic activity, it is not difficult to achieve this critical mass in many sectors. However, for low density regions, this can only be achieved by specialising in a few selected sectors.

The policy implications of this result go beyond the finding that less dense regions benefit from greater specialisation. More generally, it suggests that a region's optimal degree of specialisation cannot be determined without a thorough understanding of a region's specificities. Beyond density, other characteristics are likely to play a role, such as the degree of polycentricism, geographic characteristics, workforce characteristics and so on.

Diversity and resilience

The diversity of the economic structure of a region has consequences beyond the growth performance of a region - a sufficient degree of diversity can also strengthen a region's resilience to economic shocks. Regions that rely on a single cluster of firms or even on a single firm are at risk of a severe negative downturn if a shock hits the cluster or the firm (OECD, forthcoming[18]). In contrast, if regions are diversified and rely on various economic sectors and many different types of firms, the likelihood that all of them are simultaneously affected by negative shocks is much smaller. As a consequence, diversification can protect regions from severe downturns that are not caused by systemic events that affect all parts of the economy.

Box 3.5. From clusters to open innovation platforms in Tampere Region, Finland

The region of Tampere has a long-standing tradition of innovation and change. It was the cradle of Finnish industrialisation in the 19th century and continued to be a manufacturing powerhouse in the 1960s. It moved towards a university-driven knowledge economy, becoming a Nokia-led global ICT hub from the 1990s to the early 2010s (City of Tampere, 2015[19]).

A technological change in the mobile phone industry obliged Nokia to change its business strategy and to downsize globally. The negative impact of this downsizing showed in the 14.4% fall in Tampere's GDP growth rate between 2008 in 2009 (Statistics Finland, 2015[20]). On the other hand, the large companies that predominantly constitute the region's machine-building sector (mechanical engineering, paper and pulp) continue to play a very important role, accounting for approximately 26% of total employment in the region in 2014 (City of Tampere, 2016[21]). Nonetheless, after the global financial crisis in 2008, this sector faced lower demand and competitive pressures, reducing investment and employment levels.

In light of this context, the region's innovation system needed review. The decline of Nokia and its related industries highlighted the need for Tampere Region to develop a new innovation policy, encouraging a move away from the previous cluster-based emphasis on sectoral specialisation towards a focus on a cross-cutting strategy for innovation. Indeed, the region gradually moved away from the regional cluster specialization policy (1994-2013) towards an open innovation platform policy (2009-present). In the platform economy, co-creation processes tighten the link between research and value creation, across widely different sectors, from administrative support to ICT technologies.

The cross-sectoral innovation strategy adopted by the Tampere region has proved successful in a number of ways. It enabled to break down silos and improve the exchange of expertise, leading to more adaptive and flexible innovation processes, the so-called open platform economy. The involvement of universities and R&D centres contributed to skilled human resource retention and fostered a culture of entrepreneurship.

Sources: Adapted from: OECD (2016[22]), *Resilient Cities,* Preliminary Report: www.oecd.org/cfe/regional-policy/resilient-cities-report-preliminary-version.pdf. City of Tampere (2016[21]), Response to the OECD questionnaire on Resilient Cities, www.tampere.fi/en/index.html; City of Tampere (2015[19]), Tampere: Open/smart/connected: Summary of the application by the city of Tampere, Finland to the contest for the European Capital of Innovation Award", available at: https://fl-cdn.scdn1.secure.raxcdn.com/files/11649/tampere-icapital-proposal.pdf; Statistics Finland (2015[20]) Annual National Accounts, www.stat.fi/til/index_en.html.

In contrast to the abovementioned related varieties argument, Frenken, van Oort and Verburg (2007[9]) show that broad diversification offers the best protection against external shocks. Regions whose economies are diversified across as many sectors as possible (and not just across related varieties) are the least affected by external shocks. Nevertheless, the benefits of such broad diversification as a protection against shocks have to be weighed against any possible negative effect on average growth rates. In many cases, the benefits from improved average economic growth rates due to some specialisation in related varieties will outweigh the risks related to a higher susceptibility to economic shocks.

Box 3.6. Concerted efforts to promote innovation in Tampere Region, Finland

The innovation strategy adopted by the region of Tampere (Finland) (Box 3.5) sets a good example of a collaborative, multi-level innovation strategy. The local, regional and national levels of government have a clear and aligned long-term vision to promote innovation. Universities, public institutions and businesses are closely involved in this process, too.

The city of Tampere has adopted the new Open/Smart/Connected (O/S/C) strategy. It is based on three key elements: open innovation platforms, open data and interfaces and open participation (City of Tampere, 2015[19]). It involves issues of digitalisation, smart urban living, access to information and effective public procurement. The Tampere strategy follows the priorities and activities of the European Commission Horizon 2020 Work Programme 2016-17, such as smart and sustainable cities, promotion of healthy ageing and personalised health care, and piloting of demand-driven collaborative innovation models.

The regional and city strategies benefit from the support of the national government. Finland's national "INKA-Innovative Cities" programme was launched in 2014 to create competitive, high-tech companies and foster innovation clusters. The programme aims to generate new business and new companies from high-quality competences, creating more jobs. It is based on close local co-operation and pooling of resources between science, education, companies and the government. The city of Tampere also plays a key role in the national strategy "The Six City Strategy – Open and Smart Services (2014-2020)", aimed at sustainable development for the six largest Finnish cities. Tampere leads the Six City Strategy spearhead project on open data and collaborates in the projects of open innovation platforms and open participation.

Besides the national government, the open innovation strategies for the Tampere region and city have the support of key stakeholders. The local universities and corporate R&D facilities have started to make a successful transition to a more entrepreneurial and open mode of innovation, through their involvement in various platforms. The Tampere Region Economic Development Agency (TREDEA) provides services, information and assistance to firms and individuals to invest in or start a business venture in the region. TREDEA also leads the region's international marketing on tourism, investment and innovation, through the "Tampere – All Bright!" strategy (www.tampereallbright.fi). Lastly, the Baltic Institute of Finland (BIF) promotes inter-regional co-operation. The BIF has secured a number of European projects and developed networks that support smart specialisation agenda in the Tampere region (Newcastle University, 2015[23]).

Sources: Adapted from OECD (2016[22]), *Resilient Cities,* Preliminary Report: www.oecd.org/cfe/regional-policy/resilient-cities-report-preliminary-version.pdf. City of Tampere (2015[19]), Tampere: Open/smart/connected: Summary of the application by the city of Tampere, Finland to the contest for the European Capital of Innovation Award", available at: https://fl-cdn.scdn1.secure.raxcdn.com/files/11649/tampere-icapital-proposal.pdf; Newcastle University (2015[23]), "Smart specialisation for regional innovation: WP5 regional report on Pirkanmaa (Tampere), Finland", www.regioconeixement.catedra.urv.cat/media/upload/domain_697/arxius/carpeta%20sense%20nom/tampere%20regional%20report%20-%20full%20version%20(october%202015).docx.

Encourage labour force mobility to start new clusters

Domestic and international in-migration can provide an important impetus and the human capital basis for the development of new clusters. Hausmann and Neffke (2016[24]) show that 'pioneer plants' rely heavily on experienced workers hired from other parts of the country. They define pioneer plants as those that open in a region in which no similar industry has existed previously. By definition, these regions do not have a domestic workforce with experience in the industry. Instead of training local workers, firms prefer to hire experienced workers from other regions. The authors argue that this is the case because actual experience provides crucial tacit knowledge that cannot be learned by training alone. Thus, hiring experienced workers from the outside is crucial to successfully open new plants or start new clusters.

To illustrate their point, Hausmann and Neffke (2016[24]) provide a series of historical examples to illustrate how the inflow of migrants created important and long-lasting clusters across the world. The beer brewing industry in the Czech Republic was started by immigrants from Bavaria. Likewise, wine-making in South Africa was introduced by immigrants from France. More recently, high-tech clusters in the People's Republic of China ("China" herafter), India, Israel and other countries were founded by diasporas returning from the U.S. Rhee (1990[25]) shows how Bangladeshi garment workers trained in Korea created the seeds of Bangladesh's successful garment industry.

These examples show that the skills brought by migrants to regions can provide the seeds for new clusters to emerge. More importantly, they also offer the possibility for diversification beyond related varieties into sectors that are completely unrelated to existing clusters. Such diversification is difficult to achieve based on endogenous factors alone, but if successful it offers a large potential for regions. It creates a new economic foundation from which further innovation can evolve and new clusters can be spun off.

A regional perspective on global value chains

The emergence of global value chains

The term global value chains (GVCs) describes production processes that take place in several stages across various countries around the world. GVCs are characterised by production processes that are split into several stages and distributed across countries. Throughout each stage of the production process, value is added, for example by producing a new good out of several intermediate goods or by refining an intermediate good. As intermediate goods and traded services used in GVCs flow from one country to another, the emergence of GVCs has contributed to growing global trade.

Value chains that divide the production process into different stages have existed for centuries even though the concept was first formally described by Porter (1985[26]). By connecting different activities that are necessary to produce a final good, they create more value than the sum of all activities contained within them would create on their own. Value chains also facilitate the division of labour and specialisation within the production process. The importance of this mechanism in fostering economic productivity has long been known and has famously been discussed by Adam Smith (1776[27]) in *The Wealth of Nations*.

Although value chains have existed for a long time, their nature started to change in the 1980s. Different steps in the production process were increasingly located within different countries. Value chains that were previously located primarily within one country became increasingly international. Initially, the production processes were often distributed across countries in close proximity, but in the late 1990s and early 2000s, they became truly global by integrating production processes over very long distances (Los, Timmer and de Vries, 2015[28]). Over the same time period, the importance of GVCs increased further, up to the point where they now form the basis of the global economy (OECD, 2017[29]).

As value chains became more prevalent, the production of more and more goods has been distributed across GVCs. Products made through GVCs range from goods requiring traditional manufacturing techniques such as textiles to technology-intensive goods such as electronics (OECD, 2017[29]). In parallel to becoming more prevalent, GVCs have also become longer and more complex. Production processes are divided into more steps that are distributed across countries. Along with the increasing flows of goods and services the economic interconnectedness of countries has increased.

Today, GVCs form the backbone of the global economy. Nevertheless, emerging evidence suggests that the importance of GVCs might have reached a peak. Global trade flows have started to decline as a share of GDP (IMF, 2016[30]); (OECD, 2016[31]). A number of structural factors – ranging from rising trade costs to new technologies that reduce the costs of small scale production – could make it more attractive to produce closer to markets. Notwithstanding these uncertainties about the future evolution of GVCs, at this point in time they are an essential element of every advanced economy (OECD, 2017[29]).

Vertical specialisation

One of the reasons behind the growth of GVCs has been so-called vertical specialisation [see (Hummels, Ishii and Yi, 2001[32])]. The term refers to an increasing division of the production process into more and more specialised steps. As vertical specialisation implies a break-up of the production process into many small steps, it is an important factor that contributes to being able to distribute production processes across countries. Not surprisingly, trade in vertically specialised intermediate goods significantly increased during the 1990s alongside the rise of GVCs (Chen, Kondratowicz and Yi, 2005[33]).

Increasing vertical specialisation in GVCs implies that an intermediate good might cross borders into and out of a country several times during the production process. In between each border crossing, the intermediate good is augmented or refined and a small amount of value is added in the process. In trade statistics, the intermediate good is registered as an export each time it leaves the country. Thus, increasing vertical specialisation and GVCs have contributed to rising gross exports in many countries.

However, rising gross exports do not necessarily indicate that a greater share of the economy relies on exports. Increasing vertical specialisation implies that the value added to an intermediate good before it is exported decreases. As a consequence, the total exported value-added can stay constant despite rising gross exports. If this effect is not taken into account, rising gross exports due to vertical specialisation and GVC integration can be misinterpreted as an increase in the overall importance of exports for the economy (Chen, Kondratowicz and Yi, 2005[33]). UNCTAD (2013[34])estimate that approximately 28% of the value-added in global gross exports has previously been imported.

Global value chains at the regional level

In contrast to the national level, where the importance of GVCs is undisputed, their role at the regional level is less well understood. While it could be expected that a greater degree of GVC integration is strongly correlated with economic performance, this is not necessarily the case. On the one hand, it is true that lagging regions are less integrated in GVCs than the average. Yet, the same is true for frontier regions as well. The most productive regions tend to be urban economies that rely heavily on an advanced service sector. As services play a comparatively small role in GVCs, frontier regions are in fact less integrated into GVCs than the average region.

More generally, the effects of GVC integration seem to vary widely across regions. Anecdotal evidence suggests that some regions benefit from GVC integration and are able to build important regional clusters around production processes within GVCs, whereas in others few connections between GVCs and the regional economy emerge.

Box 3.7. Regional GVCs

As described above, GVCs have been primarily discussed in terms of the distribution of production across different countries. Yet, they contain an important regional dimension. First, production processes are not only distributed across countries, they can also be distributed across regions. For example, R&D might take place in one part of a country whereas manufacturing might occur in another depending on the availability of workers with the right skill set. Second, GVC integration might vary significantly across regions within a country. Using only national level data would miss these regional differences.

Figure 3.4 shows a stylised value chain across four regions. Region 1 produces intermediate goods using capital and labour that get exported to Region 2 where they and other intermediate goods are used as inputs for the production of another intermediate good. Using this and other intermediate goods, a final good is produced in Region 3, which is partly consumed in Region 3 and partly exported for consumption in Region 4.

Many value chains and almost all global value chains are much more complex than the stylised structure presented in the figure below and can involve large numbers of intermediate goods being produced across many regions. Since many intermediate goods are produced from other intermediate goods that may come from different regions, they can also branch out into complex, tree-like structures instead of following a linear path.

Figure 3.4. A stylised value chain

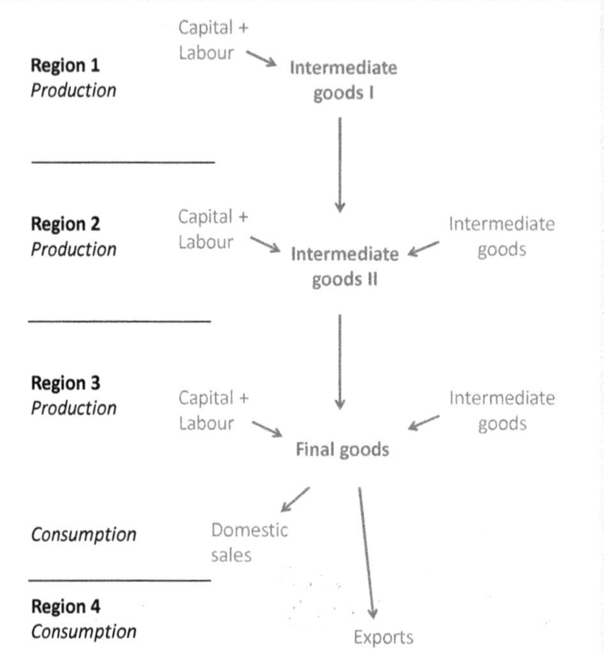

Source: Adapted from Los, B. and W. Chen (2016[35]), "Global Value Chain Participation Indicators for European Regions", Report for the OECD, December 2016 and Chen, H., Kondratowicz, M., & Yi, K. M. (2005[33]), Vertical specialization and three facts about US international trade. *The North American Journal of Economics and Finance*, *16*(1), 35-59.

Data on regional GVC integration

Data on GVCs at the regional level is derived from so-called input-output tables that document all flows of goods and services into and out of a region as well as their origins and destinations. These are large matrices with sometimes hundreds of millions of entries. By summing up inflows and outflows of goods and services and calculating the difference between the two sums, it is possible to derive several meaningful measures that describe the integration of regions into GVCs.

The first global input-output tables became available in the early 2000s, but they did not provide any information on the regional distribution of trade flows within countries. This section analyses a new dataset by Los and Chen (2016[35]) that is based on regional input-output tables and provides information on regional GVC integration.

The following measures are used as key indicators on regional GVC integration:

- **Value-added within GVCs** indicates the total value-added that is produced within GVCs in a region.
- **Regional labour income within GVCs** measures the labour income that is earned within GVCs in a region.
- **Regional gross exports** are the sum of all exports from a region. It is a measure of total trade activity. As discussed above, it includes the exported value-added

from within a region and the value of previously imported intermediate goods that are exported.

- **Regional value-added in gross exports** measures the value-added within a region that is exported. It is the difference between gross exports and gross imports. It includes value-added that is produced within GVCs and exported, but also value-added that is produced and exported in more basic trade relationships outside of GVCs.

Instead of using absolute values, many measures are more meaningful if they are expressed as shares or ratios. The following ones are used in this section:

- **Share of value-added from GVCs in total regional value-added** is the share of regional value-added that is created within GVCs. It provides a good indication of the overall importance of GVCs for the regional economy because total regional value-added is a good proxy of regional GDP.
- **Share of regional domestic labour from GVCs in total regional labour income** is another measure of the importance of GVCs for the regional economy focusing on labour income.
- **Share of regional value-added in exports in regional GDP** provides a measure of the overall importance of exports (within and outside of GVCs) for the regional economy.
- **Share of exported regional value-added in regional gross exports** is a measure of the concept of vertical specialisation that has been discussed above. The lower the share of value-added as a percent of gross exports, the greater the degree of vertical specialisation of exporters. If the share is very low, the average firm adds only little value to exports and is thus likely to work on a small and specialised step within the production process. In contrast, if the share is high, the average firm is likely to work on many steps within the production process and thus has a low degree of specialisation.

Key facts on GVCs at the regional level

GVC integration varies strongly not only across countries, but also across regions within a country. Figure 3.5 shows the value-added produced within GVCs as a share of total value added. While most national averages fall between 15% and 25%, the shares across regions within a country fluctuate by approximately 10 percentage points in many countries.

Figure 3.5. Contribution of GVCs to total regional value-added in Europe, 2010

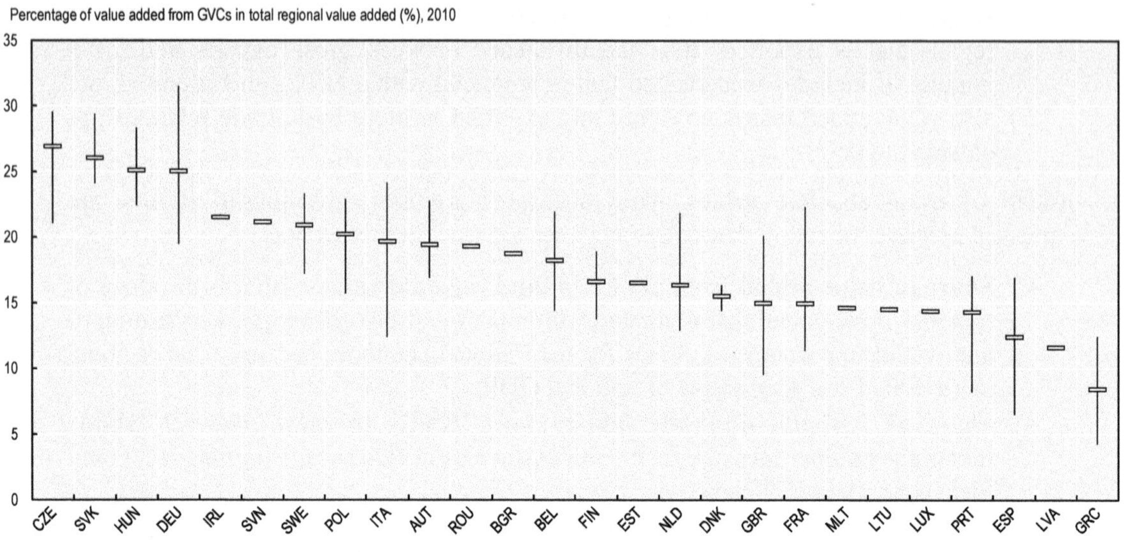

Note: Small horizontal bars denote weighted country averages, long vertical bars show the range of values across regions within a country. No regionally disaggregated data available for Romania, Bulgaria, Slovenia, Malta, Latvia, Luxembourg, Lithuania or Estonia.
Source: Calculations based on data provided by Los and Chen (2016[35]), see Thissen, Lankhuizen and Los (2017[36]) for details.

StatLink http://dx.doi.org/10.1787/888933708102

Regional GVC integration remained largely stable between 2000 and 2010

While GVC integration varies widely from region to region, few changes occur over time. Figure 3.6 shows the average contribution of value-added within GVCs to total regional value-added from 2000 to 2010. It distinguishes three groups of regions: highly integrated regions are the top 25% of regions that obtain the highest share of value-added from GVCs in 2000. Regions with low integration are the bottom 25% of regions in terms of the share of value-added from GVC participation and regions with medium integration are the 50% of regions in the middle.

The figure shows two striking facts. First, it confirms that there are large differences in GVC integration across regions. The top 25% of regions on average obtain more than 30% of their value-added from economic activities within GVCs. In contrast, the bottom 25% of regions obtains only approximately 11% of their value-added from activities that are integrated in GVCs. Second, there is little convergence occurring. The share of GDP that is obtained from GVCs has moved mostly in parallel with the GVC share of more integrated regions and declined slightly between 2000 and 2010.

The lack of convergence in GVC integration across regions is largely due to a generally high degree of persistence in the degree of GVC integration over the 2000 to 2010 period. On average, the share of value-added from GVCs that a region obtained changed by less than 2.5 percentage points during this time period.

Figure 3.6. Share of value-added from GVCs in total regional value-added over time (by group)

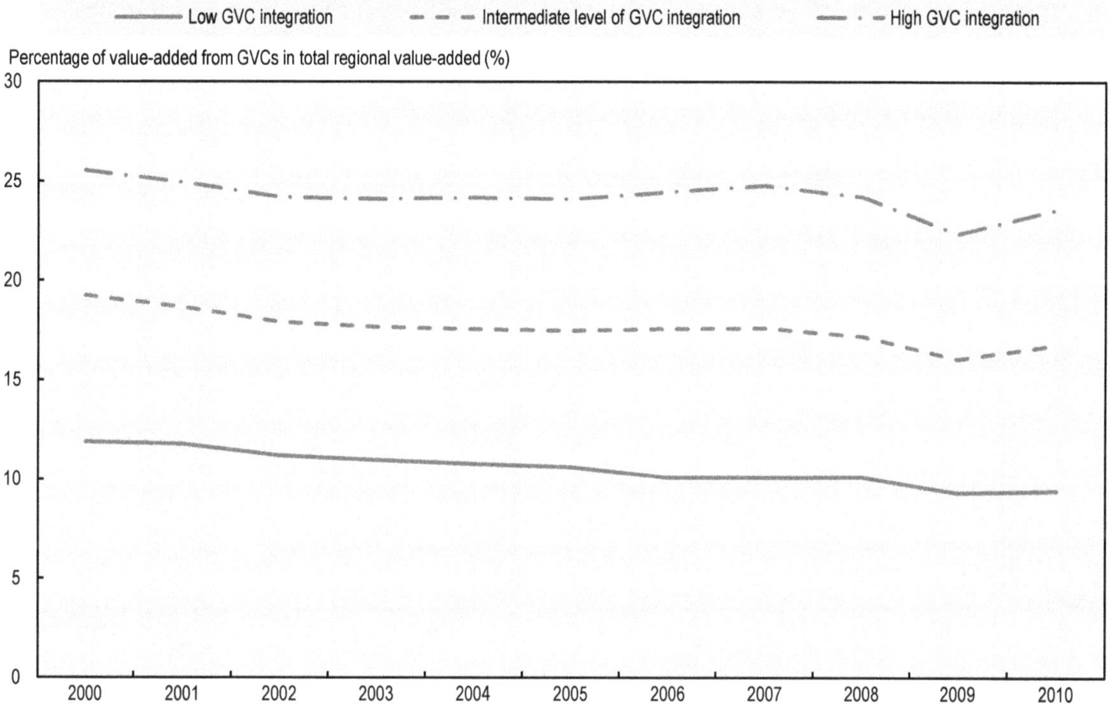

Note: Highly integrated regions are the top 25% of regions with the highest percentage of value-added from GVCs in total regional value added in 2000. Regions with low integration constitute the bottom 25%, and regions with intermediate levels of integration are the 50% of regions in between.
Source: Calculations based on data provided by Los and Chen (2016[35]), see Thissen, Lankhuizen and Los (2017[36]) for details.

StatLink http://dx.doi.org/10.1787/888933708121

The picture is similar for other measures of trade activity. Gross exports rose by 20% between 2000 and 2010 despite significant declines in the immediate aftermath of the financial crisis in 2008. However, GDP grew by approximately 10% over the same time, implying that the growth in gross exports as a share of GDP has only been half as much.

Exported value-added as a share of total value-added increased only marginally by one percentage point from 19.7% to 20.7% over the same time period. In parallel, the share of value-added in gross exports has declined somewhat from 54.2% to 51.8%, thus indicating greater vertical specialisation.

Thus, while there has been a slight increase in exported value-added in combination with greater vertical specialisation, the overall picture has been relatively stable. Apart from a severe, but brief shock in 2009, no major changes in the overall importance of regional trade occurred between 2000 and 2010.

The general absence of clear trends on GVC integration is also reflected in Figure 3.7. It shows how GVC integration and vertical specialisation changed between 2000 and 2010 in each region. Each arrow represents a region with the end of the arrow indicating the region's position in 2000 and its tip indicating its position in 2010. Panels are separated depending on whether the region is a frontier region, catching-up, diverging or lagging as defined in Chapter 1. While there is some variety across regions, a faint pattern can be discerned. On average, all groups of regions experienced a slight decline in GVC participation, as has already been mentioned above. More importantly, frontier and catching-up regions have experienced a decline in vertical specialisation, which indicates that their share of exported value-added in total exports has increased. In contrast, regions that diverge or keep pace have seen a roughly constant degree of vertical specialisation, which indicates stagnating shares of exported value-added.

Figure 3.7. GVC integration and vertical specialisation

Change in value-added from GVCs as a share of total value-added (horizontal axis) and exported value-added as a share of total exports (vertical axis) by type of region (2000-10)

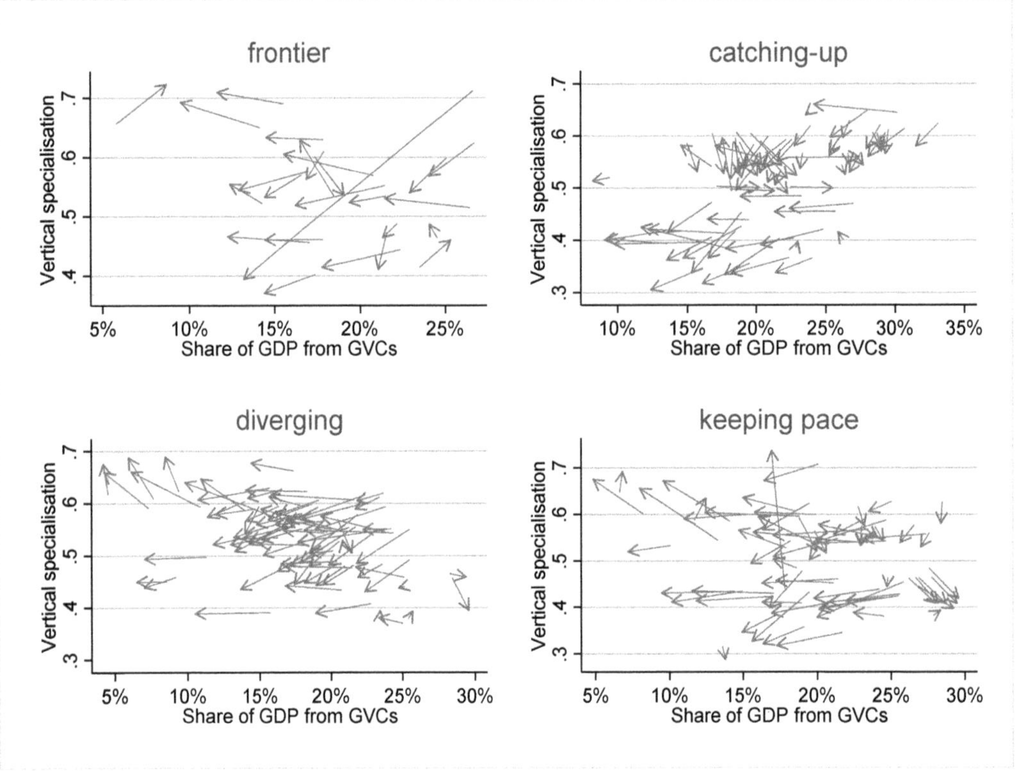

Source: Calculations based on data provided by Los and Chen (2016[35]), see Thissen, Lankhuizen and Los (2017[36]) for details.

StatLink http://dx.doi.org/10.1787/888933708140

GVCs create high value-added in the regions where they have their final production stage

GVCs can be distinguished according to where the production of the final output occurs. Perhaps surprisingly, Figure 3.8 shows that in 2010 55% of the value-added that is produced within GVCs is produced within those GVCs whose final production occurs within the same region: 14% of the value-added is produced within GVCs whose final production stage occurs in another region within the same country and 31% of value-added is produced in GVCs whose final production stage occurs in a foreign country. Since 2000, GVCs with final production stages in foreign countries have increased slightly in importance, but in general the pattern has remained largely unchanged.

Figure 3.8. Share of value-added from GVCs depending on place of final production

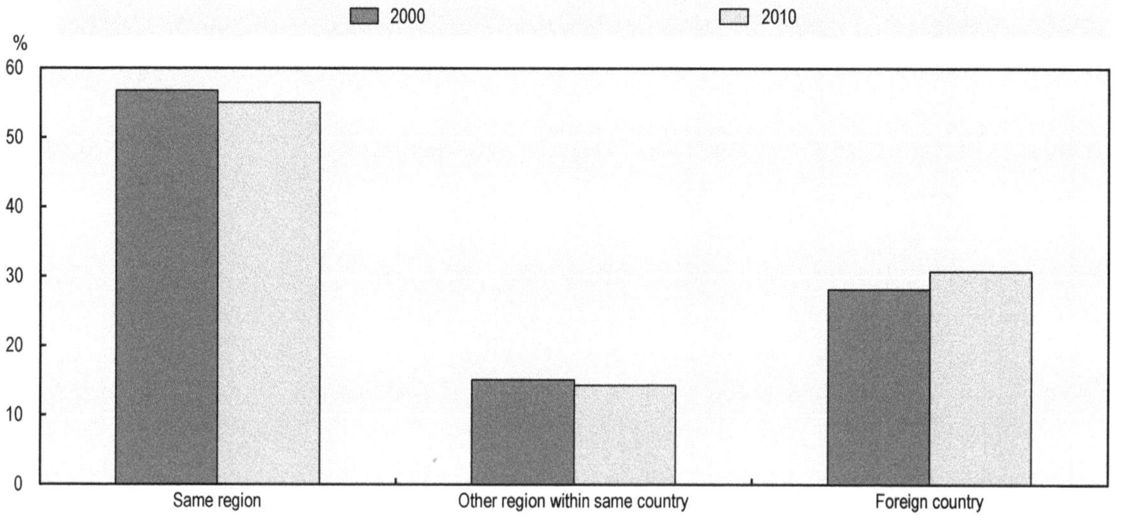

Note: This bar chart shows the share of value-added from GVCs depending on whether the final production process takes place in the same region, in another region within the same country or in a foreign country. The values refer to the average region (i.e. they reflect the unweighted average across all 242 regions).

Source: Calculations based on data provided by Los and Chen (2016[35]), see Thissen, Lankhuizen and Los (2017[36]) for details.

StatLink http://dx.doi.org/10.1787/888933708159

A likely reason behind the importance of GVCs that end in the same region is the production of the final good. The value-added in the last production stage tends to be disproportionally large (UNCTAD, 2013[34]). If a region produces the final good in a GVC, by definition the GVC ends in this region and the region is likely to create high value-added from that GVC.

Regional GVC participation varies by sector

The data provides a picture of GVCs across five different sectors: mining, textiles, fuels, machinery, and other manufacturing. Among them, machinery and other manufacturing are by far the most important sectors, contributing each to approximately 6-7% of regional value-added, of which fuels contributed roughly half (just over 3%). With slightly above 2% and 1%, respectively, GVCs in mining and textiles contributed the lowest share of total regional value-added in 2010.

Figure 3.9 shows the development over time. Several patterns are visible. First, the contributions of GVCs in machinery and other manufactured goods move in lockstep. Both fluctuated over time and were comparatively strongly affected by the financial crisis and the subsequent decline in trade in 2009. Nevertheless, their average contributions to total regional value-added remained virtually identical over the entire observation period. Second, the contribution of GVCs in fuels remained constant between 2000 and 2010. Third, the importance of mining- and textile-related GVCs has diverged. Whereas the average contribution from mining-related GVCs increased steadily from 1.8% in 2000 to 2.2% in 2010, the average contribution from textile-related GVCs steadily declined from 1.9% to 1.1%.

Figure 3.9. Average share of value-added of GVCs as a % of total value-added by sector

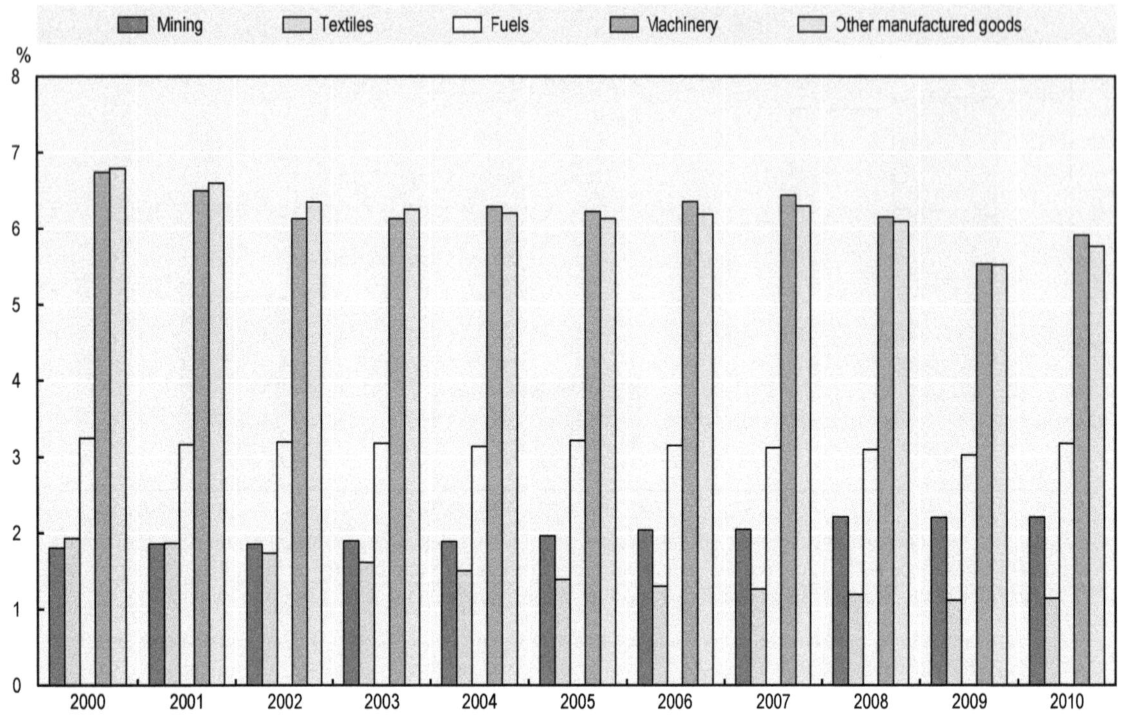

Note: The (unweighted) average contribution of GVCs to regional GDP by sector.

Source: Calculations based on data provided by Los and Chen (2016[35]), see Thissen, Lankhuizen and Los (2017[36]) for details.

StatLink http://dx.doi.org/10.1787/888933708178

Of course, averages hide significant variation across regions. In particular, regions vary considerably with respect to the importance of GVCs in the textile sector and in fuels. The coefficient-of-variation that measures the standard deviation relative to the mean of a variable is above 0.6 in both sectors in 2010. For example, the region with the lowest importance of GVCs in fuels obtains only 0.3% of its total value-added from it, whereas the region with the highest importance receives approximately 13% from it. With coefficients-of-variation of approximately 0.5, mining and machinery also show relatively strong variation across regions. In contrast, the importance of GVCs in other manufactured goods varies the least across regions with a coefficient-of-variation of approximately 0.35.

Exports' contribution to labour income is below average

Across all regions, the labour share – the percentage of GDP earned as labour income – is 48.8%, which is in line with the OECD average.[2] This is somewhat higher than the share of labour income earned from exports. Only 46.6% of the value-added that is exported is earned as labour income.

Regions with diverging labour productivity have a higher labour share in aggregate GDP and exported value-added. The labour share is 52.4% of general GDP and 49.2% of exported value-added. Assuming the return to capital equalises across regions, production in diverging regions tends to be less capital intensive than in other regions.

Figure 3.10. Labour share in GDP and exported value-added

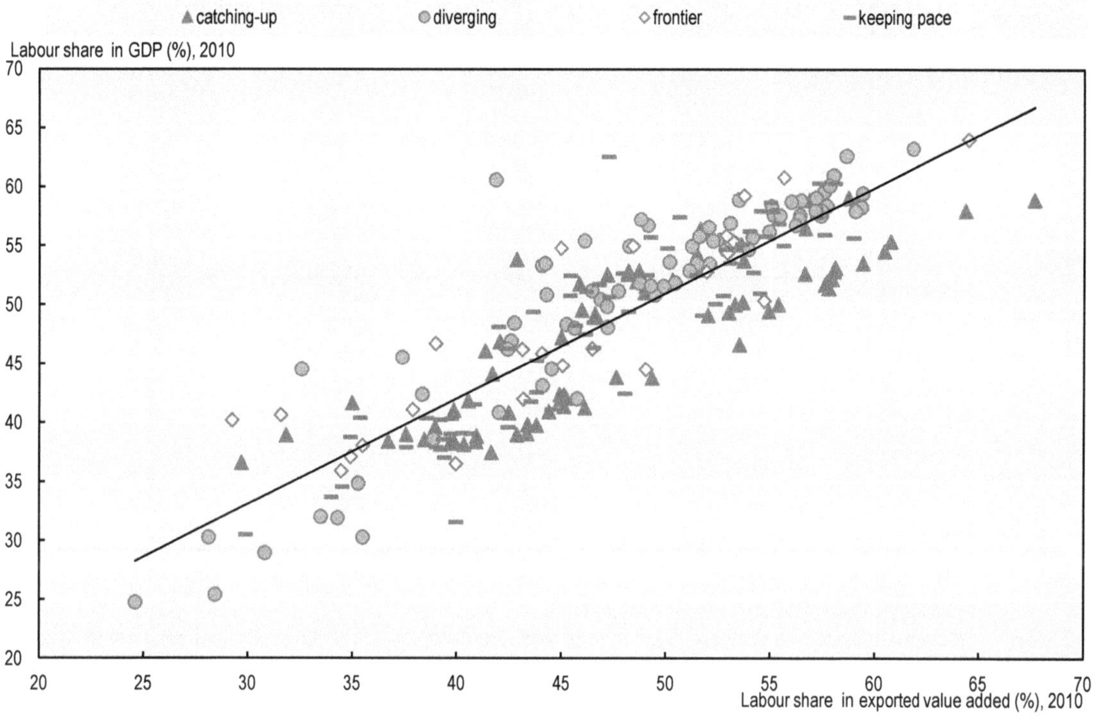

Source: Calculations based on data provided by Los and Chen (2016[35]), see Thissen, Lankhuizen and Los (2017[36]) for details.

StatLink http://dx.doi.org/10.1787/888933708197

When the labour share in exported value-added is plotted against the labour share in GDP, another pattern emerges. Diverging regions tend to have higher labour shares in their general GDP relative to the labour share in exported value-added. In contrast, regions that are catching up tend to have a lower labour share in general GDP relative to exported value-added. In Figure 3.10, this can be seen by diverging regions lying mostly above the trend line and regions that are catching-up fall mostly below the trend line.

GVC participation increases exports

Increased GVC participation is associated with greater exports. Specification 1 in Table 3.5 shows that a 1% increase in value-added produced within GVCs in a region leads to a 0.75% increase in total exports. Given that GVCs account for, on average, only half of regional exports; this implies that increased GVC participation typically goes along with increases in other exporting activities, too. This could be seen as an indication that the same factors that foster regional GVC participation are also responsible for more general export performance and vice versa.

Perhaps surprisingly, a 1% increase in value-added produced within GVCs also leads to a 0.72% increase in exported value-added as shown in specification 2, Table 3.5. Thus, the estimated increase in exported value-added is only slightly smaller than the increase in gross exports. This suggests that increasing integration into GVCs has not lead to substantial increases in vertical specialisation, which would be characterised by increases in gross exports without corresponding increases in exported value-added.

On the contrary, if regional trend-growth is taken into account (specifications 3 and 4) the estimates even suggest that regional GVC participation has led to a disproportionally high increase in exported value-added. Whereas a 1% increase in value-added from GVCs is estimated to lead to a 0.47% increase in gross exports, the effect on exported value-added is estimated to be 0.58%.

Table 3.5. GVCs and exports

	Log regional gross exports (1)	Log regional value-added in exports (2)	Log regional gross exports (3)	Log regional value-added in exports (4)
Log value-added from regional GVCs	0.75*** (0.03)	0.72*** (0.03)	0.47*** (0.03)	0.58*** (0.03)
Region fixed-effects	YES	YES	YES	YES
Year fixed-effects	YES	YES	YES	YES
Linear regional trend-growth	-	-	YES	YES
Number of regions	241	241	241	241
Number of observations	2651	2651	2651	2651

Note: ***,**,* indicate statistical significance at the 99%, 95%, and 90% confidence level, respectively. Heteroskedasticity robust standard errors in parenthesis.
Source: Calculations based on data provided by Los and Chen (2016[35]), see Thissen, Lankhuizen and Los (2017[36]) for details.

Box 3.8. A note on statistical models

This box presents a brief and largely non-technical description of the statistical models that are used for the estimations presented in this section. Unless otherwise noted, all estimates are based on so-call fixed-effects models for panel data that use annual data from 2000 to 2010 for 241 European regions. This implies that the estimates describe the consequences of changes over time within regions. In other words, the estimates are not based on comparisons of different regions with each other, but on the average effects of changes within regions over time. This eliminates the general characteristics of a region that do not change over time, such as its geographic location.

Furthermore, the estimates do not capture effects from changes over time that affect all regions similarly. This is important because the data covers the 2000-2010 time period, which includes the financial crisis of 2008 and its immediate aftermath. The severe recession during this period had exceptional effects on global trade patterns. If these effects were not excluded from the estimations, they could lead to spurious results. However, insofar as the financial crisis was a global phenomenon that affected all regions in a similar way, the estimates presented in this section are not influenced by it. Only if regions were affected in unusual ways by the crisis would it influence the results shown in the following.

Some of the estimated specifications also include variables to rule out that linear trend-growth in regions affects the results. This is important if the dependent variable and the explanatory variable grow for unrelated reasons at similar rates within regions. For example, many eastern European regions had high GDP growth rates during the early 2000s. At the same time, they also experienced strong growth in GVC participation.

While the two processes are most likely connected to some degree, it cannot be ruled out that at least partially they are due to independent catch up processes that did not affect each other. By including trend-growth terms in the estimations the results are not influenced by (linear) growth processes that occur in parallel, but for unrelated reasons.

All estimations use log-levels or ratios as variables of interests. This implies that the coefficients can be interpreted as the percentage change in the dependent variable in response to a 1%change in the independent variable (in case of log-levels) or as the percentage point change in the dependent variable in response to a 1 percentage point change in the independent variable (in case of ratios).

Formally, the following Specification is estimated:

$$y_{it} = \beta_1 x_{1,it} + \ldots + \beta_n x_{n,it} + \boldsymbol{\alpha_i} + \boldsymbol{\gamma_t} + \boldsymbol{\delta_i t} + \epsilon_{\text{it}},$$

where y_{it} indicates the outcome variable in region i and year t, $x_1 \ldots x\_n$ is a set of explanatory variables, $\beta_1 \ldots \beta_n$ are the coefficients of interest, $\boldsymbol{\alpha_i}$ is a set of region fixed-effects, $\boldsymbol{\gamma_t}$ is a set of year-fixed effects, $\boldsymbol{t}$ is a set of variables capturing linear time-trends for each region, and ϵ_{it} is the error term for region i and year t. Cluster-robust standard errors are computed to allow for arbitrary correlations of the error terms within regions.

When interpreting the estimates in this shapter, the reader should keep the maxim *correlation does not imply causality* in mind. It is generally incorrect to infer that one variable causes a change in another variable just because the two variables are correlated with each other. Much more commonly, there are many unobserved variables that cause changes in both observed variables and are the cause of their correlation.

The estimates presented in this section employ a variety of methods that prevent many of such unobserved variables from influencing the estimates. Yet, it is unlikely that they prevent all unobserved variables from influencing the estimates. In particular, region-specific factors that fluctuate over time and affect both variables of interest in an estimation (e.g. GDP and value-added from GVCs) can create correlations between the two variables that could be misinterpreted as causal effects.

As a consequence, the estimates described throughout this chapter should be carefully interpreted. They are most likely influenced by unobserved variables and therefore cannot be interpreted as showing the causal impact of a change in one variable on another variable.

The above-mentioned pattern is confirmed if the impact of increasing GVC participation on vertical specialisation is estimated directly. Specifications 1 in Table 3.6 indicates that the share of regional value-added in exports increases by 3.8 percentage points if regional GVC participation increases by 1%. This implies decreasing vertical specialisation. Once regional growth-trends are taken into account, the estimate becomes somewhat smaller but still remains statistically significant. As specification 2 shows, an increase in value-added from GVCs of 1% leads to an 1.6 percentage points increase in exported value-added as share of regional gross exports. Thus, the evidence suggests that greater GVC participation actually reduces vertical specialisation at the regional level.

Table 3.6. GVCs and vertical specialisation

	Share of exported regional value-added in regional gross exports (1)	Share of exported regional value-added in regional gross exports (2)
Log value-added from regional GVCs	3.81*** (0.53)	1.59** (0.64)
Region fixed-effects	YES	YES
Year fixed-effects	YES	YES
Linear regional trend-growth		YES
Number of regions	242	242
Number of observations	2662	2662

Source: Calculations based on data provided by Los and Chen (2016[35]), see Thissen, Lankhuizen and Los (2017[36]) for details.
Note: ***,**,* indicate statistical significance at the 99%, 95%, and 90% confidence level, respectively. Heteroskedasticity robust standard errors in parenthesis.

Some studies predict that greater GVC integration will lead initially to greater vertical specialisation, which is followed by a subsequent decline in vertical specialisation as regions develop and increase their exported value added [e.g. (UNCTAD, 2013[34])]. However, no evidence for such a u-shaped relationship between GVC integration and vertical specialisation can be found in the data, either.

GVC integration goes hand in hand with better economic performance

Greater GVC integration is strongly positively correlated with better economic performance at the regional level. A 1% increase in value added from GVCs is associated with a 0.52% increase in GDP levels (Table 3.7, Specification 1). Given that on average, GVCs create less than 20% of a region's value-added, this implies that for each additional euro created within GVCs, another 1.5 euros of value-added is created outside of GVCs.

Specification 2 in Table 3.7 takes the effect on value-added in exports into account. This reduces the effect of a 1% increase in GVC participation to 0.41%, whereas a 1% increase in exported value-added increases GDP by 0.32%. The estimates imply that an increase in value-added that gets exported through GVCs has an impact on GDP that is more than twice as big as an increase in exported value-added that is exported outside of GVCs. Whereas a 1% increase in the former is associated with a GDP increase of 0.41% + 0.33% = 0.74%, the latter is associated with an increase of only 0.32%. Thus, while increases in exported value-added are positively associated with GDP, the effect appears much stronger when those exports occur through GVCs.

In contrast, gross exports are only very weakly and negatively correlated with GDP once the effects of value-added from GVC participation and exported value-added have been taken into account. This indicates that exports per se create little benefits. Unsurprisingly, it is the value-added contained in those exports that matters for economic performance.

Table 3.7. GVC integration and GDP levels

	Log GDP (1)	Log GDP (2)
Log value-added from regional GVCs	0.52*** (0.04)	0.41*** (0.042)
Log value-added in exports	-	0.33*** (0.094)
Log gross exports	-	-0.17* (0.10)
Region fixed-effects	YES	YES
Year fixed-effects	YES	YES
Linear regional trend-growth	YES	YES
Number of regions	241	241
Number of observations	2651	2651

Note: ***,**,* indicate statistical significance at the 99%, 95%, and 90% confidence level, respectively. Heteroskedasticity robust standard errors in parenthesis.
Source: Calculations based on data provided by Los and Chen (2016[35]), see Thissen, Lankhuizen and Los (2017[36]) for details.

Increasing labour income from GVCs is negatively correlated with GDP

Although the estimates suggest that GVCs generally have positive effects on economic performance, there are signs that not every kind of GVC integration is positive for the regional economy. In particular, an increasing share of labour income from GVCs relative to the value-added produced within GVCs is correlated to lower GDP levels. A one percentage point increase in the ratio of labour income from GVCs relative to value-added produced within GVCs is associated with a 0.2% decrease in GDP levels.

This finding provides evidence that some forms of increasing regional GVC integration can actually harm economic performance and labour productivity. GVC integration in labour intensive sectors tends to reduce productivity and GDP. This can most likely be explained by the fact that GVC participation in labour intensive sectors frequently involve activities that create low value-added. Furthermore, these activities offer little potential for innovation and are often disconnected from other parts of the economy. In contrast, no statistically significant correlation between GVC integration and the employment rate of a region can be found if regional and year fixed-effects are taken into account.

Box 3.9. Who are the losers from trade?

This chapter provides tentative evidence that trade and GVC integration can benefit regions. However, it is important to acknowledge that trade also has downsides for some regions. Regions lose from increasing trade if economic activities in which they have specialised are replaced by traded products from other regions or countries.

The estimates in this chapter do not show if and to what degree the positive effects of trade and regional GVC integration occur at the expense of other regions. This is primarily due to the difficulty in identifying where economic decline is due to trade and where it is due to other factors. Data on GVCs show in which regions trade and value-added from GVCs have grown, but that data does not show if this growth has raised overall economic output or simply displaced economic activity from one region to another. Thus, the data can show which regions are the winners from trade and how they benefit from it, but they are less useful in identifying the losers.

Recent evidence by leading scholars such as Autor, Dorn and Hansen (2016[37]) and Acemoglu et al. (2016[38]) shows that growth in international trade can indeed have strong negative effects on some economic sectors even if it benefits national economies in aggregate. Facing new competition from businesses abroad, some industries have declined strongly in OECD countries. Since these industries are often not evenly distributed across countries, but concentrated in specific regions, the negative impact from increasing trade can outweigh the benefits in these regions. Chapter 5. discusses policies to respond to trade's downsides.

The economic benefits of GVC integration depend on the position within the GVC

Different activities within GVCs create different amounts of value-added. In particular, production steps at the beginning and the end of a GVC tend to create greater amounts of value-added than production activities in the middle of the GVC. This pattern is well documented and is sometimes called the 'smile curve' because of its characteristic shape when plotted on a graph.

Early stages in a GVC include research and development activities, which tend to be high in value-added. Likewise, resource extraction can create very high amounts of value-added.[3] In contrast, manufacturing and fabrication processes that are in the middle of a GVC are often low in value-added, especially when they include mass production. Lastly, the final stages of the GVC often create high value-added again, which is also reflected in the previously discussed Figure 3.8. They include activities such as branding and services related to the final product.

Thus, the benefits that regions derive from GVC participation will depend on where in the value chain the activities are located. Regions that are initially only able to attract low value-added activities in the middle of the GVC should try to expand upstream or downstream along the GVC into activities that create more value-added.

Policies to maximise the returns from GVC participation

Due to the global nature of GVCs, production processes that are integrated in them can lack connections to the regional economy. Intermediate goods used in the production process might be imported, knowledge and intellectual property used at a production facility is often created outside the region and marketing and after-sales services are potentially provided from somewhere else, too. In such situations, little value is created by a GVC within the region and there is a risk that greater GVC participation will create few benefits for the broader economy operating outside of GVCs. This section provides suggestions about how to avoid such situations and maximise benefits from GVC integration.

Linking GVCs to cluster policy

Policies to integrate GVCs into the regional economy are closely linked to cluster policies. Clusters can create distinct absolute advantages for regions if they offer access to services or time-critical intermediate goods that are not available in other regions. They can also contribute to the development of particular skill sets among regional workers. Through all these factors, clusters can attract investments linked to GVCs that rely on the availability of these services. In the best case, virtuous cycles can develop in which existing regional clusters attract investments linked to production stages within GVCs, which in turn strengthen the existing clusters by increasing the demand for the goods and services produced by them.

Clusters and GVCs are governed in opposing ways. Humphrey and Schmitz (2000[39]) show that clusters are characterised by strong horizontal inter-firm co-operation and active co-ordination from public institutions. In contrast, GVCs are characterised by strong inter-firm governance along the value chain. Due to their fragmented nature across borders, national or regional institutions play only a limited role in governing GVCs. Compared to cluster policies, they have fewer possibilities to intervene directly and to shape the GVCs active in their region.

Yet, regional authorities are not powerless when facing GVCs. Regional institutions and governance structures play a crucial role in shaping how GVCs are integrated in the regional economy. They can influence the degree to which firms are willing to link their production processes with the regional economy and facilitate knowledge transfers. However, the bargaining power with respect to central firms in GVCs can vary widely, depending on aspects such as regional characteristics and the national institutional framework. This can influence the degree to which policy makers can compel firms to link their GVCs into regional economies. To negotiate effectively with large firms it is particularly important that policy makers be well-informed about characteristics related to GVCs and the regional economy (Coe et al., 2004[40]). The four following criteria are especially important.

First, policy makers need to have clear and detailed knowledge about the characteristics of their regions, in particular concerning the location-specific factors that make the region attractive for investments. Second, policy makers need to be aware of the sectoral specificities of the firms they are negotiating with. Firms in different sectors have different requirements and policies should be targeted at the specific requirements of firms. Third, policy makers need to be aware of their own institutional environments and the motivations and incentives of all relevant actors. Finally, policy makers need to understand which economic activities are most beneficial for their regions and target their policy interventions accordingly, for example by compelling firms to maximise the value-added within their regions (Coe et al., 2004[40]).

Strengthen the service sector connected to GVCs

GVCs are often portrayed as being primarily about the flow of goods from one country to another. Yet, this oversimplification risks distorting their nature and may lead to focusing on the wrong policy priorities. The OECD (2016[31]) emphasises that governments should not only focus on the core activities within a value chain (usually the manufacturing part), but pay attention also to business activities that support core activities. These activities may be located upstream (e.g. R&D, engineering) or downstream (e.g. transport, distribution, marketing, aftersales services) and often feature less prominently in the public debate on trade and global value chains, despite their growing importance over time.

Policies targeted at GVCs should take these activities into account. Some countries have succeeded in building significant clusters around these activities, whereas others rely more on offshore services. Regions that try to strengthen clusters around GVCs should not prefer manufacturing over the service sector. The value-added generated by an activity matters more for economic performance than the sector in which the activity occurs. Both the service sector and the manufacturing sector include activities that create high value-added and activities that create low value-added. Instead of focusing on the sector, policy makers should take the value-added in an activity as a yardstick when deciding whether or not to support it.

Develop complementary policies to address the downsides of increasing trade

While GVC integration offers significant potential gains to regions, these gains do not accrue automatically. The OECD (2016[31]) highlights the importance of complementary policies that can address the potential downsides of GVC integration. Trade increases specialisation and changes the structure of the economy. While this tends to be beneficial in aggregate, it can potentially create significant losses for specific groups of workers or economic sectors that are potentially concentrated in specific regions.

Several different policies are necessary to address the losses that trade and GVC integration can create. In particular, skill and education policies are crucial to reduce the impact of workers. Only when workers are able to adapt their skill profile to the changing demand for labour can they find new opportunities when economic sectors disappear. However, it is unlikely that skill and education policies alone will be enough.

Many skills policies are generic in the sense that they do not target the workers who are most affected by trade shocks. Due to the strong geographical concentration of the losses from trade and GVCs in some regions, skill and education policies are often not enough to compensate for the negative effects. Since trade can lead to a decline in the number of firms in a region, it is important to address not only labour supply but also labour demand. This includes, for example, policies to foster firm creation or to attract foreign direct investment into a region. Furthermore, workers should be supported to find jobs in other regions where unemployment rates are lower. These policies will be discussed in Chapter 5.

Regional employment shocks from trade and automation

Economists have long argued that trade is mutually beneficial for the countries involved in it. The theory of comparative advantage developed by Ricardo (1817[41]) states that by trading with each other, two countries can both increase their production and consumption because each country can focus on the production of the good it is comparatively more specialised in. Even today, gains from comparative advantage are a centrepiece of many of the most important theories of international trade, e.g. (Krugman, 1979[42]). Furthermore, economists have identified expanding markets as an important benefit from trade because it increases innovation (Grossman and Helpman, 1993[43]) and creates economies of scale. More recently, Melitz (2003[44]) argued that trade benefits more productive firms, which gain international market share at the expense of less productive firms. This process is beneficial in aggregate because it increases the average productivity level of a country by shifting resources from less productive firms to more productive firms.

Yet, trade theories also acknowledge that trade can generate losers. Theories of comparative advantage have distributional implications, which predict that trade harms the owners of the comparatively scarce production factors. Furthermore, trade creates losers among the less productive firms that cannot compete anymore (Melitz and Trefler, 2012[45]). Both effects eventually have an impact on some workers, who see their wages reduced due or their jobs disappear.

In light of the benefits from trade, the negative effects of trade on some workers were less of a concern if they occurred gradually and if the affected workers were evenly distributed across a country. In such an ideal scenario, jobs in unproductive firms that go out of business would be replaced quickly by more productive jobs in more productive firms. Workers would find new jobs in these firms and benefit from the turnover because rising productivity would be reflected in higher wages.

However, recent empirical evidence suggests that job losses from trade can be concentrated in some regions, occur rapidly and take a long time to be offset by job growth in other firms or sectors (OECD, 2017[46]). As documented by Autor, Dorn and Hanson (2016[37]), the rise of imports from China has led to a decline in employment in the manufacturing sector in many OECD countries. Since the industries that have been affected by import competition were often clustered in specific regions, the employment losses are equally concentrated in those regions [see Autor, Dorn and Hanson (2013[47]); Dauth, Findeisen and Suedekum, (2014[48]); Donoso, Martin and Minondo, (2015[49]); and Balsvik, Jensen and Salvanes, (2015[50])].

Even job losses that are located in one specific geographic location and sector would not pose a major problem if workers could easily find jobs in other sectors in the same region or in other regions. Yet, laid-off workers in affected regions struggle to find other jobs because affected regions lack dynamic sectors, which would create jobs that would offset those trade-related job losses. As a consequence, unemployment rates remain persistently high over long periods of time in regions that have suffered from negative trade shocks (Autor, Dorn and Hanson, 2016[37]).

Thus, policy makers face the conundrum that trade – while overall beneficial for national economies – can have important and lasting negative effects in some regions. This is an important point to understand. Previous theories of trade assumed that the effects of trade would be equally spread across all regions so that the aggregate benefits dominate everywhere and no specifically place-based policy response would be needed to address the downsides. However, given that the negative effects are predominantly concentrated in specific regions, policies to help those regions are much more important than previously thought.

In contrast, protectionist policies that restrict trade with other countries to help affected regions are likely to do more harm than good. They would reduce productivity gains from specialisation and slow down innovation. As a consequence, they would reduce living standards in the long run. Furthermore, they would harm consumers across the country that would have to pay higher prices on many goods that could be imported more cheaply than produced domestically if protectionist measures were not in place. While they could be beneficial for regions that are most affected by negative trade shocks, the downsides for the rest of the country would outweigh those benefits.

Automation increases wage disparities between low- and high-skilled workers

In parallel to the rise in trade, a second global trend has had strong effects on regional employment in manufacturing. Automation in manufacturing has made jobs obsolete by replacing workers by machines. While this process has been going on over centuries (e.g. weavers' jobs were replaced by mechanic looms in the 19th century), it has been receiving increasing attention recently because of increasing computerisation. Growing use of computers and robots has made it possible to use robots for a wide range of manufacturing processes that previously had to be performed manually.

In order to estimate the impact of automation on jobs, economists distinguish between jobs that primarily involve routine tasks and those that involve primarily non-routine tasks. Routine tasks tend to be repetitive and occur in controlled environments. Compared to non-routine tasks, they can easily be performed by machines or computers. In contrast, non-routine tasks require adaptive responses to changing environments. They are difficult to automate (Autor, Levy and Murnane, 2003[51]). Not surprisingly, many routine tasks are predominantly low-skilled whereas non-routine tasks are more frequently high-skilled. Nevertheless, the routine-content and skill-level of a task are not identical and some high-skilled tasks are mostly routine, whereas some low-skilled tasks are non-routine (OECD, 2015[52]).

In contrast to trade, automation seems to have had less of an impact on unemployment up to now. Instead, it has shifted employment towards non-routine jobs (Autor, Dorn and Hanson, 2015[53]). In other words, jobs that are made obsolete due to automation tend to be replaced by jobs in other sectors. While automation has had, at most, a moderate impact on unemployment, it has probably contributed to greater wage inequality (Autor, 2015[54]). The jobs that have replaced those that disappeared due to automation are frequently service sector jobs. They tend to be either disproportionally high-paying (e.g. many intellectual services) or disproportionally poor-paying (e.g. many manual services) (OECD, 2017[55]).

Thus, the effects of trade and automation on regional employment can appear similar, but they are not identical for two reasons. First, trade shocks have increased unemployment whereas automation has led to increasing labour market polarisation and potentially to greater inequality. Second, jobs that are vulnerable to trade shocks are often clustered in different regions than jobs that are vulnerable to automation.

Why trade and automation shocks differ

A potential reason for why trade and automation affect employment patterns differently is that they have different effects on firm performance. Foreign competition is generally negative for local firms. It is well documented that it can force firms out of business and can lead to the disappearance of entire industries in extreme cases, e.g. (Underhill, 2016[56]). In contrast, the effects of automation on firms are more ambiguous. Rapid technological change creates challenges for firms and requires them to adapt quickly. Yet, it also offers important upsides for those firms that are able to use technological advances to improve the efficiency of the production process (Bharadwaj, 2000[57]). Thus, automation is less likely to homogenously harm all firms across a region.

As a consequence, automation leads to job losses among workers whose jobs get automatized, but does not destroy the underlying fabric of firms within a region. Labour demand from these firms will still exist, even though they are likely to demand a different and more advanced set of skills from their workers. This is reflected by the abovementioned fact that automation leads to labour market polarisation that tends to benefit high-skilled workers in particular.

Importantly, the evidence on the regional impact of trade and automation is very recent and is still evolving. Most of the papers cited in this section have been written by a small group of authors. Furthermore, most of the results are focused on the United States. Additional research by other authors might yield insights that add important nuances or affect the interpretation of the findings that have been presented in this section.

Looking forward, it appears likely that automation will have greater labour market impacts than trade. As mentioned previously, GVC integration and trade is stagnating and is unlikely to increase in considerable proportions in the future. In contrast, the nature of automation is changing. Where in the past it affected mostly manufacturing, there are signs that it will have stronger impacts on service sector jobs in the future (OECD, 2017[55]).

The effect of future automation on labour markets might very well differ from the effects observed in the past. It is possible that it will rapidly affect a larger group of workers than previous waves of automation. For example the ITF (2017[58]) estimates that up to 4.4 million out of a total of 6.4 million truck drivers could be replaced by 2030 if autonomous vehicles become available quickly. If this materialises, the consequences might go beyond wage polarisation and could have important employment effects. Given that future waves of automation could occur in the intermediate future, regional policy should try to anticipate any region-specific consequences and proactively plan ahead.

Notes

1. "Low-income" and "low-growth" regions have been defined as part of the EU Lagging Regions Initiative (European Commission, 2017[5]). Low-income regions are those with less than 50% of the EU-average per capita GDP in 2013 and are located in Bulgaria, Hungary, Poland and Romania. Low-growth regions are those classified as "less-developed" or "transition" regions, i.e. with less than 75% or 90% of EU-average per capita GDP and with growth that was less than the EU average over the 2000-13 period.

2. The labour share reported here is the so-called unadjusted labour share because it does not include income earned by the self-employed. Including the income earned by the self-employed increases the labour share by approximately eight percentage points (ILO and OECD, 2015[59]).

3. Though depletion of resources makes the benefits created through resource extraction temporary. See alsoChapter 0. "Not all gaps will close, but persistent and growing differences raise concerns" in Chapter 1.

References

Acemoglu, D. et al. (2016), "Import competition and the great US employment sag of the 2000s", *Journal of Labor Economics*, Vol. 34/S1, pp. S141-S198. [38]

Arrow, K. (1962), "The economic implications of learning by doing", *Review of Economic Studies*, Vol. 29, pp. 155-173. [12]

Autor, D., F. Levy and R. Murnane (2003), "The Skill Content of Recent Technological Change: An Empirical Exploration", *The Quarterly Journal of Economics*, Vol. 118/4, pp. 1279-1333. [51]

Autor, D., D. Dorn and G. Hanson (2013), "The China Syndrome: Local Labor Market Effects of Import Competition in the United States", *American Economic Review*, Vol. 103/6, pp. 2121-2168. [47]

Autor, D. (2015), "Why are there still so many jobs? The history and future of workplace automation", *The Journal of Economic Perspectives*, Vol. 29/3, pp. 3-30. [54]

Autor, D., D. Dorn and G. Hanson (2015), "Untangling trade and technology: Evidence from local labour markets", *Economic Journal*, Vol. 125/584, pp. 621-46. [53]

Autor, D., D. Dorn and G. Hanson (2016), "The China shock: Learning from labor-market adjustment to large changes in trade", *Annual Review of Economics*, Vol. 8, pp. 205-240. [37]

Balsvik, R., S. Jensen and K. Salvanes (2015), "Made in China, sold in Norway: Local labor market effects of an import shock", *Journal of Public Economics*, Vol. 127, pp. 137-144. [50]

Bharadwaj, A. (2000), "A resource-based perspective on information technology capability and firm performance: An empirical investigation", *MIS Quarterly*, Vol. 24/1, pp. 169-196. [57]

Boschma, R. and S. Iammarino (2009), "Related variety, trade linkages, and regional growth in Italy", *Economic Geography*, Vol. 85/3, pp. 289-311. [10]

Caragliu, A., L. de Dominicis and H. de Groot (2016), "Both Marshall and Jacobs were right!", *Economic Geography*, Vol. 92/1, pp. 87-111. [17]

Chen, H., M. Kondratowicz and K. Yi (2005), "Vertical specialization and three facts about US international trade", *The North American Journal of Economics and Finance*, Vol. 16/1, pp. 35-59. [33]

City of Tampere (2015), *Tampere: Open/smart/connected: Summary of the application by the City of Tampere, Finland to the contest for the European Capital of Innovation Award*, https://fl-cdn.scdn1.secure.raxcdn.com/files/11649/tampere-icapital-proposal.pdf. [19]

City of Tampere (2016), *Response to the OECD Questionnaire on Resilient Cities*, http://www.tampere.fi/en/index.html. [21]

Coe, N. et al. (2004), "'Globalizing' regional development: A global production networks perspective", *Transactions of the Institute of British Geographers*, Vol. 29/4, pp. 468-484. [40]

Dauth, W., S. Findeisen and J. Suedekum (2014), "The rise of the East and the Far East: German labor markets and trade integration", *Journal of the European Economic Association*, Vol. 12/6, pp. 1643-1675. [48]

Delgado, M. et al. (2012), "The determinants of national competitiveness", No. w18249, National Bureau of Economic Research. [8]

Delgado, M., M. Porter and S. Stern (2016), "Defining clusters of related industries", *Journal of Economic Geography*, Vol. 16/1, pp. 1-38. [4]

Donoso, V., V. Martin and A. Minondo (2015), "Do differences in the exposure to Chinese imports lead to differences in local labour market outcomes? An analysis for Spanish provinces", *Regional Studies*, Vol. 49/10, pp. 1746-1764. [49]

European Commission (2017), *Smart specialisation*, https://ec.europa.eu/jrc/en/research-topic/smart-specialisation (accessed on 4 September 2017). [16]

European Commission (2017), "Competitiveness in Low-Income and Low-Growth Regions: The Lagging Regions Report", *European Commission Staff Working Document*, European Commission. [5]

Frenken, K., F. Van Oort and T. Verburg (2007), "Related variety, unrelated variety and regional economic growth", *Regional Studies*, Vol. 41/5, pp. 685-697. [9]

Glaeser, E. et al. (1992), "Growth in cities", *Journal of Political Economy*, Vol. 100/6, pp. 1126-1152. [6]

Grossman, G. and E. Helpman (1993), *Innovation and Growth in the Global Economy*, MIT Press. [43]

Hausmann, R. and F. Neffke (2016), "The Workforce of Pioneer Plants". [24]

Herfindahl, O. (1950), *Concentration in the Steel Industry*, Columbia University. [7]

Hummels, D., J. Ishii and K. Yi (2001), "The Nature and Growth of Vertical Specialization in World Trade", *Journal of International Economics*, Vol. 54/1, pp. 75-96. [32]

Humphrey, J. and H. Schmitz (2000), "Governance and upgrading: Linking industrial cluster and global value chain research", *Institute of Development Studies*, Vol. 120. [39]

ILO and OECD (2015), *The Labour Share in G20 Economies*, Report prepared for the G20 Employment Working Group, 26-27 February, http://www.oecd.org/g20/topics/employment-and-social-policy/The-Labour-Share-in-G20-Economies.pdf. [59]

IMF (2016), *Global Trade: What's Behind the Global Slowdown*, IMF, Washington DC. [30]

ITF (2017), "Managing the Transition to Driverless Road Freight Transport", *International Transport Forum Policy Papers*, No. 32, OECD Publishing, Paris, http://dx.doi.org/10.1787/0f240722-en. [58]

Jacobs, J. (1969), *The Economy of Cities*, Vintage Books. [14]

Ketels, C. and S. Protsiv (2016), "European Cluster Panorama 2016", *European Cluster Observatory*. [3]

Krugman, P. (1979), "Increasing Returns, Monopolistic Competition, and International Trade", *Journal of International Economics*, Vol. 9/4, pp. 469-79. [42]

Los, B., M. Timmer and G. de Vries (2015), "How Global are Global Value Chains? A New Approach to Measure International Fragmentation", *Journal of Regional Science*, Vol. 55, pp. 66-92. [28]

Los, B. and W. Chen (2016), "Global Value Chain Participation Indicators for European Regions", *Report for the OECD*, No. December 2016. [35]

Marshall, A. (1890), *Principles of Economics*, MacMillan, London. [11]

Melitz, M. (2003), "The impact of trade on intra-industry reallocations and aggregate industry productivity", *Econometrica*, Vol. 71/6, pp. 1695-1725. [44]

Melitz, M. and D. Trefler (2012), "Gains from trade when firms matter", *The Journal of Economic Perspectives*, Vol. 26/2, pp. 91-118. [45]

Newcastle University (2015), *Smart specialisation for regional innovation: WP5 regional report on Pirkanmaa (Tampere), Finland*, http://www.regioconeixement.catedra.urv.cat/media/upload/domain_697/arxius/carpeta%20sense%20nom/Tampere%20Regional%20Report%20-%20full%20version%20(October%202015).docx.. [23]

OECD (2007), *Competitive Regional Clusters: National Policy Approaches*, OECD Reviews of Regional Innovation, OECD Publishing, Paris, http://dx.doi.org/10.1787/9789264031838-en. [1]

OECD (2013), *Innovation-driven Growth in Regions: The Role of Smart Specialisation*, Preliminary report, OECD, http://www.oecd.org/sti/inno/smart-specialisation.pdf. [15]

OECD (2015), *Data-Driven Innovation: Big Data for Growth and Well-Being*, OECD Publishing, Paris, http://dx.doi.org/10.1787/9789264229358-en. [52]

OECD (2016), *Resilient Cities, Preliminary Report*, http://www.oecd.org/cfe/regional-policy/resilient-cities-report-preliminary-version.pdf. [22]

OECD (2016), *OECD Regional Outlook 2016: Productive Regions for Inclusive Societies*, OECD Publishing, Paris, http://dx.doi.org/10.1787/9789264260245-en. [2]

OECD (2016), "Global Value Chains and Trade in Value-Added: An Initial Assessment of the Impact on Jobs and Productivity", *OECD Trade Policy Papers*, No. 190, OECD Publishing, Paris, http://dx.doi.org/10.1787/5jlvc7sb5s8w-en. [31]

OECD (2017), "The Future of Global Value Chains: "Business as Usual" or a "New Normal"?", *unpublished manuscript*. [29]

OECD (2017), *OECD Employment Outlook 2017*, OECD Publishing, Paris, http://dx.doi.org/10.1787/empl_outlook-2017-en. [55]

OECD (2017), "How to make trade work for all", in *OECD Economic Outlook, Volume 2017 Issue 1*, OECD Publishing, Paris, http://dx.doi.org/10.1787/eco_outlook-v2017-1-3-en. [46]

OECD (forthcoming), "Indicators for Resilient Cities", *OECD Regional Development Policy Working Papers*. [18]

Porter, M. (1985), *Competitive Advantage: Creating and Sustaining Superior Performance*, Simon and Schuster. [26]

Rhee, Y. (1990), "The catalyst model of development: Lessons from Bangladesh's success with garment exports", *World Development*, Vol. 18/2, pp. 333-346. [25]

Ricardo, D. (1817), *On the Principles of Political Economy, and Taxation*, London. [41]

Romer, P. (1986), "Increasing returns and long-run growth", *Journal of Political Economy*, Vol. 94/5, pp. 1002-1037. [13]

Smith, A. (1776), *An Inquiry into the Nature and Causes of the Wealth of Nations*, Project Gutenberg. [27]

Statistics Finland (2015), *Annual National Accounts*, http://www.stat.fi/til/index_en.html. [20]

Thissen, M., M. Lankhuizen and B. Los (2017), *Construction of a Time Series of Fine-Grained Detailed Nuts2 Regional Input-Output Tables for the EU embedded in a Global System of Country Tables*, PBL Netherlands Environmental Assessment Agency, The Hague. [36]

UNCTAD (2013), *Global Value Chains: Investment and Trade for Development*, UNCTAD. [34]

Underhill, G. (2016), *Industrial Crisis and the Open Economy: Politics, Global Trade and the Textile Industry in the Advanced Economies*, Springer. [56]

Chapter 4. Macroeconomic frameworks and institutional factors for regional economic performance

Beyond regional policies, territorial economic outcomes are also affected by factors that are beyond the control of regional actors. These include national or global macroeconomic trends, as well as certain national policies and frameworks that may have a specifically important spatial dimension. This chapter first explores how macroeconomic frameworks and national structural policies have contributed to differences in regional economic performance. It thereafter explores more generally how institutional and governance settings affect regional economic outcomes.

Chapter synopsis

At the national level the 2007-08 crisis has led to a renewed focus on sound macroeconomic framework conditions and the role of structural reforms in ensuring that economies are competitive and resilient to adverse shocks. At the same time there is much less attention in the debate on the role that national policy frameworks play in reducing or reinforcing interregional disparities.

Within countries or single-currency areas such as the euro area, wage growth that is disconnected from productivity growth can lead to imbalances in regional competitiveness. If regional wages grow faster than productivity, unit labour costs rise and the competitiveness of the tradable sector is reduced. In contrast, regions where wages grow slower than labour productivity enhance their competitiveness, which can negatively affect other regions within the fixed exchange-rate area. This effect can be indirect, i.e. rising wages in the non-tradable sector that are not supported by productivity growth lead to higher prices for non-tradable services both for consumers and (tradable) firms.

The analysis of economic performance at the regional levels shows that a 1 percentage point increase in the growth rate of unit labour costs is, on average, associated with a 0.3 percentage point decrease in the growth rate of value added per capita and 0.4 percentage point decrease in exports per capita. One of the reasons why unit labour costs can differ across regions of the same country is centralised wage-setting mechanisms, in combination with persistent differences in productivity growth. For example, wage bargaining at the national level can lead to wage levels that are too high for regions with low productivity growth and too low for regions with high productivity growth. Sufficient flexibility in centralised wage bargaining, including opt-out clauses for struggling firms, can help to bring wages in line with productivity levels.

Flexible regulations that account for the needs of workers, the unemployed and firms in different regions are particularly important for productivity growth in lagging regions. European regions with the lowest per capita gross domestic product (GDP) and those with low per capita GDP growth benefitted more than other European regions from reforms to employment protection of regular contracts in terms of productivity growth over the 2000-13 period. Similarly, product market regulations in wholesale and retail trade appear to have particularly negative impacts on the productivity growth of a country's least productive regions. Structural reforms should be undertaken preferably during periods of high economic growth. However, as many recent reforms occurred during a period of severe economic weakness, these reforms created higher social costs in terms of job losses than they would have if they had been implemented during a boom period.

Governance and the efficient functioning of public administration can contribute to narrowing productivity gaps. A barrier to the well-functioning of cities is a fragmented administrative structure. A doubling of the number of municipalities within the boundaries of a metropolitan area is associated with 3-6% lower productivity of its workers. This penalty is alleviated by about half when metropolitan governance arrangements exist. The adverse effect of fragmentation is not limited to the city itself, as economic growth in highly urbanised regions with a larger number of municipalities per capita is lower than in less fragmented regions. Judicial efficiency can also play a role. Evidence shows that employment and turnover in Italian firms and thee likelihood of participating in global value chains are lower for firms located in jurisdictions where legal proceedings take longer than in firms located in more efficient jurisdictions.

Macroeconomic framework and structural reforms: accounting for regional differences

Regions are affected by a range of nationwide economic policies and national or even global macroeconomic trends. Policies that are designed to ensure equal treatment across space, e.g. rules that govern the dismissal of workers or the licensing of new firms, can have dissimilar economic effects in different regions. Economic structure, levels of economic development, characteristics of the local labour force and the availability of natural resources are all among the factors that may contribute to the unequal impact of policies on different regions. Macroeconomic developments such as exchange rates and nominal interest rates are – by definition – also out of the control of the individual firm or even region. Regional price competitiveness will hence typically fluctuate – at least in the short run – with changes in nominal exchange rates and relative levels of inflation in the country (or monetary zone, i.e. euro area) to which it belongs. Similarly, if inflation in a region is different from inflation rates in other parts of its country (or its monetary zone), this will affect regional price competitiveness. Depending on their economic structure, the reliance of regions on pure price competitiveness differs greatly – and effects from the aforementioned macroeconomic developments will hence affect them to different degrees.

Regional variations in the impact of policies and macroeconomic trends are amplified by the disinclination of many people to move. Even though there are no legal barriers for people to move to another region in their country, doing so typically has social costs (at least initially), and also requires solving many practical issues. The result is that people tend to prefer to stay in the region where they live. In a recent study in the United States, for example, 89% of applications sent through an online job portal were found to have been sent to firms in the state where the applicant resided (Marinescu and Rathelot, 2016[100]). Estimates for other countries, e.g. for the United Kingdom, suggest that this "distaste" for distant jobs may be even stronger outside of the United States (Manning and Petrongolo, 2017[101]). From a well-being perspective, it is easy to understand why the vast majority of people choose to stay as close to home as possible when looking for work. It implies, however, that people are not necessarily moving to the places where they could be the most economically productive, and also that forces that would tend to equilibrate a potentially uneven impact of national policies or macroeconomic developments among regions can at best be partially effective.

Misalignment between wage and productivity growth - Unit labour costs as a measure of imbalances

Chapter 2. described how regions with a larger tradable sector have been more successful in achieving sustainable economic and productivity growth. However, tradable sectors – by definition – are also directly exposed to international developments – in particular changes in exchange rates and trade shocks. This can be a particular challenge for regions that are highly dependent on production in "mature" sectors, i.e. those producing standardised goods for which technological replication is relatively easy, e.g. textile manufacturing. Cost competitiveness is often essential for such sectors and for the economic vitality of the regions where they are located. Without innovation and the introduction of new products or processes, firms need to rely on keeping unit costs in line with international competitors to remain profitable.

A good example of this is Portugal's Norte region. The appreciation of the euro, which occurred at the same time as The People's Republic of China ("China" hereafter) joined the World Trade Organization, jolted the textile manufacturing sector. As a consequence, Portugal's Norte region was seriously affected; China's textile exports were directly competing with many of the producers in Norte, and the appreciation of the euro meant that exports from Norte were becoming relatively more costly. The result of the loss in its competitive position was a slow decline in manufacturing employment in the Norte region (c.f. "Is a large tradable sector more risky for a region?").

Among the different factors that affect production costs, a main focus in the public debate often centres on the cost of labour, including workers' basic wages or employers' additional social contributions. While this obviously is a key factor in industries that mainly compete on price, other factors also contribute to a firm's production costs. These include purchasing and maintenance of machinery, rent for office space, electricity and other utility costs, the time it needs to deal with administrative requests, interest rates at which the firm can borrow, and the cost of imported intermediate products.

A measure that captures the development of personnel costs in relation to productivity is "unit labour costs". It is calculated as the ratio between personnel costs per employee and labour productivity (i.e. real output per worker). Unit labour costs increase if the compensation of employees rises faster than their productivity and decrease if productivity gains outpace compensation. In the popular debate, the focus is often on rising labour costs. What unit labour costs highlight is that rising labour costs are not necessarily a concern, quite the contrary as they reflect rising incomes and living standards. But if rising labour costs are not offset by productivity gains, increases become easily unsustainable. Unit labour costs can therefore serve as a possible warning sign for accruing imbalances in an economy.

Unit labour costs growth before the 2007-08 crisis

The European countries hit hardest by the 2007-08 crisis were the ones where unit labour costs had risen steadily and in many cases rapidly in the run-up to the crisis (c.f. "The global 2007-08 crisis uncovered some unsustainable growth models "in Chapter 1). While some growth in unit labour costs is natural and driven by inflation, excessive growth is red flag that imbalances are accruing. Annual increases in worker remuneration typically compensate for inflation. But in many countries, personnel costs appear disconnected from productivity growth and inflation. For example, the 3-year growth in unit labour costs in Greece, Spain or Romania exceeded the 9% threshold (12% for non-euro area countries) set by the European Macroeconomic Imbalance Procedure (MIP) Scoreboard in each year between 2003 and 2007.

Over the same time period, the opposite process took place in Germany and other northern European countries. From 2000 to 2007, labour productivity in Germany grew by 11% whereas real wages increased by only 1%. This widened the gap in labour unit costs across European regions and worsened the competitive position of regions with high unit labour cost growth.

Recent empirical OECD work confirms that increasing unit labour costs can be detrimental to regional growth. Over the period 2000-13, regions' growth in income and export per capita is negatively associated with increases in unit labour costs. A 1 percentage point increase in the growth rate of unit labour costs is, on average, associated with a 0.3 percentage point loss in growth of gross value added per capita and a 0.4 percentage point loss in exports per capita.[1] This effect can also be seen for regions in individual countries. For example in Portugal (excluding Lisbon)[2] per capita exports in each region increased faster than the country average in years where its unit labour costs were declining, but saw a relative export decline in years when its unit labour costs were rising (Figure 4.1).

Figure 4.1. Rising unit labour costs and falling exports in Portuguese regions (excluding Lisbon), 2000-10

Annual average export growth per capita vs annual average growth in unit labour costs

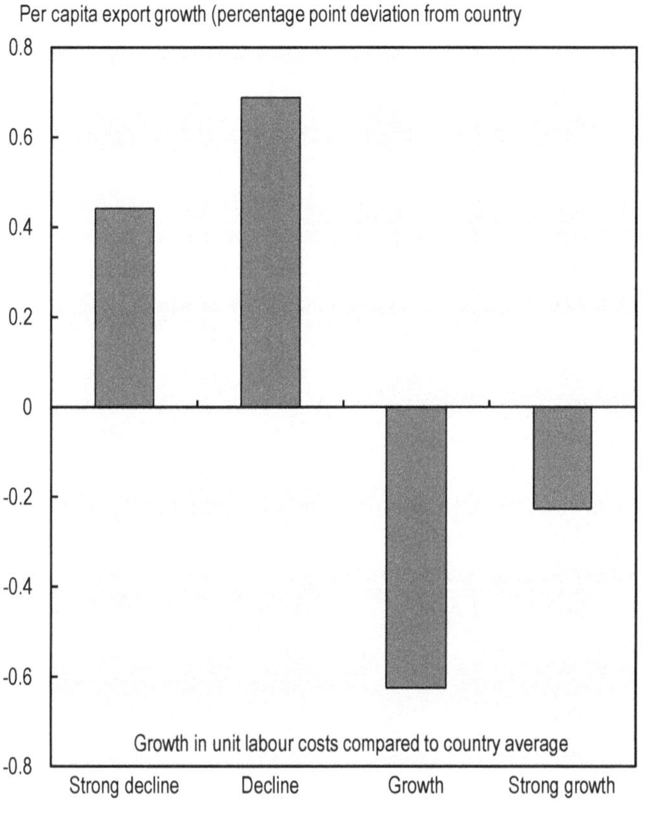

Note: Relative growth in per capita exports is the difference between the unweighted average of growth rates across regions within the group and the country average growth rate. Growth rates are classified as "strong decline" or "strong growth" are those deviating by more than 1 percentage point from the country average growth rate in unit labour costs, growth rates within 1 percentage point are classified as "decline" or "growth".

Source: Lembcke, Oliveira Martins and Wolf (forthcoming) based on Eurostat Regional Statistics [Database] and data provided by Los and Chen (2016[76]).

StatLink http://dx.doi.org/10.1787/888933708216

Wages grew faster than productivity, eroding unit labour costs in southern European regions

Changes in unit labour costs in southern European regions prior to the crisis were driven by wages that grew faster than productivity. In this respect, the distinction between tradable and non-tradable sectors turns out to be essential in understanding both the drivers of increases in unit labour costs and the challenge regions face in supporting tradable activities. In regions in Greece, Italy, Spain and Portugal, it was the unit labour costs in non-tradable sectors that drove aggregate unit labour costs.[3] In these countries, unit labour costs tended to be not only high in non-tradable sectors, but also tended to grow faster than in tradable sectors.

Strong growth in the costs for staff that are not supported by productivity growth, tend to be particularly damaging in countries that have a fixed exchange rate regime. In a fixed exchange rate regime, such as the euro area, rising unit labour costs cannot be compensated by a depreciation of the nominal exchange rate. Instead, they directly translate into changes in the real effective exchange rate, i.e. a decrease in the country's cost competitiveness.

Labour costs in non-tradable and tradable sectors tend to move in tandem

Considering separately the two constituent elements of unit labour costs, labour costs and labour productivity, sheds further light on the origins of low regional performance. First, while productivity in tradable sectors in southern and Eastern Europe had been growing before the 2007-08 crisis, productivity in non-tradable sectors had been stagnant, if not declining. These patterns should have been reflected in, at best, moderate labour costs increases, and if anything higher increases in the tradable sector (as workers can move between the two sectors, wages tend to increase in tandem in both sectors). This was indeed the case in most European regions where labour costs for tradables and non-tradables increased at similar rates by and large (see Figure 4.2, left panel). However, the reality was very different in southern European regions with low growth where labour costs in the non-tradable sector increased in line with the rest of the country, and in particular much faster than labour costs in the tradable sector (Figure 4.2, right panel). In such a situation, workers tend to move from the tradable to the non-tradable sector, resulting in a decline in the tradable sector while the non-tradable sector increases strongly – usually in an unsustainable fashion.

Figure 4.2. Labour costs in tradables and non-tradables strongly diverged in some regions

Relative labour costs in low growth and low income regions compared to other regions in the country separated for tradable and non-tradable sectors (100=non-tradable sectors in 2000 in regions that are not low income or low growth), 2000-13

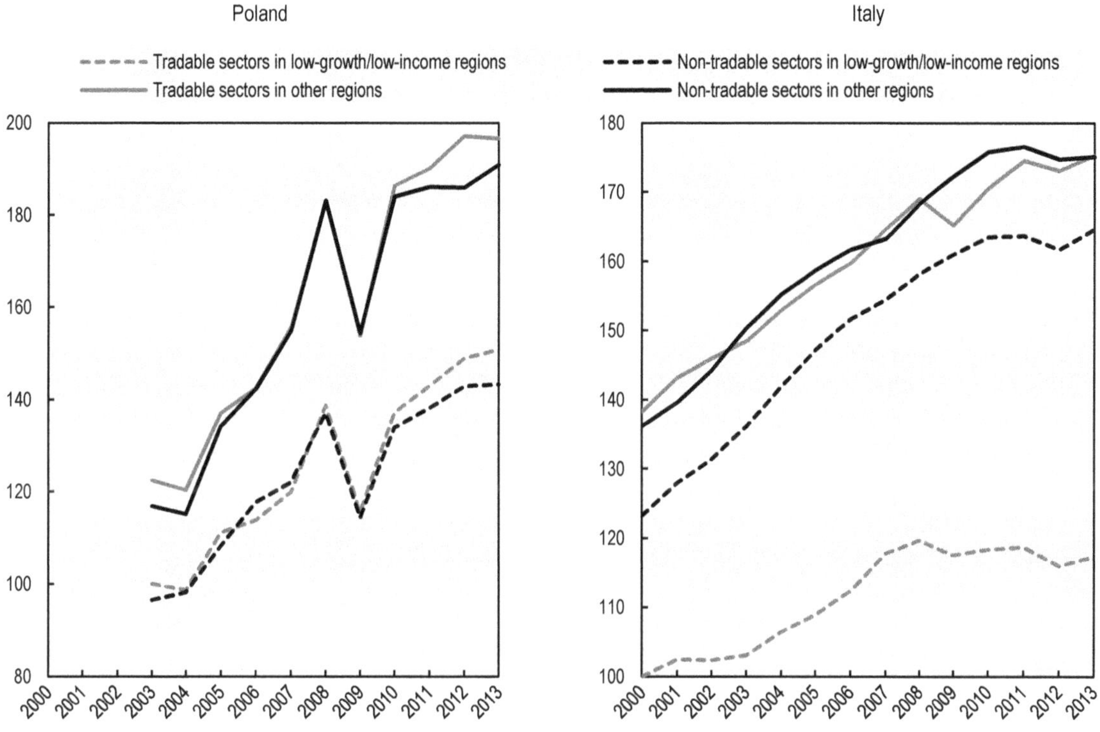

Note: Personnel costs are the total compensation of employees from regional accounts.
Source: Lembcke, Oliveira Martins and Wolf (forthcoming) based on Eurostat Regional Statistics [Database].

StatLink http://dx.doi.org/10.1787/888933708235

Labour cost misalignments can be driven by capital flows, but labour market institutions may also play a role

Normally, market forces contribute to the alignment of non-tradable and tradable labour costs in a given labour market. It is hence somewhat surprising to see stark divergences in labour costs for the non-tradable and tradable sector within the same region. To understand such a situation, it first needs to be acknowledged that prices in the tradable sector need to take international prices for the same goods and services into account, which does not give companies much flexibility in wage setting. International competition implies that if wages increase too much (i.e. significantly above increases in productivity), such companies will go out of business. As a result of this competition, tradable firms' wages should reflect the productivity of their employees.

In contrast, firms in non-tradable sectors are (at least in the short- to medium-term) unconstrained by international or global prices since these firms do not face competition from competitors in other regions. In situations of strong demand for non-tradables – such as when demand is driven by strong capital inflows into a country or region – prices and wages in the non-tradable sector may hence see significant increases, even if those often turn out to be unsustainable in the medium- to long-term. Such increases may then become self-perpetuating, as in a situation of comparatively higher inflation in a given region (or country within a monetary union), real interest rates may become negative and – through fuelled credit demand – further inflate an already booming non-tradable economy. Such a boom can go on for some time until eventually capital flows into the region or country dry up and a tightening credit supply ends the party.

Furthermore, if wages are sectorally negotiated for a whole country (as is the case in many European countries) and do not account for local cost of living differences, the real wage in non-tradable sectors – including the public sector – can easily become too high in low cost regions and too low in high cost regions.[4] The same is not necessarily true for tradable sectors. The reason is that every place needs hairdressers, kindergarten teachers or construction workers, but the production of textiles, cars or development of computer programmes is not spatially bound. Thus, whereas economic activity in the tradable sector will move to other regions in the long run if unit labour costs are too high, firms in the non-tradable sector will stay in the region.

The difference in wage setting regimes between the south and the east of Europe is a potential explanation for the differing growth performance of southern and eastern European regions. Across countries and industries there is evidence that the misalignment of wage and productivity developments is greater where wages are not set at the firm level (ECB, 2015[102]). In contrast, centralised bargaining might have dampened the adverse employment effects following the 2007-08 crisis. There is some evidence that employment in countries with stronger centralisation of collective bargaining fell less as wages in these countries adjusted quicker to the shock (OECD, 2017[96]).

Flexible institutions and structural reforms might be particularly relevant in lagging regions

Flexible labour market regulations that account for the needs of workers, the unemployed and firms in different regions are particularly important for lagging regions. Increased flexibility in wage setting and reforms of Germany's social security and welfare system have been credited with the expansion of employment and a decline in unemployment since 2003, dubbed the "German labour market miracle" (Burda, 2016[103]). Estimates show that rigid employment regulations can hurt productivity growth more in lagging regions than in regions that are already more productive and less able to cope with more rigid labour market regulations (D'Costa, Garcilazo and Oliveira Martins, 2016[104]).

Low-income and low-growth regions experienced stronger productivity growth than other European regions following labour market reforms (Figure 4.3). However, major labour market reforms are rare and changes often piecemeal or targeted at fixed-term contracts. The OECD strictness index for employment protection legislation (EPL) in Italy, for example, did not change for more than 20 years until the contentious "Monti-Fornero reform" was introduced in June 2012. Despite the political effort involved in passing the reform, only three out of the 25 constituent indicators considered in the OECD Indicators of Employment Protection changed.

Figure 4.3. Flexibility in the labour market can boost productivity growth

Cumulative impact of a decrease in the stringency of Employment Protection Legislation on productivity growth

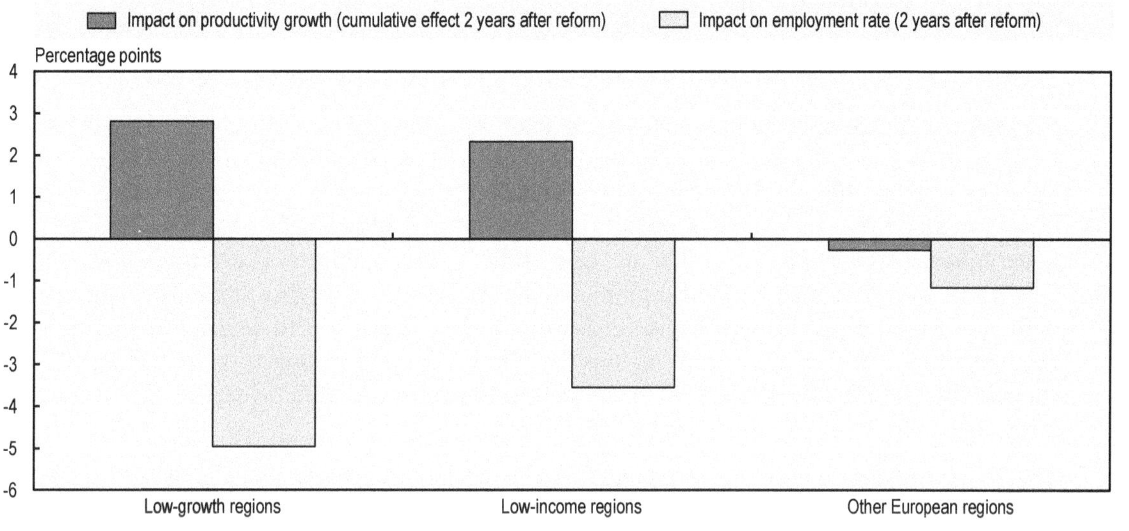

Note: Estimates based on multivariate regression allowing for a delayed impact of reforms to the labour market up to two years.
Source: D'Costa, Lembcke and Oliveira Martins (forthcoming).

StatLink http://dx.doi.org/10.1787/888933708254

Similarly, product market regulations in wholesale and retail trade appear to have particularly negative impacts on the productivity growth of a country's least productive regions (those farthest from the leading region of the country in terms of GDP per worker), which includes Europe's lagging regions. Conversely, trade openness appears to help less productive regions disproportionately more than other regions, particularly in low-growth countries (D'Costa, Garcilazo and Oliveira Martins, 2013[105]). It is therefore important to consider not only the aggregate impact of nationwide structural policies, but their impact on different types of regions and particularly on lagging regions.

Institutions and governance: Constraints and catalysts

Beyond national macroeconomic trends or structural reforms, regional growth and productivity is also more generally affected by a country's institutional and governance settings. These settings can be a facilitator or barrier to regional economic performance. Institutions and, more generally, social norms provide the foundation for the interactions of firms, workers and consumers among each other and with the government. Of particular importance are institutions that guide these economic interactions, such as the rule of law and low levels of corruption.[5]

While much of the evidence on the effect of institutions is focused on developing countries, differences in the quality of government across European regions – and in particular low levels of corruption and a high degree of accountability – seem to be highly relevant in explaining per capita GDP growth.[6] The European Quality of Government Survey provides several waves of data on good governance in the public sector and illustrates that the difference in governmental quality can be stark, not only across but also within countries.[7] For example, the best-performing Spanish and Italian regions rank among Europe's highest scoring regions, but other regions in the countries fall below the EU average. Low quality of government in a region is highly correlated with the level of economic development in the region, but also with levels of social trust (Charron, Dijkstra and Lapuente, 2014[106]).

Fragmented governance curtails productivity of cities and urban regions

Fragmented governance arrangements can curb productivity and economic growth in cities and regions. Ahrend et al. (2017[107]) estimated that a doubling of the number of municipalities within the boundaries of a metropolitan area was associated with 3-6% lower productivity, but that this penalty is alleviated by about half when metropolitan governance arrangements exist. The adverse effect of fragmentation is not limited to the city itself, but affects the whole region. Economic growth in highly urbanised regions with more municipalities per capita is lower than in regions with less administrative fragmentation; for regions with a mostly rural population there is, however, no statistically significant impact of increased administrative fragmentation (Bartolini, 2015[108]).[8]

The impact of administrative fragmentation on productivity most likely arises through inefficiency in policies that require co-ordination across different local or regional governments, examples being transport and land-use planning, which also should be aligned with tax and environmental policies (OECD, 2017[109]) or growth-promoting policies in general (Cheshire and Magrini, 2009[110]). For example, administrative fragmentation in the Chicago Metropolitan Area has been one of the factors behind an overly complex and not particularly efficient governance structure of public transit providers in the metropolitan agglomeration. This, in turn, has been reflected in relatively low levels of integration of the public transit system, and has also contributed to underinvestment in its infrastructure (OECD, 2015[111]).

Improving administrative efficiency has significant economic returns

Barriers to productivity growth and trade integration can extend to judicial efficiency. The length of legal proceedings can vary significantly between jurisdictions. In Italy, the average length of civil proceedings in southern regions was twice that of courts in the north for cases in the 2002-07 period.[9] But even in Italian cities like Milan or Rome, the average time to reach a ruling is more than double that in Madrid (Spain) or that in Polish regions.[10] But even within the north and the south, judicial efficiency varies significantly. Employment and turnover of manufacturing firms has been estimated to increase by 2% for a 10% reduction in the length of court proceedings (Giacomelli and Menon, 2017[112]). Firms in less efficient jurisdictions are also less likely to participate in global value chains. The probability of a manufacturing firm supplying specialised inputs abroad increases by about 0.4 percentage points for a 10% reduction in average trial length (Accetturo, Linarello and Petrella, 2017[113]).

The ease of doing business varies not only across, but also within countries

Judicial aspects are not the only factor that varies across regions. The World Bank's "Ease of Doing Business" indicators show that national frameworks and general business conditions can limit business dynamics, with obvious negative effects on growth and productivity. For example, in countries with low growth regions, the most recent range of indicators stresses how firms struggle to access credit, enforce contracts and to deal with issues involving minority investor protection. In Europe's eastern countries with low-income regions, insolvency regimes and contract enforcement are key challenges (World Bank, 2016[114]). For several countries, data on the business environment at the subnational level have recently become available, confirming the existence of major differences not only across countries, but also across regions within countries.[11]

Notes

1. Cited results from Lembcke, Oliveira Martins and Wolf (forthcoming) account in the regression for time-invariant regional characteristics, the change in the skill composition of the local labour force and trends at the country level. Gaulier and Vicard (2013[188]) assess the impact of unit labour cost increases at the country level and find little relationship with exports, but a strongly negative relationship with the current account deficit.

2. Excluding the archipelagos.

3. The three-year growth rate in non-tradable regional unit labour costs was higher than the national average growth rate in all years between 2000 and the 2007-08 crisis. Greece is the only exception where over the period 2000-03 non-tradable unit labour costs in regions not classified as "low-growth" was below the national average.

4. Public sector wages are often also determined centrally and might play a role in explaining the patterns found in this study. Utilising a more stringent definition of "non-tradable" that is dominated by public and related sectors (public administration, defence, health care and social services) shows an even stronger alignment of personnel costs than in the main delineation used here and in the OECD Regional Outlook 2016 (OECD, 2016[1]). The benefits are not necessarily passed on to workers. A decrease in public employment between 2001 and 2011 in Italy increased private sector employment, especially in southern regions (Auricchio et al., 2017[215]). Spatial segregation of low-wage/low-productivity jobs and sectors in some regions and high-productivity/high-cost ones in others can partly circumvent the stringency of centralised wage setting. Another solution is that wage bargaining only constitutes a wage floor, with better-performing firms paying their workers an additional premium. Firms in Portugal have used these "wage cushions" extensively (Cardoso and Portugal, 2005[204]). Firms might also simply not comply with regulations. For instance, Garnero (2017[189]) estimated that about 10% of Italian workers are paid below the minimum wage set by their collective bargaining agreement. This share is higher in Italy's south where the cost of living is less than in the north where prices are high. The disparity ranges from 8.5% of the workforce being underpaid in the northeast to 18.5% in the country's south. Instead of aiming to alleviate poverty through general increases in nominal wages (or minimum wages), targeted strategies (such as living wages that account for local cost of living) are likely to be more successful in targeting low-income households and have less adverse effects on employment, as found for the United States (Neumark, Thompson and Koyle, 2012[168]). Direct measures, such as transfers via earned income tax credits that benefit low-income households can directly result in better distributional outcomes for low-income households (Neumark and Wascher, 2011[169]). A further advantage of this type of support is that it ties work incentives to an increase in income without disconnecting employer wages from worker productivity.

5. Acemoglu, Johnson and Robinson (2001[224]) made the seminal contribution that empirically linked institutions and economic development. See Acemoglu and Robinson (2012[223]) for a summary of the literature detailing the characteristics of institutions that support growth.

6. Low levels of corruption and a high degree of accountability are associated with good performance in terms of economic growth in European regions (Ketterer and Rodríguez-Pose, 2016[178]).

7. It surveys residents on their experience and interaction with the public sector in areas such as corruption, accountability (in case of corruption), rule of law and effective service delivery (in education and health care). See Charron, Dijkstra and Lapuente (2015[203]) for a description of the survey.

8. Based on data for the 1996-2011 period on per capita GDP growth and administrative fragmentation in 250 TL2 regions from 23 OECD countries. The regression includes education, density and innovation controls, as well as country fixed effects.

9. See Giacomelli and Menon (2017[112]) and related sources.

10. See the discussion by the European Commission (2017[11]) based on subnational reports on the ease of doing business for Italy (World Bank, 2013[161]), Poland (World Bank, 2015[160]) and Spain (World Bank, 2015[159]).

11. Reports are available for Italy (World Bank, 2013[161]), Poland (World Bank, 2015[160]) and Spain (World Bank, 2015[159]). The assessment of the business environment focuses on the main cities in different countries. In aggregate, the three countries with available indicators form a clear ranking. Polish cities tend to have a more conducive business environment, followed by Spanish and Italian regions. With regard to certain indicators, however, there are substantial differences across countries and regions. Starting a business or registering property takes longer in Polish regions than in Italy or Spain, but receiving a construction permit is significantly faster.

References

Accetturo, A., A. Linarello and A. Petrella (2017), "Legal enforcement and Global Value Chains: Micro-evidence from Italian manufacturing firms", *Occasional Papers (Questioni di economia e finanza)*, No. 397, Banca D'Italia. [16]

Acemoglu, D., S. Johnson and J. Robinson (2001), "The Colonial Origins of Comparative Development: An Empirical Investigation", *The American Economic Review*, Vol. 91/5, pp. 1369-1401. [31]

Acemoglu, D. and J. Robinson (2012), *Why Nations Fail: The Origins of Power, Prosperity and Poverty*, Profile Books, London. [30]

Ahrend, R. et al. (2017), "What Makes Cities More Productive? Evidence From Five OECD Countries on the Role of Urban Governance", *Journal of Regional Science*, Vol. 57/3, pp. 385-410. [10]

Auricchio, M. et al. (2017), "The consequences of public employment: evidence from Italian municipalities", *Working Papers*, No. 1125, Banca d'Italia. [29]

Bartolini, D. (2015), "Municipal Fragmentation and Economic Performance of OECD TL2 Regions", *OECD Regional Development Working Papers*, No. 2015/2, OECD Publishing, Paris, http://dx.doi.org/10.1787/5jrxqs60st5h-en. [11]

Burda, M. (2016), "The German Labor Market Miracle, 2003 -2015: An Assessment", *SFB 649 Discussion Paper*, No. 2016-005, Humboldt -Universität zu Berlin. [6]

Cardoso, A. and P. Portugal (2005), "Contractual Wages and the Wage Cushion under Different Bargaining Settings", *Journal of Labor Economics*, Vol. 23/4, pp. 875-902. [28]

Charron, N., L. Dijkstra and V. Lapuente (2014), "Regional Governance Matters: Quality of Government within European Union Member States", *Regional Studies*, Vol. 48/1, pp. 68-90. [9]

Charron, N., L. Dijkstra and V. Lapuente (2015), "Mapping the Regional Divide in Europe: A Measure for Assessing Quality of Government in 206 European Regions", *Social Indicators Research*, Vol. 122/2, pp. 315-346. [27]

Cheshire, P. and S. Magrini (2009), "Urban Growth Drivers in a Europe of Sticky People and Implicit Boundaries", *Journal of Economic Geography*, Vol. 9/1, pp. 85-115. [13]

D'Costa, S., E. Garcilazo and J. Oliveira Martins (2013), "The Impact of Structural and Macroeconomic Factors on Regional Growth", *OECD Regional Development Working Papers*, No. 2013/11, OECD Publishing, Paris, http://dx.doi.org/10.1787/5k451mplq9lw-en. [8]

D'Costa, S., E. Garcilazo and J. Oliveira Martins (2016), "Impact of Structural Reforms on Regional Growth: Distance to the Frontier Matters", *SERC Discussion Paper*, No. 203, Spatial Economics Research Centre. [7]

ECB (2015), "Economic Bulletin", No. 08/2015, European Central Bank. [4]

European Commission (2017), "Competitiveness in Low-Income and Low-Growth Regions: The Lagging Regions Report", *European Commission Staff Working Document*, European Commission. [26]

Garnero, A. (2017), "The Dog That Barks Doesn't Bite: Coverage and Compliance of Sectoral Minimum Wages in Italy", *Discussion Paper*, No. 10511, IZA. [25]

Gaulier, G. and V. Vicard (2013), "The signatures of euro-area imbalances: Export performance and the composition of ULC growth", *CompNet Policy Brief*, No. 02/2013, European Central Bank. [24]

Giacomelli, S. and C. Menon (2017), "Does weak contract enforcement affect firm size? Evidence from the neighbour's court", *Journal of Economic Geography*, Vol. 17/6, pp. 1251–1282. [15]

Ketterer, T. and A. Rodríguez-Pose (2016), "Institutions vs. 'first-nature' geography: What drives economic growth in Europe's regions?", *Papers in Regional Science*. [23]

Los, B. and W. Chen (2016), "Global Value Chain Participation Indicators for European Regions", *Report for the OECD*, No. December 2016. [3]

Manning, A. and B. Petrongolo (2017), "How Local Are Labor Markets? Evidence from a Spatial Job Search Model", *American Economic Review*, Vol. 107/10, pp. 2877-2907. [2]

Marinescu, I. and R. Rathelot (2016), "Mismatch Unemployment and the Geography of Job Search", *NBER Working Papers*, No. 22672, National Bureau of Economic Research, Cambridge, MA. [1]

Neumark, D. and W. Wascher (2011), "Does a Higher Minimum Wage Enhance the Effectiveness of the Earned Income Tax Credit?", *Industrial and Labor Relations Review*, Vol. 64/4. [22]

Neumark, D., M. Thompson and L. Koyle (2012), "The effects of living wage laws on low-wage workers and low-income families: What do we know now?", *IZA Journal of Labor* [21]

Policy, Vol. 1/1, pp. 1-34.

OECD (2015), *Governing the City*, OECD Publishing, Paris, http://dx.doi.org/10.1787/9789264226500-en. [14]

OECD (2016), *OECD Regional Outlook 2016: Productive Regions for Inclusive Societies*, OECD Publishing, Paris, http://dx.doi.org/10.1787/9789264260245-en. [32]

OECD (2017), *The Governance of Land Use in OECD Countries: Policy Analysis and Recommendations*, OECD Publishing, Paris, http://dx.doi.org/10.1787/9789264268609-en. [12]

OECD (2017), *OECD Employment Outlook 2017*, OECD Publishing, Paris, http://dx.doi.org/10.1787/empl_outlook-2017-en. [5]

World Bank (2013), *Doing Business in Italy 2013: Smarter Regulations for Small and Medium-Size Enterprises*, World Bank Group, Washington, DC. [20]

World Bank (2015), *Doing Business in Spain 2015*, World Bank, Washington, DC. [18]

World Bank (2015), *Doing Business in Poland 2015*, World Bank, Washington, DC. [19]

World Bank (2016), *Doing Business 2016: Measuring Regulatory Quality and Efficiency*, World Bank, Washington, DC. [17]

Chapter 5. Policy lessons: Productivity and growth in regions

This concluding chapter presents policy lessons to drive productivity growth and job creation in all types of regions. Building upon the analyses of the previous chapters and previous OECD research, this chapter offers somewhat concise answers to three different issues that have long surrounded regional development policies: an over-reliance on non-tradable sectors, a focus on "exogenous" growth stimuli rather than on local strengths and the challenge of diffusion of knowledge and innovations beyond the frontier.

Chapter synopsis

What policies can support productivity and growth in regions? Levers in three broad areas are among those that help regions seize the opportunities of cities and tradable sectors, while addressing the possible adverse repercussions that increased openness and international competition can bring. These levers are better policy co-ordination, a focus on regional strengths and regional links to support knowledge diffusion.

To realise the potential of cities and the tradable sector in regions, policies should be co-ordinated across administrative boundaries and across policy fields. In particular the link between cities and the surrounding rural areas can provide "agglomeration benefits" to less densely populated areas, while alleviating congestion costs in cities. Links include physical transport connections but are not limited to them. For example, firms in rural regions should be connected to universities and research institutes that are often found in cities. Likewise, access to financing often depends on connections to financial institutions that also tend to be located in cities.

A holistic approach that brings together actions from different policy fields is particularly relevant to address adverse shocks from trade. Education and training for displaced workers are critical, but without firms to hire them, even the best skilled workers will not find jobs. Thus, regions where trade shocks caused substantial harm to the fabric of firms need policies that foster firm creation and recovery. Such policies can include cluster policies, programmes to support start-ups and business creation or policies to attract foreign direct investment. They need to be adapted to place-specific factors and make use of the particular strengths of a region. Too many trade adjustment programmes focus solely on retraining workers and neglect this important dimension.

Regions should build on their particular strengths to attract firms. Many successful regional development strategies identify unique characteristics of their region and focus on how businesses can use them to grow. Unique regional characteristics can include natural features, such as location, particular geography or the abundance of resources, or man-made features, such as the availability of specific infrastructure, highly specialised research institutes, or already existing economic clusters. Instead of creating a "race-to-the-bottom" in which different regions try to undercut each other, for example at the expense of tax revenues or environmental and labour standards, such approaches can encourage a race-to-the-top, helping regions to perform better while lifting the economic performance of the entire country.

An essential asset for a region's economy is the knowledge embedded in its workers, firms and academic institutions. But the diffusion of knowledge and innovation is often difficult. Public authorities can contribute to the diffusion of productivity-increasing knowledge across firms. Innovation agencies and business support centres can help small businesses to implement effective production and management practices. Such training programmes can be combined with other relevant assistance, for example advice on how to enter foreign markets. Industry associations can help firms to learn from each other's experiences and can co-ordinate joint research activities between businesses. Governments can support such co-ordinated efforts by businesses as long as they do not lead to collusion. Effective university-industry collaboration is another successful strategy to create and spread innovation. In return for industry-relevant R&D, universities benefit from private sector research grants. To further encourage knowledge transfer, technology centres that aim to connect university research with firm R&D can play a vital role in translating abstract research into innovative new products.

Policy lessons for three persistent challenges in regional development

The prior chapters discussed the challenge of combining productivity growth and job creation in a globalised world, highlighted the role of tradable sectors and well-functioning cities in supporting the catching up of regions to their country's most productive region, how sectoral clusters in regions and their integration in global value chains are linked to regional economic performance and how the macroeconomic framework and national-level regulations affect regions. Building on this analysis, the discussion in this concluding chapter puts the spotlight on three different issues that have long surrounded regional development policies.

The first issue is the over-reliance of many policymakers on non-tradable sectors, even though tradable sectors tend to be more productive and not necessarily riskier (c.f. Chapter 2.). The next section presents evidence supporting this assertion, and provides additional guidance about how to incentivise tradable sector development. The section also discusses how territories can invest in trade adjustment programmes that protect workers and firms alike from global shocks.

The second issue is that many regions still seek "exogenous" ways to grow. They provide subsidies and require lower environmental and labour standards to attract firms from elsewhere. They try to mimic the successful productive sectors of other regions. Instead, it is argued in the third section of this chapter that regions should build on regional strengths and invest in human capital development to promote productivity growth. Thereby, rather than a "race to the bottom", competition among regions can lead to a "race to the top".

The third issue is that dissemination of innovation from leading firms to firms that lag behind the productivity frontier appears increasingly difficult. This issue is addressed in the fourth section of this chapter by presenting different actors, processes and instruments that can help laggard firms in this endeavour. Other firms in the supply chain, even in global ones, can transfer knowledge to these firms. Universities and research-oriented organisations can generate innovation to support firms, and many different instruments exist to support collaboration. The public sector can conduct innovation-friendly procurement, which can stimulate innovation in firms.

There is no single solution to "save" places, and there is no single recipe that can be copy and pasted into other places, given their different contexts and characteristics. Whatever regions can do, it will not be simple and definitive. The good news is that there is a lot that they can do. This is reflected in the multi-faceted structure of this chapter. Indeed, the key to achieving convergence is the multi-faceted nature of the strategies that regions can adopt in their quest for productivity growth and job creation.

Realising the potential of the tradable sector

Policy co-ordination across regions and cities

Most policies are created by governments for specific jurisdictions – national, regional or local. For regional policies, the region is naturally the focus of attention for policy makers. Yet, it is important to keep in mind that no region exists independently from its surrounding environment. Regions within a country are connected through inter-regional trade, the flows of people and capital and fiscal transfers. Through these links, regions influence each other constantly.

Policies implemented in one region inevitably affect all other regions in a country, even if the effects are often indirect and cannot be clearly attributable to the policy. For example, a policy that creates new jobs in one region would attract unemployed persons from other regions, which positively affects the unemployment levels in these regions. While the effects of a single regional policy on other regions are often so small that they are close to imperceptible, taken together the spillover effects from many regional policies can be substantial.

In some instances, regional spillovers are unequivocally positive. If a region becomes a hub for R&D, it can create innovations from which all regions benefit. In other instances, spillovers can be unequivocally negative. For example, a region might use subsidies to convince a business to relocate from another region to it. This situation (which is discussed in the section, "Productive ways to compete among regions: A race to the top" below) creates economic growth in one region at the expense of another region.

In most cases, spillovers include positive and negative elements, and it is the task of policy makers to ensure that positive spillovers dominate. Thus, regional policies should also be evaluated with respect to their effects on surrounding regions, and national governments should provide policy frameworks that make it attractive for regions to pursue policies that have positive spillovers on other regions.

Related to the issue of policy spillovers is the question of policy co-ordination across regions. In many instances, the optimal geographic scope of policies is above the regional level but below the national level. A basic example of such a policy would be investment in regional public transport. Even though it does not need to be co-ordinated at the national level, regions have to ensure that their regional public transport systems are well connected to those of neighbouring regions. Thus, policy makers need to work with neighbouring regions to ensure effective inter-regional policy co-ordination.

Co-ordination of policies is particularly important between urban areas and surrounding rural regions. Cities serve as hubs that provide essential services for businesses in rural areas. By ensuring that rural areas are well-connected to cities, policy makers can help rural regions benefit from the opportunities that cities offer. Importantly, being well connected in this context should not be understood narrowly, as in the context of transport infrastructure. Non-physical connections are equally important. For example, businesses in rural regions should be connected to universities that create innovation and to banks that provide financing for investments.

This implies that the region in which a policy is implemented and the full extent of the area where benefits arise are not necessarily one and the same. Using the previous example, a policy to better connect research institutions with businesses in rural areas could be implemented in the urban region where the research institutions are located with the goal to help businesses in a neighbouring rural region.

More generally, the examples above show that regional policy makers need to think beyond regional boundaries even if their sole focus is on their own region's economic improvement. Spillovers and interregional dependencies imply that the solutions to increase one region's productivity can often be found in another region. To identify and use these opportunities, regions need to exchange information, discuss and co-ordinate policies with each other.

Incentives for tradable sector development

The tradable sector is important if regions are going to "catch up" to their country's most productive frontier regions (OECD, 2016[1]). As demonstrated in Chapter 2. of this report and prior OECD research, regions and countries with a higher share of economic activity in tradable sectors innovate more, are more productive, have higher wages and narrow the "productivity gap" faster (OECD, 2016[1]). Despite this solid evidence, many regions and countries still focus support on non-tradable sectors, to "play it safe". This puzzling paradox merits attention.

For one, excessive reliance on non-tradable sectors has limited economy-wide productivity growth. Investments in the construction sector, increased access to credit and stimulus of consumption have fostered cycles of artificial demand that subsequently failed to sustain long-term growth, as the first two chapters of this report argue. At the same time, it is important to acknowledge that non-tradable sectors account for the largest contribution to the regional economy, and investments in infrastructure, personnel and housing are often needed. However, investment decisions in these sectors should not be made with the goal of providing a temporary boost to economic growth in the short term. Instead, they should be based on long-term needs and be supported by objective cost-benefit analyses.

The second aspect is the erroneous but widespread belief that the tradable sector is more volatile to shocks and thus riskier, while the non-tradable sector would be safer to invest in. This belief arises from the assumption that shocks that hit a particular sector are the dominant source of volatility. Recent evidence shows, however, that country-specific shocks, which strike all sectors in a certain country, are as damaging as sector-specific shocks with regards to volatility patterns (Caselli et al., 2015[2]).

Another misleading belief is that openness to trade leads to higher sectoral specialisation, which would make countries and regions more vulnerable to shocks. However, regions where employment shifted most strongly towards non-tradable sectors suffered the most in terms of employment losses following the global 2007-08 crisis (c.f. Chapter 2.). Non-tradable sectors are not only indirectly linked to global volatility trends, but they also have had a hard time recovering from the shock of the crisis, since their activity depends solely on local demand.

In fact, the effect of trade openness on volatility depends on the level of economic diversification. That is, if the economy is diversified enough, openness to trade lowers volatility, while, if the economy is not sufficiently diversified, it increases volatility.[1] Hence, tradable sectors not only yield higher economic returns, they can also reduce volatility levels, as long as there is enough economic diversification.

For being more productive and less volatile to shocks, tradable sectors should attract more attention from public officials and there are different sets of policies that can help. Beyond policies that can affect non-tradable and tradable sectors alike (e.g. investment in human capital, infrastructure development and support to innovation), this report sets out three sets of policies that can specifically assist tradable sectors.

Well-designed cluster policies can support the formation of economic hubs in selected tradable sectors. When a dominant cluster already exists, regional policy should strive to facilitate the development of related activities. Clusters can provide services and inputs to each other in a complementary rather than competitive fashion, within the same region or across regions (Box 5.1). Indeed, diversification into related varieties is likely to facilitate knowledge spillovers and stimulate innovation, as pointed out in Chapter 3. Policies that succeed in achieving this can spur growth in a region, while also reducing exposure to external shocks.

Box 5.1. Regional clusters in the Netherlands

Regional policy in the Netherlands supports R&D to stimulate the competitiveness of key Dutch sectors. Top Sector priorities are supported by regional development institutions, in line with regional and national development strategies. The rationale is that investment in sectors with highest R&D&I intensity can foster economic growth, create jobs and increase competitiveness.

More concretely, R&D&I support is provided to several different high-tech clusters, across different regions. The different clusters are regarded as unique yet complementary. That is, by supporting clusters across different economic activities, the Dutch economy becomes more diverse and less volatile to shocks. It also benefits more from innovation processes and can generate higher productivity growth overall.

The main clusters in the Netherlands are named around the themes of ports and valleys:

- Mainports: Amsterdam-Schiphol (airport) and Rotterdam Seaport. Connection points for multiple transport networks create opportunities for regional economic development as well as national and international economic competitiveness.
- Brainport: The high-technology complex emerged from Philips industries around Eindhoven, and is considered one of Europe's most innovative areas. This knowledge-intensive manufacturing region specialises in 'high tech systems' and 'design'. It is supported by a triple-helix structure of university, industry and public sector collaboration.
- Greenports: These are physical locations where particular elements of agriculture and horticulture cluster. There are six greenports in the Netherlands: Westland-Oostland (greenhouses), Venlo (flowers, food & logistics), Alsmeer (cut flowers), Duin en Bollenstreek (bulbs and flowers), Boskoop (trees and bushes), and Enkhuizen (seeds and breeding).
- The Energy Valley, located in the province of Groningen, consists of a cluster of companies that produce energy from gas (including biogas and green gas) and wind.
- The Food Valley is located in the province of Gelderland and consists of a well-integrated network of international food companies, research institutes and universities. It seeks to create conditions for food manufacturers and knowledge institutes to join forces in order to develop innovative food concepts.
- The Health Valley, also located in the province of Gelderland, aims to bridge knowledge between the biomedical and healthcare sectors. It is an opportunity for businesses and care institutions to operate in an innovative way and support each other.

Source: OECD (2014[31]), *OECD Territorial Reviews: Netherlands 2014*, OECD Publishing, Paris, http://dx.doi.org/10.1787/9789264209527-en.

Governments can also support industries in tradable sectors via negotiated deals. In the British model of *Sector Deals*, the government works with specific sectors, e.g. the life sciences, that organise themselves behind strong leadership (EEF, 2017[4]). The model is based on existing sector strategies in the aerospace and automotive industries. The deal can involve: addressing regulatory barriers; aligning policies on skills and training around a sector; creating institutions to support innovation creation and diffusion; and working together to increase exports and to commercialise research. Sector Deals are supposed to create a close relationship between the government and firms that are members of the deal (EEF, 2017[4]). They have limited geographic scope, i.e. they are localised to some extent. Sector Deals require a firm commitment from both sides, without overlooking the interests of smaller companies or companies that are not part of the deal. This relationship can help regions and industry sectors to better address challenges and foresee changes.

Lastly, the tradable sector can also be supported by facilitating exports led by specific agencies or networks. It can be particularly challenging for small and medium-sized enterprises (SMEs) to access external markets, given bureaucratic barriers, language challenges and even issues of scalability.

Export promotion agencies assist firms in entering external markets and overcoming foreign trade barriers. They can also help solve asymmetric information problems regarding tastes of foreign consumers, quality standards and regulations in other markets and business opportunities. A study across 103 countries finds that export promotion agencies have a positive effect on exports (Lederman, Olarreaga and Payton, 2010[5]).

Even though – as previously argued – developing tradable sectors is generally a less risky strategy than expanding the non-tradable sector, economies that export more and that are more open to trade should, nonetheless, be prepared for eventual trade shocks. Benefits from trade are also unevenly distributed, with some sectors benefitting more than others, which can have significant repercussions for employment in specific industries or specific regions. Trade adjustment programmes can provide assistance to such areas. This point will be addressed in more detail in the following section.

The territorial dimension of trade adjustment programmes

Trade adjustment programmes assist workers and enterprises that are negatively affected by trade policy reforms or changes in trade flows. Evidence confirms that some groups of workers face temporary unemployment and lower income when they lose their jobs due to heightened international competition (François, Jansen and Peters, 2011[6]).

These programmes offer temporary assistance to specific groups of workers. Often, workers need to file a collective petition demonstrating that the globalisation shock disproportionally affected their group in order to benefit from governmental assistance. Assistance can include unemployment subsidies, training and counselling. It is important to notice that these measures complement existing policies to support workers in general, such as employment assistance, skills retraining and lifelong learning.

One example of a programme that supports trade-affected workers is the Trade Adjustment Assistance (TAA) programme developed by the U.S. Department of Labor. The programme is implemented through partnerships with state agencies. It provides income support, assistance with health insurance premiums, job search and relocation allowances, and skills training. Workers who file the collective petition are on average 46 years old and have at most a secondary education degree. They often have obsolete skills in the manufacturing sectors, with on average over 12 years' experience in jobs that frequently no longer exist.

Other country-wide programmes operate in parallel. The Economic Adjustment Assistance Program of the Department of Commerce targets communities in distress. It provides technical, planning and infrastructure assistance to regions experiencing economic stress that may occur suddenly or over time. These economic changes include, but are not limited to, shocks from trade or automation. The Partnerships for Opportunity and Workforce and Economic Revitalization (POWER), a joint initiative of the U.S. Economic Development Administration and the Appalachian Regional Commission, assists workers impacted by changes in energy policy, notably those in coal mines and coal-fired power plants.

Box 5.2. Relocation allowances in trade adjustment programmes

The U.S. Trade Adjustment Assistance programme provides relocation allowances to workers who want to move elsewhere for jobs. Mobility has declined in the United States lately, and one reason for that are high moving costs. It covers not only the cost of physically moving a family and its belongings, but also includes the costs of transitioning to a new job, finding a house, etc. Moreover, health insurance plans cannot always be kept when moving to a different state, and diverse school curricula across states make it more difficult for students to adjust to new schools. Limited savings and limited access to credit may further restrict the moving opportunities of laid-off workers. Relocation allowances help offset the costs of moving.

Relocation allowances benefit not only workers who move and who will likely find better jobs in more productive regions, but can benefit those who stay, too. If workers in a profession that has high unemployment rate move away, then the labour market in the region becomes less competitive. That is to say, people who move away generate a positive externality on the local job market (Moretti, 2012, p. 162[7]). Those who stay have a higher probability of finding a job if they have fewer contenders, considering that they are competing for similar positions. At the same time, regions that receive an influx of workers are likely to have a high demand for labour and would therefore benefit from the inflow of workers.

Source: Moretti, E. (2012[7]), *The New Geography of Jobs*. Houghton Mifflin Harcourt, 294p.

In the European Union, the main trade-adjustment instrument is designed to assist workers made redundant by the effects of globalisation. The European Globalisation Adjustment Fund (EGF), established in 2006, co-funds active labour market policies such as job search assistance, training, and knowledge-transfer for start-ups (Cernat and Mustilli, 2017[8]). EU member states provide the other part of the funding and are responsible for implementing the defined measures. The programme has successfully increased support in cases where restructuring programmes are already well-established.

Even though these adjustment efforts are fairly comprehensive and important, there is room for improvement. One criticism is that they are reactive, providing help after the fact, i.e. after a plant has shut down or workers have been laid off. The programmes could provide counselling, assistance and training to workers at an earlier stage, e.g. before a shock hits, or when a given firm makes plans for restructuring.

One example of proactive assistance, this time offered by a firm, is the case of Saab Automobile in Sweden (Eurofund, 2014[9]). The downsizing of the firm was accompanied by social programmes to inform and prepare workers for the new circumstances. The firm offered regular counselling, psychological guidance and training for workers while they were still working at Saab. These measures could assist workers in transitioning to a new position faster, which not only brings financial benefits but can also improve their self-esteem and well-being. Proactive programmes give more time for workers to plan ahead and move forward.

Trade adjustment programmes can also support firms. Shocks from foreign competition can cause substantial harm to the regional fabric of firms. Policies should be designed to rebuild and sustain this fabric. By helping firms to thrive where they are and preserve their local roots, policymakers can strengthen the link that these firms have with the territory and ensure that local workers keep their jobs.

The Trade Adjustment Assistance for Firms (TAAF) of the U.S. Department of Commerce exemplifies this assistance to trade-affected firms. The programme aims at assisting firms affected by import substitution to develop and implement projects to expand markets, strengthen operations, increase profitability and regain global competitiveness. This assistance usually comes in the form of technical assistance, which is used to develop business recovery plans. In fact, federal funds are used to pay third-party consultants who, in turn, develop a customised business recovery strategy. Manufacturing, production and service firms are equally eligible to receive assistance. Firms do not receive funds directly and share costs with the administration.

Another strategy to rebuild the regional fabric of firms is to encourage firm creation. That is, besides supporting existing firms to stay in the market, programmes can also support new firms to enter it. These programmes can further operate as a combination of firm and worker support, via entrepreneurship and start-up assistance. By supporting trade-affected workers in becoming self-employed, these programmes would at the same time help expand the regional fabric of firms.

For instance, the Austrian Steel Foundation, formed by a group of firms in the steel sector, assists steel workers affected by structural changes in the industry. Assistance for creating a new business is one of the different types of training offered..[2] The Foundation hosts an administrative centre where office space and basic infrastructure such as telecommunication services are provided. It also hires business consultants to carry out market analyses and develop business plans for workers who seek to start their own business. More than one hundred firms have been successfully created in the field of consulting and services, machinery and energy and environmental technology (Winter-Ebmer, 2001[10]).

Building on regional strengths

The discussion on support to the tradable sector in the previous section has stressed the importance of fostering a favourable business environment. Support to innovation, investment in infrastructure, education and skills, export promotion, deregulation of markets, simplification of bureaucratic procedures were all mentioned as policy mechanisms that can help firms thrive.

However, this does not mean facilitating business at any price, in disregard of social and environmental consequences. It also does not mean luring business to a region with massive subsidies at the expense of others. As argued above, the fact that regions are part of a connected system entails that they should collaborate with each other, and that the national government should address imbalances.

Bearing these remarks in mind, this section emphasises productive and innovative ways to support regional economies. The first subsection discusses how regions should build on their own strengths and specific assets, developing regional strategies that are unique and tailored to their context. This approach calls for smart specialisation strategies and other instruments, with the goal of promoting productivity growth.

Moreover, as it will be argued in the second subsection, regions can make the most of territorial branding opportunities, by connecting them to productive aspects of their economy. In this overarching scheme for regional development, human capital is fundamental. It requires not only solid government policies on education, but also the active involvement of employers and education institutions in skills development and utilisation, as the third and fourth subsections discuss.

Productive ways to compete among regions: A race to the top

A typical approach to economic development has been to attract firms from elsewhere (OECD, 2009[11]). This approach calls for tax exemptions, fiscal incentives, wage restraints, flexible environmental and labour regulations and cheap land availability. After all, lower costs of relocation and operation could be enough of an incentive for firms to move into a certain region, in the absence of other desirable characteristics such as skilled labour markets, dense transport networks or a large base of suppliers or customers.

However, this approach has proven to have modest effects. The mere concentration of resources in a place does not automatically translate into economies of agglomeration. Instead, they are conditioned on the existence of a pooled labour market, linkages among firms and knowledge spillovers (OECD, 2009[11]). Moreover, this approach can translate into a "race to the bottom", leading to revenue losses and weaker labour and environmental standards. Lastly, from a regional (national) standpoint, if existing economic activity is simply transferred from one location to another within the same region (country), net benefits are at best zero, and usually negative.

Instead of competing for existing economic activity, regions should grow by tapping into underutilised potential and maximising their own advantages. Accordingly, competition among regions should occur in the form of positive-sum games rather than zero-sum games. In other words, competition should improve the general economic conditions and increase economic activity in general rather than just relocating existing economic activity from one place to another. The difference between positive-sum competition and zero-sum competition can be illustrated as follows.

In a positive-sum game, regions can seek to attract businesses by providing better services and infrastructure. In such cases, even regions that lose the competition to attract a business are likely to benefit in the long term. By improving their general business environment, they foster the growth of existing businesses and are more likely to attract additional ones in the future. If the region has better infrastructure, skilled labour and more knowledge spillovers, new firms will seek to take part in this vibrant ecosystem.

In contrast, zero-sum competition does not lead to generally improved conditions. For example, regions can try to attract businesses by providing indirect subsidies by selling land at below market prices. They can also offer direct tax incentives, as the section below explains. This benefits businesses at the expense of taxpayers, without increasing the capacity of the economy. Even though the region that manages to attract a business might benefit, overall economic growth would not occur. No overall increase in economic activity is expected as a consequence of zero-sum competition.

One example of a policy instrument that supports "productive" competition across regions is the *Core Regional Growth Areas* in Germany (OECD, 2012[12]). The Brandenburg Region selected 15 Core Regional Growth Areas to receive preferential financing, providing that they display growth potential and develop integrated development strategies with the territories in which they are located. This policy intended to create a pool of knowledge that many firms can benefit from, hence stimulating innovation and productivity growth. It has brought about a new spirit of competitiveness, in which different territories are stimulated to become growth centres while at the same time benefitting from co-operation arrangements amongst themselves. The growth centres have been a key element in weening the region off subsidies and transfers and becoming more focused on development growth (OECD, 2012[12]).

To this point, regions benefit from solidifying their competitive advantage, rather than emulating or attracting success from elsewhere. Regions have to identify their distinct strengths and create a vibrant ecosystem around them that supports productivity growth (OECD, 2016[1]). Smart specialisation strategies could promote development, in advanced and more traditional sectors alike.

One example is the incorporation of Information and Communication Technology (ICT) and innovative technologies to support the production of a local distinctive cheese, *La torta del Casar*, in Extremadura, Spain. The Shepherding School aims to keep the tradition of producing the cheese alive by training highly professional shepherds, embracing ICT and the latest technological advances in the field. This strategy aims to address a weakness of the territorial production system, which is the capacity to incorporate knowledge-based innovation. So far, innovation at the local level has received a boost, and a more rounded perspective on rural development is being fostered.[3]

Another example of a smart specialisation strategy that builds upon existing industries is found in Emilia-Romagna (Italy), which combines an automotive cluster with investment in R&D and higher education and promotion of automobile-related tourism. The higher education institutions in the region successfully train high-skilled workers and promote the knowledge economy (Ortega-Argilés, 2012[13]). The region also supports collaborative research projects for SMEs through research laboratories and innovation centres (Ortega-Argilés, 2012[13]). The region further leverages the strength of traditional automobile industries in advertising itself as the "Motor Valley" of Europe and attracts related tourism, having created thematic museums across the region, organised fairs and festivals, and partnered with tourism agencies to offer specialised tours (Alberti and Giusti, 2012[14]).

Regions can also invest in "niche" sectors based on location-specific advantages, geographic characteristics or natural resources (see also Chapter 1.). Regions benefit from unlocking this potential, especially rural ones. The most productive rural areas benefit from natural resources they can leverage through promoting solid industrial sectors and investing in human capital to work on extractive, ideally regenerative, technologies and related services (OECD, 2016[1]).

To illustrate, the natural characteristics of the northern regions of Sweden, Finland and Norway have resulted in the development of particular competences and technologies (OECD, 2017$_{[15]}$). The Arctic climate in the area combines extremely cold winters, short summers, low precipitation levels, and high levels of radiation. The region is abundant in natural resources, such as hydrocarbons, rare minerals, forests, and fresh water. These advantages have been leveraged by many different businesses, with research institutions also making valuable contributions. Some key activities include cold weather vehicle testing, data storage centres, energy saving technologies and construction solutions.

The cases of satellite launching in New Zealand (Box 5.3) and an optical cluster in Wales exemplify how location-related advantages can be used to promote economic niches. In New Zealand, it is the combination of natural characteristics, low population density and low sea and air traffic that makes it safe for frequent satellite launches. In Wales, an optical cluster of compound semiconductors is being developed, thanks to the stable and vibration-free ground soil in the area, which is an advantage for the production of advanced optical instruments.[4]

Box 5.3. Satellite launching in New Zealand

New Zealand is promoting a sector-based approach to innovation, based on specific location-specific advantages. Satellite launching from New Zealand has certain comparative advantages. Proximity to the ocean, low sea and air traffic and low population as well as its geographic location make it suitable for frequent launches at a range of launch angles. In addition, New Zealand has a business and innovation friendly environment with a skilled workforce, a globally competitive economy with exports accounting for 30% of GDP. It is also politically stability, with an open political system and the least corrupt public sector in the world (Transparency International 2016 Corruption Perception Index).

The economic value-added to the New Zealand economy from becoming a spacefaring nation has been quantified by the government's economic review commission at USD 415-1 073 million over 20 years. While most of the benefits are likely to accrue to the company exploring this sector, Rocket Lab, and a handful of their key suppliers, the wider range of benefits include additional employment, construction and launch activities, space tourism, cluster effects (e.g. satellite manufacturing, carbon composite, 3D printing), knowledge and technology spillovers, aspiration effects (motivating students, researchers and "garage inventors") and national prestige effects. Further upside potential exists from new companies choosing to operate out of New Zealand and new, unforeseen opportunities brought on by the other spacefaring nations looking for partners.

New Zealand has established a legal framework to regulate Rocket Lab's activities and to attract participation from other space players in niche areas of the space economy where New Zealand has a comparative advantage. The new law, called the Outer Space and High-Altitude Activities Act (OSHA Act), is intended to establish a licencing regime to regulate all the activities related to high altitude activities. Implementation of activities is being monitored by the Ministry of Environment, to ensure that satellite launching activities do not cause significant pollution, particularly damage to the seabed caused by rocket debris.

Sources: New Zealand (2017), *Outer Space and High-altitude Activities Bill;* Fryberg, E (2017), *Rocket Lab faces government environmental checks,* Radio New Zealand News, retrieved from: www.radionz.co.nz/news/national/337505/rocket-lab-faces-government-environmental-checks.

When developing a regional strategy, regions should be aware of what the neighbouring regions are doing, to prevent the duplication of strategies.[5] Duplication can lead to lower effectiveness and increased competition for the same markets, reducing profitability. For instance, research investments have been plagued by a "me too" syndrome, in which regions make investments in similar and fashionable areas such as ICT, nanotechnologies and biotechnologies (Sörvik and Kleibrink, 2015[16]). Hence, a region's specialisation strategy should consider in which promising niches and knowledge-creation activities other regions are investing (OECD, 2015[17]).

Beyond openness and awareness, regions can collaborate with each other by having complementary strategies. Regions with interrelated competences and strategies can innovate together and expand their markets. As argued in Chapter 3. , regions do benefit from producing a variety of goods and services in related sectors, as this generates more knowledge spillovers. In this way, when productivity is enhanced by innovation the benefits are shared across the broader economy.

For instance, in the European Union, there is room for co-operation in smart specialisation strategies. Co-operating regions combine related strengths, invest in joint research initiatives and leverage access to global value chains. They can, for example, operate in complementary niche sectors that share technologies or generate inputs for one another. Moreover, a macro-regional strategy can be developed whereby different regions come together to develop a shared smart specialisation strategy. In this type of collaboration, stakeholders from across the macro-region join forces, align strategies and pool common resources, to promote their common prosperity through research and innovation.[6]

How relocation incentives work (or not)

One of the clearest signals of how much competition across regions shapes policymaking is the widespread adoption of incentives to firms. These incentives include subsidies, tax breaks, subsidised loans, grants and infrastructure improvements. The main goal of such incentives is to influence firms' location choices and hence contribute to local job creation. Given the widespread adoption of incentives as local economic development tools, positive and negative examples abound (Jensen, 2017[18]).

One positive example of incentives is investment subsidies given to manufacturing firms in economically disadvantaged areas in the United Kingdom (Criscuolo et al., 2016[19]). The programme awards discretionary grants to manufacturing firms, to spend on property, plant or machinery, with the expectation of job creation that would not happen otherwise – the so-called "additionality criteria".

It has been shown that subsidies have a statistically significant impact on job creation (Criscuolo et al., 2016[19]). Importantly, the positive effect is not attributed to job relocation but appears to come from the pool of unemployed living in the area. However, the positive effects of this UK programme are mitigated for large firms, which are more able to "game" the system (i.e. taking the investment subsidy without making additional investments that would have not been made otherwise). The effect of business support was thus stronger on smaller firms (under 50 workers).

One negative example of tax incentives to firm relocation is the one in the metropolitan area of Kansas City in the United States. Kansas City is divided between the states of Kansas and Missouri, which both offer tax breaks and subsidies for firms to locate in their jurisdiction, as long as they create and sustain jobs. Given that the functional urban area of Kansas City extends over both states, it is relatively easy for firms to move from one side of the border to the other.

In Kansas City's "border war", firms have accepted substantial fiscal advantages to periodically move their headquarters or plants to the other side of the urban area. From 2009 to 2013, 3 289 jobs were added to Kansas from Missouri, at a cost of $140 million in tax incentives. At the same time, 2 824 jobs moved to Missouri from Kansas, at a cost of $72 million. Together, these two states spent $212 million on job relocation across the four-year period, with Kansas achieving a net gain of a meagre 465 jobs (McGee, 2015[20]).

This simple example shows that jobs have been mostly shifted across administrative borders, at high costs for the public budget. If each state is considered separately, a significant number of jobs were added from 2010 to 2015. However, given that most jobs were eventually shuttled out of one state to the other, the total gain was lower than job creation statistics divided per state indicate.

Moreover, many of these jobs cannot be directly attributed to the programme. Very few beneficiary firms in Kansas affirmed that job creation would not have occurred without the programme, and statistical analysis shows no significant evidence in this direction (Jensen, 2017[18]). In all, relocation incentives in Kansas City illustrate the type of competition that lowers standards and benefits firms, at the expense of public budgets.

Location incentives for private firms are subject to criticism. One critique is that incentives are redundant and fail in changing the behaviour of firms. Extensive research shows that firms typically praise the incentives, but say that they would have moved to a certain place even without the subsidy (James, 2013[21]). Once the location decision is made, firms negotiate or look for tax breaks and subsidies to "sweeten" the deal. This argument corroborates the notion that location matters more than temporary financial incentives. Ultimately, firms choose their location based on access to key inputs, suppliers and customers, not on tax breaks.

Another critique is that the majority of incentives are reaped by large firms, while research shows that their impact is more socially beneficial when small firms receive them (Criscuolo et al., 2016[19]). An evaluation of state aid programmes in three US states (Florida, Missouri and New Mexico) showed that 68% of state economic development spending goes to large firms, while only 19% are targeted at small firms and 13% have flexible eligibility criteria.[7] To avoid this, states should gear eligibility criteria towards small firms.

Thirdly, requirements for job creation that are tied to incentives can be too low. Moreover, requirements are not always linked to the quality and long-term viability of jobs. In the Start-Up NY programme, for instance, firms are required to create one new full-time job and to not reduce employment in subsequent years. In exchange, they are exempt from a range of taxes for up to a decade.[8] The first evaluation of the programme in 2014, the first year of the programme, showed that 76 jobs had been created by 30 participating companies, at a cost of USD 56 000 in tax benefits, by 2016 the programme had expanded and a total of 722 jobs been created since the inception of the programme with tax benefits in the year amounting to just over USD 3 million.[9] The appeal of incentives based on tax reductions is that they only arise after the firm operates and little risk is involved for the public sector. But the tax breaks do not include the personnel cost in the administrating agency, nor the significant marketing cost that the agency had to spend on the programme, which amounted to more than USD 45 million between October 2013 and October 2014.[10]

On the other hand, defenders of financial incentives to firms claim that targeted location incentives spur economic growth. The attraction of major firms to a given area can catapult economic development, due to real estate values, wage growth and by attracting other firms. If a tax incentive can make one key firm relocate to the area, the private investments that follow can easily outweigh the costs borne by the public sector (Kline and Moretti, 2014[22]).

It is important to highlight that – as previously stated – regions can use other policies beyond tax incentives to encourage firms to move to their region. For example, simplifying administrative and legal procedures can make regions more attractive to firms because complicated and burdensome administrative procedures can create high costs. In this sense, improving business licensing processes, simplifying tax codes at all levels of government and streamlining requirements are all good measures to improve the ease of doing business and to attract firms, without foregoing tax revenues.

Another set of policies that can be adopted to support local job creation regards supporting local entrepreneurship, and investing in skills and education. As argued in this report, human capital development and support aimed at helping the creation of new businesses are important factors in promoting local growth.

Taking advantage of opportunities for territorial branding

Territorial branding can be a useful tool for regional development, if well-articulated and well-promoted. Places have their own characteristics, products and people, i.e. economic, geographic and cultural attributes that can be identified as unique or special. Branding is a way to promote the uniqueness of places, and today a commonly explored route for policy makers.

One lesson from place-branding is that a clearly identifiable brand is more beneficial than many different, segmented ones. Investing in several different brands for the same place can limit the impact of the marketing strategy and create market confusion. Oliveira (2015[23]) notices that, in the case of Portugal, the proliferation of tourism brands has created a cacophony of names and slogans. What is more, these brands have been promoted with little attention to the economic and social issues behind place-making.

In this sense, brand creation needs follow-up action to consolidate it. The literature has extensively noted that logos and slogans alone have little significance in fostering economic restructuring and social cohesion (Oliveira, 2015[23]). Places should follow up on actions that can transform the region, in order to realise the potential of the brand. The place makes the brand; the brand does not make the place. From the different accounts of territorial branding, key lessons emerge.

The case of the brand *Produit en Bretagne* (Made in Brittany) in France shows how shared values and collective efforts to expand and solidify the brand can yield positive results (Donner, 2016[24]). The oldest regional food brand in Europe, *Produit en Bretagne* was created in 1986 to strengthen regional solidarity and employment. Since then, an association of producers was created, which includes today members of the service sector such as hotels, restaurants as well as the cultural and creative sectors. The association is in charge of quality controls on products and coordinates a marketing strategy with an array of stakeholders. The association successfully created a business incubator to support innovative projects, too (Donner, 2016[24]).

This example also signals the importance of participatory territorial branding, i.e. of involving local stakeholders in brand development and consolidation. Promoting synergies and consensus among regional stakeholders has been identified as one of the key elements in keeping a brand alive and well in the long run.

Box 5.4. The positive effects of the Cherry Festival in Fundão, Portugal

The municipality of Fundão, located in the rural area of the Beira region in Portugal, has around 32 000 inhabitants. It is characterised by a shrinking and ageing population, a predominance of primary sector activities and lower purchasing power than the national average. In this context, local stakeholders started to invest in the production of cherries. The climatic conditions provided by the fertile land, high altitude and exposure to the sun make cherries from the region unique.

To capture attention and attract infrastructure, the local authorities created the Cherry Festival. During the festival, cherry producers receive visitors in small taverns where products derived from cherries (jam, liquor, chocolate) and other regional products such as wine, cheese and handicrafts are sold. Activities - from cherry harvesting to mountain biking, garden tours, street fairs, concerts and exhibitions - also take place.

The festival has had a positive impact on the regional economy. Hotels and restaurants operate with twice the normal occupancy rate and cherry production has received a boost. By promoting the unique quality of cherries in the region, high value-added products can be developed. Studies confirm that there is a monetary premium on products that are associated with specific locations and production processes (Lorenzini, 2011[25]).

In addition, residents and suppliers have noticed that the Cherry Festival has contributed to community pride and to enhancing the region's image (Alves, Cerro and Martins, 2010[26]). They nonetheless expressed concerns about traffic congestion and pressure on local services, albeit limited to the festival days. In the long run, for events such as the Cherry Festival to continue flourishing, the buy-in of the local community and key partners is fundamental.

To conclude, through cultural events, places may attract not only tourists but investments, too. Event-related tourism generates employment and economic diversification. It can improve service provision and local infrastructure, if enough revenues are generated, and if locals demand. It can also help to preserve the local heritage and foster social cohesion. The Cherry Festival contributes to creating new job and businesses opportunities and to improving the overall quality of local life.

Sources: Alves, H. M. B., A. M, C. Cerro and A. V. F. Martins (2010) "Impacts of small tourism events on rural places", Journal of Place Management and Development, Vol. 3 Issue: 1, pp.22-37, https://doi.org/10.1108/17538331011030257; Lorenzini, E. (2011), *Territory branding as a strategy for rural development: experiences from Italy*, Proceedings of the 51st Congress of the European Regional Sciences Association, Barcelona, Spain, http://hdl.handle.net/10419/120139.

Successful territorial branding strategies are not just about marketing a territory. They require the creation of an identifiable brand, linked to the specific socio-cultural and economic context of the region. But they also demand investments in productive activities that are related to the brand, be them tourism, agri-business, industry clusters or even natural resource preservation. Furthermore, the promotion of common values, the involvement of local stakeholders and public-private co-operation are key factors in this process. In the long run, the level of local embeddedness will determine if a branding strategy can have long-term success.

A place-based approach to skills development

OECD research over the past ten years shows that human capital is a robust determinant of regional growth.[11] Several policy sectors can contribute to increasing human capital in regions. For instance, reforms of tertiary education systems to enhance access and improve quality have been recommended (OECD, 2010[27]). Lifelong learning via skills training and innovative workplaces has also been advocated. Supporting international mobility of labour, research and education is another valid recommendation (OECD, 2010[27]).

These recommendations need to be enhanced by awareness of the different stakeholders operating in a given territory. A place-based approach to skills and human capital development requires that regional economic development strategies be connected with education and labour policies for local skills development (OECD, 2016[28]). This has been challenging for regions in an array of countries, as the examples below indicate.

The region of Geelong, in Australia, has developed a strategic regional development strategy. A multi-stakeholder alliance was formed to identify local strengths and promote a co-ordinated approach to regional growth (OECD, 2013[29]). One of the main aspects of this strategy is the transition from traditional manufacturing sectors to new and more dynamic sectors, including niche tourism as well as innovative tech-food and agri-business practices. However, very little in the regional strategy refers to developing the skills that workers will need to adjust to this new environment. Consequently, the OECD (2013[29]) has recommended to the Geelong region that it would be better to invest in human capital development, and link it closely with its regional strategy.

In the case of the region of Pomurje in Slovenia, employment and labour market instruments were adopted to address structural changes, without the backup of a regional development programme (Eurofund, 2014[9]). As a result, few jobs were available in the region and retrained, skilled workers ended up commuting to Austria to access jobs. Also, the Pomurje region continued to show the poorest economic and labour market indicators across the country. In response, the region launched a regional development programme to foster competiveness, support employment creation and facilitate private investments. The existing labour-market instruments were coupled with business support strategies, and were anchored in a clear understanding of regional needs.

By helping would-be entrepreneurs to start their own businesses and develop their skills, regional policies are made more effective, as it is the case in Pomurje. As the above section on trade adjustment programmes discusses, by assisting firms to locate and thrive in a given territory, policymakers are also supporting workers. Without a solid regional fabric of firms, even well-trained workers would not find jobs or their skills would remain underutilised.

Furthermore, social policy should include regional development strategies. Social policy programmes can advance the employability of marginalised and vulnerable groups, which is an integral part of inclusive growth. Housing policies, in particular supply-side ones, can contribute to keeping housing costs at reasonable levels. They can also help reduce the spatial job mismatch of low-skilled workers. Public childcare facilities help reconcile work and family life and are a tool to increase female labour force participation (OECD, 2017[30]).

One example of a policy instrument that effectively addresses this link is the *Territorial Employment Pacts* in Austria.[12] The Pacts function as contractual partnerships signed between public authorities at the regional and local levels. The authorities develop integrated projects, co-ordinate policies and streamline processes across different departments that deal with employment and social inclusion. Their main goal is to provide co-ordinated measures to improve the integration of marginalised groups into regional labour markets. The measures include employment assistance, social advice, counselling, crisis intervention, housing, and recovery and health issues.

These cases demonstrate that regional development programmes should address labour, skills and social policy while also supporting innovation and business creation if they are to effectively promote productivity growth (OECD, 2016[28]). Under a place-based approach to skills development, training workers also means trying to ensure that there are firms where they can find work and assuring that their surrounding environment is safe and healthy.

Skill development and utilisation: A shared responsibility

Skill development has to be a central priority for governments, especially when facing the challenges brought on by globalisation, migration and digitalisation (European Commission, 2017[31]). Moreover, equal access to high-quality education and training is a powerful way of reducing inequality in societies. As the section above indicates, there are many different policies that governments can invest in, from employment assistance to skills training and social counselling.

That said, other actors should get involved in the aim of improving skills development policies. Public offices responsible for employment assistance and related up-skilling activities can only do so much. Their role is to provide temporary support to unemployed workers in order to find a new job, and often training is restricted to "recycling" skills or to acquiring skills that are industry-specific. In this sense, employers and educators can have an important and comprehensive to play in skills development.

Employees' or employers' associations should play an active role in skills development to ensure skills are fully utilised at the workplace. There are potentially high returns from investing in workers' skills, since better-qualified workers are more productive, are more flexible to undertake new tasks, and earn higher wages. Workforce development should hence be a functional part of an enterprise's business model in order to be sustainable in the long run (OECD/ILO, 2017[32]). The workplace should be a place of continuous learning and training. Employers could offer on-site qualification and courses on a regular basis.

Employers can also encourage their employees to take part in practice-based learning. They can communicate with educators about the skill sets they need, helping them to refine their programmes. They can host students from these programmes in their firms, to carry-out practice-based projects and train for specific skills.

In addition, in the event of firm restructuring, employers bear responsibility towards workers. To the fullest extent possible, employers should plan the scaling-down in advance. With the aim of supporting the transition to new jobs, employers or other entities can provide education and training, or fund education facilities. Matching services could further address the challenges of skills mismatch and of economic restructuring. Box 5.5 contains a few examples of such initiatives.

Box 5.5. Firm restructuring and skills development

- **Revitalisation agreements in France aid territorial employment**: The revitalisation agreements (*contrats de revitalisation*) make private funds available for local economic development. Companies of 1 000 or more employees that undertake collective redundancies for economic reasons have to sign such an agreement, within six months after the regional authority is notified of the planned layoffs. The company's financial contribution is intended to foster economic activity and create jobs, thus mitigating the effects of the restructuring within the territory. This innovative financing programme allows for investments in infrastructure, innovation and human capital to be made, ultimately reinforcing employment in the territory.
- **Work foundations in Austria, public and private join forces to support workers**: Work foundations (*Arbeitsstiftungen*) are a general restructuring support instrument based on legislation and jointly funded by the company that is restructuring and public authorities to provide redundant workers with comprehensive career reorientation, reskilling, matching and psychological support. They operate by using a regional approach, i.e. they are linked to the territory and the workers affected by the firm that is restructuring. If restructuring affects several regional SMEs, which by themselves would lack a critical mass of affected workers, a regional work foundation (*Regionalstiftung*) can be set up, with strong involvement from the employers, the regional public employment service and social partners.

Sources: Eurofund (2014), *Effects of Restructuring at Regional Level and Approaches to Dealing with the Consequences*; Zapalski, E. (2015); *Conventions de revitalisation: quel impact réel sur les territoires en difficulté?*, Localtis, 2014, https://goo.gl/p7ocCx.

Skills development strategies should be adapted to the needs of a region. Different regional economic specialisations can require very different skills profiles from the workforce. Furthermore, structural changes within the regional economy can create specific challenges, such as the need for retraining a large number of workers with a skills profile that has suddenly become obsolete (Box 5.6).

Vocational training and apprenticeship systems that combine workplace-based learning with classroom-based learning are one of the most important ways to safeguard the provision of a well-trained workforce at the regional level. Different types of vocational training and apprenticeships target different skill levels. They can range from basic post-secondary education in trade schools to advanced higher education in universities.

Vocational training is important for regions because it can provide close links with regional and local businesses (OECD/ILO, 2017[33]). By relying strongly on workplace-based training and inputs from firms for curriculum design, vocational training programmes ensure that transferred skills match the needs of the regional industry. Since one of the key characteristics of vocational training programmes is close collaboration between the education sector and regional firms, measures enabling regional authorities to become actively involved in the process will need to be set up.

In Germany, the curricula of post-secondary vocational training programmes are developed in partnership with unions and industry associations, who also contribute to the funding of the programmes. They define a common set of standards for a given trade, but offer sufficient flexibility to adapt the content of programmes to regional needs. The possibility to adapt vocational programmes to specific challenges has also been proven to be effective in other countries (Box 5.6).

Classroom-based education in vocational training programmes often takes place in trade schools, but can also involve higher education institutions. Polytechnics, community colleges and universities of applied sciences frequently provide joint classroom-based and workplace-based programmes. At the same time, they offer stand-alone undergraduate and graduate degree programmes.

Furthermore, universities of applied sciences and similar institutions can have an important place-based dimension. They exist in many mid-sized towns and are important regional centres for the training of specialised high skilled workers. In contrast to many regular universities that are predominantly located in larger cities, students do not have to move outside the region to study and are more likely to look for work in the region later on. In this sense, it has a strong regional dimension of retaining skilled workforce and firms in a given territory.

Professors should be well-qualified to teach industry-relevant skills, and even higher education institutions that do not specifically focus on teaching job-related skills can benefit from links with non-academic institutions. A possible approach is to hire professors with cutting edge industry experience, or create research centres affiliated with the university that link researchers with public or private sector projects. Moreover, educational institutions should show flexibility to part-time and non-exclusive job contracts, for teachers to work in the industry in parallel if desired. It is of course critical in this context that academic standards are upheld.

Lastly, higher education institutions can invest in practice-based research, in partnership with businesses and industry sectors. Instruments of practice-based research include internships and work-study contracts, but also collaborative research projects, open labs and business incubators. The latter will be further explained in the section below on "Effective university-industry collaboration".

Taken together, skills development requires an effective partnership between government, employers and educational institutions. It is far from being an easy task. Complex, fragmented and frequently unresponsive systems that fund and deliver education and workforce training will need to be connected and co-ordinated (Liu, 2016[34]). This requires different instruments for training and education, which have to be flexible enough to adapt to a changing world but concrete enough to guarantee prompt access to the labour market.

Box 5.6. Countering the economic crisis with vocational education and training in Sweden

After the bankruptcy of the large car manufacturer Saab in 2011, more than 3 000 people lost their jobs in the town of Trollhättan, in southern Sweden. In light of this context, the public sector provided temporary support for the unemployed to address immediate needs. At the same time, forward-looking measures in the fields of education, skills training, entrepreneurship and business creation were adopted, aiming at the long-term renewal of the local economy.

Major investments were made in education and training. Since 2011, approximately 3 750 new spots have been created in universities, higher vocational education institutions and municipal adult education programmes. Given that workers were offered the possibility to study while keeping their unemployment benefits, many of them accepted the offer and began to train for a new career.

In addition, workers who had been made redundant received assistance. They qualified for skills training and in-firm counselling. Saab also co-ordinated with suppliers to hire some of their former workers in the near future. After all, workers who are highly specialised in car manufacturing have skills that can be put to good use along other points of the supply chain.

Public authorities also developed initiatives to support entrepreneurship. One example is Innovatum's project to develop electric car use. With the diversification of the local economy in sectors such as building, transport and aerospace, many new companies have been launched, employing today around 1 000 people. By 2014, unemployment was even lower than it was before the bankruptcy declaration, dropping from 16% to 12%.

Sources: Eurofund (2014), *Effects of Restructuring at Regional Level and Approaches to Dealing with the Consequences*; European Commission (2017), "Reflection Paper on Harnessing Globalisation", https://ec.europa.eu/commission/sites/beta-political/files/reflection-paper-globalisation_en.pdf.

Supporting knowledge diffusion

The gap in productivity between frontier and lagging firms has grown since the mid-1990s (2015[35]), as has the gap between the most productive regions and the rest of the country (OECD, 2016[36]). One way to look at the divergence across firms and regions in the global economy is to track innovation patterns. As firms at the productivity frontier continue to push the envelope, a significant challenge for the global economy is not necessarily the lack of innovation in general, but insufficient innovation diffusion (OECD, 2015[35]). This harms aggregate productivity growth and inclusiveness, because workers in some regions and industries are left behind.

Structural policies can support innovation diffusion through three main approaches. One is to enable a market environment conducive to more productive firms, which are expected to be more innovative. This means reducing barriers to firm entry and exit, and fostering an overall environment that has better management practices and does not keep inefficient firms artificially in the market. Importantly, it requires fair bankruptcy legislation, adequate intellectual property rights frameworks and incentives to invest in R&D.

The second approach relates to matching more effectively workers' skills and jobs, which can be achieved by increasing labour mobility, with flexible employment regulations, portable health and pension benefits and social safety nets (OECD, 2015[35]). It can also be promoted by developing skills, via training and lifelong learning, which can help ensure that workers are sufficiently flexible so they can adapt to shifting market demands (see the section, "Effective university-industry collaboration").

Besides promoting better labour market matching, which per se increases productivity and wages, another important contribution is the transfer of knowledge. People with specific sets of skills and experience can transfer this expertise to firms elsewhere. Especially for new firms, experienced workers are an asset that cannot be replaced by workers with formal education but little practical experience in the field (Hausmann and Neffke, 2016[37]).

The third approach refers to supporting innovation. Innovation support can, for instance, take the form of measures that facilitate trade and stimulate entrepreneurship (see the section on "Innovation diffusion across the supply chain"). Nonetheless, it is not a given that every firm in the tradable sector will be innovative on its own. For this reason, firms have to invest in knowledge creation, which can be supported by public incentives or public investment in R&D and partnerships with universities (see the section on "Effective university-industry collaboration").

Innovation diffusion can happen along the supply chain and across firms that offer similar products but are not direct competitors. Collaborative relationships across firms and the involvement of research institutions and industry associations can help to foster knowledge transfer in these instances (see the section on "Effective university-industry collaboration").

In other cases, innovation diffusion occurs across firms that compete with each other. Intellectual property rights laws should be flexible enough to allow the spread of innovation among competitors while protecting innovations sufficiently to encourage firms to invest in R&D. Likewise, non-competition clauses in employment contracts that prevent employees from working for competitors in the future should be carefully regulated, in order to prevent abuses that can, in the end, curtail competition.

Innovation diffusion across the supply chain

Regional clusters can be, among other reasons, beneficial for regional economic development, because they offer possibilities for different actors within the region to learn from each other and thereby benefit from "innovation spillovers". Participation in production along Global Value Chains (GVCs) add an important international dimension to this process (c.f. Chapter 3.). By linking regional businesses to firms from across the globe, they can potentially facilitate knowledge spillovers from advanced regions in other countries.

If and how learning occurs within GVCs depends on how firm-to-firm relations are structured within them. In GVCs that are built on arm's length transactions, learning is primarily based on unstructured knowledge spillovers. In GVCs that are based on relational interactions, learning can occur through regular contact among employees from different firms. In GVCs based on hierarchical or captive relations between firms, learning is potentially most structured. Dominant firms within the GVC might employ targeted knowledge-transfer or training programmes to help subordinate firms to acquire the knowledge and skills they need to perform their role within GVCs (Pietrobelli and Rabellotti, 2010[38]). While such direct knowledge transfer can be highly effective, it is often also narrow in its scope. As a consequence, the transferred knowledge might be of limited use for expanding a firm's activities beyond its role in the GVC.

However, innovation diffusion along the supply chain does not always take place. For one, competitive relationships in the supply chain can undermine innovation. Sporadic interactions with little or no trust do not encourage the supplier to search for innovative solutions to present to the customer. The customer refrains from transferring technology to this type of supplier, too. On the flip side, collaborative relationships build trust between actors, thus enabling technology transfer and increasing supplier-driven innovation.[13]

Second, it can be difficult for innovation to travel along the supply chain. Firms do not always share technologies, and knowledge spillovers are greatly facilitated by spatial concentration. To overcome these barriers, research-oriented institutions that work closely with the private sector can be of great value. They can generate innovation that is shared along a whole industry sector, and transfer technology from one sector to another. They can foster networks and joint product development, too. Their role is explained in the section below on "Effective university-industry collaboration".

Furthermore, regional firms should diversify across different customers in different GVCs in order to increase productivity (Humphrey and Schmitz, 2002[39]). Thus, instead of selling to one customer within a single value chain, firms perform better if they have multiple customers in multiple GVCs. By learning from differences in internal production processes, firms can innovate and increase productivity. Regional authorities can help this process by providing support to firms seeking to diversify across markets.

In order to strengthen learning, it is recommended that governments seek partnerships with dominant firms within GVCs to encourage knowledge sharing along the GVC (UNCTAD, 2013[40]). In contrast, if dominant firms within a GVC try to prevent regional firms from diversifying their customer base, governments should use antitrust policies to prevent or penalise any anti-competitive behaviour of dominant firms within GVCs and ensure that weaker firms are not prevented from seeking business opportunities outside the GVC.

Effective university-industry collaboration

The benefits of linking universities and firms are widely acknowledged today. They include – but are not limited to – higher productivity, improved innovation processes, skills training to students, creation of spin-off companies and higher patenting rates. Given these benefits, most OECD countries have adopted strategies and programmes to promote university-industry collaboration, albeit some of them have been considered fragmented, uncoordinated and limited in scope (OECD, 2016[41]).

To promote a more integrated approach, regional governments should adopt several knowledge transfer and R&D tools (Table 5.1). They can support businesses by offering grants, contract opportunities and innovation vouchers, for instance. With new technologies, businesses can develop innovative products and innovative organisational practices. They can support universities by providing strategic funding to patent development and creation of spin-off companies, among other tools. They can support both firms and universities by launching programmes to encourage student hiring by industry and by establishing collaborative, open research laboratories (Table 5.1).

Table 5.1. University-industry commercial knowledge transfer tools

Channels / Tools	Description	Examples
Collaborative research and research partnerships	Scientists and private companies jointly commit resources and research efforts to projects; research may be co-funded (unlike contract research). The level of co-operation varies from individual to institutional, from small-scale projects to strategic partnerships with multiple members and stakeholders (i.e. public-private partnerships).	- Open Innovation Policy Platforms, e.g. Finland and Catapult Centres (UK). - Matching grants, e.g. University of California (IUCRP) - CARL programme in Ireland to develop practical results with non-profit organisations - Austrian Competence Centre Program (COMET) and laboratories by Christian Doppler Research Association (CDG).
Consulting and Research contracts	Research or advisory services provided by researchers to industry clients to pursue a solution to a specific problem.	- Innovation vouchers, adopted in several countries, create opportunities for firms, notably SMEs, to benefit from academic expertise (HEI or PRO).
Student hiring by industry	A graduate student is hired by a firm to develop research in-house, while being supervised by a university laboratory. Benefits for all: high thesis completion rate, significant rates of patent creation and enhanced employability.	- CIFRE convention (France)
Patenting and Licensing	Patents are one indicator of prospective commercialisation efforts. Academic researchers may appear as inventors in firms' patent filings as a result of them being a contract research or through academic consulting. However, not all academic inventions are owned by PROs. It may depend on IPR regulations, the institutional profile of the national research system and national specificities of industry-science relationships.	- Knowledge Transfer and IPR commercialisation offices in Germany (Fraunhofer Institute), Austria (Technology Transfer Offices in several universities) and Japan (e.g. SACI, Tokyo University) - Innovation Offices in Sweden
Public Research Spin-offs	Spin-off firms or organisations are created to commercialise university research by developing marketable products.	- Programmes to support university spin-offs, such as EXIST (Germany), SBIR (USA), AplusB Centres (Austria)

Source: Adapted from OECD (2013) *Commercialising Public Research: New Trends and Strategies*, OECD Publishing, Paris, doi: 10.1787/9789264193321-en. *Source:* OECD (2016), *Knowledge Triangle: Case Study Summaries,* background document to the OECD High Level Event on the Knowledge Triangle.

Besides these commercial tools, there are also purely knowledge-related tools, such as publications, conferences and standards, which can be valuable ways to transfer knowledge, regardless of direct commercial output. Conferences and networking events can allow informal connections to be formed, thereby enhancing trust. Trust has been found to be one of the key elements to jump start formal collaborations between researchers and entrepreneurs (Vallance et al., 2017[42]).

For university-industry collaborations to work, certain structural conditions should be in place. Beyond creating a certain programme or adopting a certain tool, policymakers should invest in a framework enabling these tools or programmes to operate successfully, including consistent funding, clear property rights and confidentiality issues, career incentives for professors to be involved in industry collaboration and trust among actors (Edmondson et al., 2012[43]).

Piecemeal funding has been a characteristic of several programmes. Ad hoc, project-oriented funding is flexible and can be adapted to different circumstances. Yet, this type of short-term funding can halt the development of a more all-encompassing, long-term strategy, focused on priority areas. Enduring university-firms partnerships can have positive results, such as increased levels of knowledge transfer and greater trust among actors, which can facilitate future collaboration.

In this sense, consider the example of innovation vouchers. Under this programme, SMEs receive vouchers that can be used to consult academic expertise for a specific purpose. The purpose can be accessing a new technology, developing a marketing strategy, altering the organisational structure of the firm – anything that can generate innovation and requiring external expertise. SMEs may particularly lack the expertise and the resources to generate innovation without such support.

The voucher programme in Lombardy, Italy has yielded positive results. Vouchers increased the competitiveness of local firms and strengthened the dynamics among actors of the Regional Innovation System, providing grounds for future collaboration.[14] Vouchers can raise awareness among SMEs regarding the benefits of collaborating with academia (OECD, 2011[44]). Still, given that vouchers are a one-off funding opportunity, future collaboration will depend on the initiative of regional actors.

Box 5.7. Limits to entrepreneurial culture

If links between university and industry are desirable for boosting innovation and productivity, universities should not be reduced to only serving business needs. Universities have the valuable role of advancing purely scientific, fundamental research, as well as the humanities and social sciences, regardless of clear, direct commercial application. They also teach skills and values that go beyond the needs of specific industries in a given time period. Tertiary education should educate citizens and not limit itself to merely training future workers for whatever industry happens to be thriving at a given time.

In this sense, regional systems should have different types of universities. Frontier and discovery research, vocational and education training and outreach to the local community are all functions that universities need to fulfil. The diversity of higher education institutions in a region can ensure a balance between the different roles they need to play. A more comprehensive view of higher-education systems can ensure that different institutions complement each other. This may mean that no region falls behind in research and education, while also ensuring that entrepreneurial culture becomes a valuable, albeit not dominant, feature of the system.

Universities need to engage their faculty in such partnerships. To do so, universities could broaden their performance evaluation criteria, beyond publication track records. Activities such as co-ordinating innovation labs, filing patent applications and developing innovative products for industry partners or spin-offs could be used as additional performance criteria. This could encourage more professors and research staff to engage in partnerships with industry without harming their careers.

Another challenge is that the different tools for partnerships between university and industry seem to be disconnected. France, for instance, has witnessed a proliferation of different agreements, contracts, partnerships and scholarships. The lack of co-ordination between mechanisms and the parties involved is a handicap, since it does not allow the

State to provide a coherent range of mechanisms or avoid overlapping supervision roles and responsibilities (OECD, 2014[45]). One exception to the French system is the long-lasting CIFRE convention of student hiring by industry (Box 5.8).

Box 5.8. Student hiring by industry: The case of CIFRE convention in France

The CIFRE convention, created in 1981, is one of the key mechanisms linking French businesses with universities and doctoral students. The student is granted a research mandate within the business, supervised by the university laboratory. A CIFRE contract has a term of three years, with a minimum gross salary of EUR 23 484 per year. The partner business receives a subsidy of EUR 14 000 per year to partially offset that salary from the National Association for Technological Research (ANRT).

CIFRE agreements cover all scientific disciplines and sectors of activity and are concluded with large companies as well as with SMEs. They operate primarily in the sectors of electronics, communications and information technology, transport and energy, and to a much lesser extent in the construction, banking and insurance sectors.

Measured in terms of publications, CIFREs are a force to be reckoned with in research (at least 1 037 highly ranked international publications in 2012) and development (2 000 patents filed between 1981 and 2012). The thesis defence rate is 90% across all disciplines. Employment rates for CIFRE students are 96% within a year and 70% within one month after graduation (ANRT data).

The mechanism remains relatively straightforward for the various signatories to CIFRE; the project evaluation mainly consists in determining whether the business and laboratory are relevant to the doctoral student's field of competence. The processing time (around three months) is another key to the success of this mechanism. Between 1981 and 2016, CIFRE grants contributed to training 25 400 doctoral students and brought together 9 000 companies and 4 000 laboratories (ANRT data).

By hosting a doctoral student, the business is a location for and an ally in the student's training. The agreement creates or reinforces strong links between these two worlds, with their sometimes differing methods and cultures (Levy, 2005[46]). CIFRE doctoral students receive steady funding and are able to combine their scientific and professional development.

Adapted from: OECD (2014), OECD Reviews of Innovation Policy: France. http://dx.doi.org/10.1787/9789264214026-en.
Sources: Levy (2005), "Les doctorants CIFRE: médiateurs entre laboratoires de recherche universitaires et entreprises", Revue d'économie industrielle, Vol. 11, No. 111, pp. 79-96, www.persee.fr/doc/rei_0154-3229_2005_num_111_1_3083; Ministère de l'Enseignement supérieur, de la Recherche et de l'Innovation, France (n.d.), Les CIFRE www.enseignementsup-recherche.gouv.fr/cid22130/les-cifre.html/?menu=6.

University-industry partnerships should have clear rules and regulations, notably concerning patent and ownership issues. For that to happen, universities can create specialised offices to manage collaborations with industry. These offices can serve as "one-stop shops" for private partners looking to work with the different university departments, in different research fields. The offices develop expertise in signing agreements, commercialising products and forming partnerships. They become especially knowledgeable on matters of licensing and intellectual property, which further allows the university or regional consortium of universities to have a single policy for patenting and product commercialisation.

For instance, the Society-Academia Collaboration for Innovation (SACI), established in 2007, works as a one-stop shop for companies interested in collaborating with Kyoto University. SACI provides up-to-date information on technology developed or under development by the university. SACI also promotes entrepreneurship education in the university community via the Venture Support programme, which offers educational programmes and funding to help inventors and innovators make their ideas and concepts more commercially successful (OECD, 2016$_{[41]}$).

In Austria, the regional Knowledge Transfer and Intellectual Property Rights Exploitation Centres promote co-operation between universities and companies. Their main areas of activity are: educating university personnel in practical intellectual property rights matters, invention spotting, filing and management of university patents, marketing of university inventions, and assisting the establishment of spin-off companies. They also boost strategic patent funding and provide funding for prototypes. The patent promotion scheme awards funding for universities to strategically develop patents for which successful commercial exploitation can be expected. This centralised approach has strategic benefits, fuelling the industry's pipeline while also generating long-term revenue streams for the university.[15]

The role of technology centres in knowledge transfer

Research and technology organisations (RTOs), also called "technology centres", "industrial research centres" or "public research organisations" are non-profit organisations that provide research and development technology and innovation services to enterprises and governments. They function mainly as a support platform for companies, generating and facilitating the use of technological knowledge, providing local companies with research, development and innovation services.

RTOs can fulfil their role through a variety of instruments. Partnerships with regions can be developed to test new technologies and help regions to design innovation strategies. RTOs can facilitate cluster interactions among firms and support collective activities such as the structured monitoring of technology trends. They can support a whole industrial sector, by functioning as an R&D centre whose main role is to transfer technology to the sector. They can work with individual firms by subcontracting research and developing accelerators or incubators.

RTOs funded by an industrial sector develop and share technology across the firms within this sector, or across complementary sectors. One example is the AIMEN Technology Centre in Spain. Created in 1967, AIMEN promotes and executes R&D activities and technological services promising high value-added. AIMEN supports several industrial areas, from aeronautics to chemical and petrochemical, automotive, shipbuilding, construction, energy, and more. Besides providing technological services to individual firms, the fact that innovation can be shared across sectors facilitates cross-sectoral collaboration. The EURAC research centre in Italy and the VTT Technical Research Centre of Finland are other examples of cross-sectoral research and technology organisations with a broad mandate.

The Fraunhofer Institute is one of the most successful examples of a RTO, and also the largest of its kind in Europe. The institutes are embedded in universities, with the director of the Fraunhofer Institute who also occupies a faculty chair at the same time. The model maintains separation between the university and RTO functions, but organically links the two elements. It offers opportunities for postgraduate students to engage in practice-oriented research. At the same time, it allows innovation in firms and industries to be guided by cutting-edge research, while granting important revenue streams to the university.

Innovation-friendly procurement

Public procurement can be used to encourage innovation in a market-friendly way.[16] Because of their purchasing power, governments can foster innovation in firms, directly or indirectly, and create a signalling effect as a lead user, influencing the diffusion of innovation. First, regular public procurement can be made "innovation-friendly" by incorporating innovation-related criteria in the tender specifications and in the evaluation of proposals. This can work for different products and services purchased by public authorities, from construction and energy to catering services.

Second, public procurement can also be strategic, such as when the government requests specific technologies for the delivery of public services in sectors such as transport, healthcare or defence. It involves the acquisition of a product, service or system that does not exist yet but could be developed within a reasonable timeframe by companies responding to the call for tender. The purchasing authority should specify the requirements of the desired product or service.

Third, the public sector can use public procurement to stimulate technological advances that require R&D, before any market solution can be launched. This type of procurement is called pre-commercial, because it is directed to support research, not to purchase a given product in the market. In some cases, pre-commercial procurement is used to offset biases against innovation driven by new and small companies. In Korea, for example, this instrument is used to guarantee innovations developed by SMEs will be purchased, offsetting the costs of research (OECD, 2011[47]).

Innovation in the service sector

The importance of innovation in services has often been underestimated or neglected in favour of technological change in the manufacturing sector. Services were long regarded as activities that did not need innovation. For one, it is true that the service sector had been lagging in the use of advanced technologies. Secondly, in manufacturing innovation often results in a new product (at least for measurement purposes), while in the service sector products are often intangible, and innovation is more likely to be measured as changes in the production process or organisational aspects (Morrar, 2014[48]). Today, with the rise of the service economy and of the so-called "servitisation" of firms in manufacturing, it is extremely important to understand and measure innovation in the service sector.

One way that innovation often occurs in the service sector is by generating new technologies or incorporating technologies that are already used in the manufacturing sector. For example, the adoption of information and communication technologies in service activities can make services more innovative and productive.

In this sense, technological innovation in the service sector can be stimulated by the traditional mechanisms that support innovation in the manufacturing sector. As argued above, governments can do so by promoting entrepreneurship, investing in R&D, offering specific assistance to SMEs and linking research centres and firms, among other mechanisms.

Another way to innovate is via non-technological incremental changes that are specific to services. Innovation can occur in marketing strategies, organisational structures, service customisation and problem-solving approaches. Innovation in the workplace can also occur by making better use of the workers' skills. Besides better matching them to jobs, the way in which the service delivery processes are organised can be made more efficient. This perspective stresses firm organisational structure and human resource management.

Policies to support non-technological innovation in the service sector can include support for entrepreneurship, creation of leadership centres and technology agencies, and soft mechanisms such as awards for workplace innovation, as indicated in the examples below.

Support for entrepreneurship can come in the form of innovation vouchers. In Barcelona, the FAD-INS programme gives vouchers to SMEs in the sectors of fashion, design and audio-visual technologies to contract external expertise with a view to improving their business.[17] This expertise can involve a new marketing strategy, more efficient organisational processes or better human resource management. This voucher programme effectively supports SMEs to generate innovation that is not necessarily attached to high-technology advances.

One example of a public agency working on service sector innovation is *Tekes*, the Finnish Funding Agency for Technology and Innovation. Unlike more traditional innovation agencies, the Finnish one focuses on workplace development, through the *Liideri* programme. In particular, the agency helps to develop management practices and forms of working that promote the active utilisation of the skills and competences of employees. It reflects an emphasis on demand and user-driven innovation (OECD/ILO, 2017[32]).

In addition, public authorities can assist businesses in making better use of the skills that their employees already have, with actions such as leadership centres and awards for workplace innovation. In Australia, for instance, the Centre for Workplace Leadership supports capacity building in leadership and promotes a high performance work culture. In Europe, the Workplace Innovation Network stimulates awareness and knowledge-sharing regarding workplace innovation. Awards such as the Australian Training Awards and the Productivity Olympics in the Philippines recognise small and medium enterprises that have developed best productivity practices (OECD/ILO, 2017[32]).

There is no panacea for regional development and each of these policies to foster innovation will create only small increases in productivity if implemented separately. Yet, if they are implemented in combination with other policies discussed throughout this report, they can generate substantially higher productivity growth. By pursuing policies to strengthen the tradable sector, to become more innovative, to support knowledge diffusion, to raise skill levels and to utilise their unique advantages, regions will not only ensure they remain competitive, but will raise living standards for all residents.

Notes

1. Findings by Haddad et al. (2013[53]) and Caselli et al. (2015[2]) support this argument.

2. For more information on the types of assistance offered to workers by the Austrian Steel Foundation, refer to Hofer, Weber and Winter-Ebmer (2013[51]).

3. Based on http://s3platform.jrc.ec.europa.eu/-/a-territorial-perspective-on-smart-specialisation (accessed on 22 November 2017).

4. More information about the optical cluster in Wales can be found at: www.ft.com/content/7b986bec-349e-11e7-99bd-13beb0903fa3 and www.compoundsemiconductorcentre.com/.

5. Duplication can also occur across different institutions operating at the regional level or across government levels, as well as across policy fields (OECD, 2014[55]).

6. As of 2017, 4 macro-regional strategies have been formed: Baltic Sea Region, Danube Region, Adriatic and Ionian Region, and Alpine Region. More information available at: http://s3platform.jrc.ec.europa.eu/eu-macro-regional-strategies [Accessed Nov 10, 2017].

7. The state aid programmes have been evaluated by Tarczynska, Cafcas and LeRoy (2016[49]).

8. The programme is advertised to accumulate exemptions up to all business-related taxes. See the statutes of the Start-Up NY programme for details on eligibility criteria. https://esd.ny.gov/sites/default/files/SNY_Statute_06232015.pdf (accessed 01 January 2018).

9. A full list of firms can be found in the 2014 and 2016 reports for the programme. https://cdn.esd.ny.gov/reports/2014_startupny_report.pdf and https://esd.ny.gov/sites/default/files/news-articles/2016_STARTUPNY_Report.pdf (both accessed 1 January 2018).

10. Data can be found in the Marketing and Service Performance Monitoring report by the New York State Office of the State Comptroller. www.osc.state.ny.us/audits/allaudits/093015/14s10.pdf (accessed 01 January 2018).

11. See, for example, OECD (2009[11]) and OECD (2016[1]).

12. Information retrieved from Austrian Partnership Practice (2015[54]).

13. Henke and Zhang (2010[52]) found evidence of this when investigating supplier-driven innovation in the US automobile sector.

14. The evaluation of the voucher programme in Lombardy and its effects was carried out by Sala, Landoni and Verganti (2016[50]).

15. Information retrieved from: https://wissenschaft.bmwfw.gv.at/home/research/national/knowledge-transfer-centres-and-exploitation-of-ipr/ and https://transfer.univie.ac.at/fileadmin/user_upload/d_transfer/Inventions_at_the_University_of_Vienna.pdf (accessed 10 November 2017).

16. For more information on this matter, see OECD (2011[47]).

17. Information retrieved from: http://fad-ins.cambrabcn.org/?lang=es (accessed on 10 November 2017).

References

Alberti, F. and J. Giusti (2012), "Cultural heritage, tourism and regional competitiveness: The Motor Valley cluster", *City, Culture and Society*, Vol. 3/4, pp. 261-273. [14]

Alves, H., A. Cerro and A. Martins (2010), "Impacts of small tourism events on rural places", *Journal of Place Management and Development*, Vol. 3/1, pp. 22-37, http://dx.doi.org/10.1108/17538331011030257. [26]

Austrian Partnership Practice (2015), *Overview of TEPs as a Policy Instrument in ALMP/Active Labour Market Policy: 1999-2014*, APP, http://vtr.istra-istria.hr/site_media/media/uploads/files/news/TEPs_Overview_09122015_en.pdf. [54]

Caselli, F. et al. (2015), "Diversification through Trade", *NBER Working Papers*, Vol. 21498. [2]

Cernat, L. and F. Mustilli (2017), "Trade and Labour Adjustment in Europe: what role for the European Globalisation Adjustment Fund?", *Chief Economist Note, Trade, European Commission* 2. [8]

Criscuolo, C. et al. (2016), "The Causal Effects of an Industrial Policy", *CEP Discussion Paper*, No. 1113, Centre for Economic Performance. [19]

Donner, M. (2016), *Understanding place brands as collective and territorial development processes*, Wageningen University, Montpellier SupAgro. [24]

Edmondson, G. et al. (2012), *Making industry university partnerships work: lessons from successful collaborations*, Science|Business Innovati on Board AISBL. [43]

EEF (2017), "Unlocking Business Ambition Through an Improved Sector Deal Framework", EEF. [4]

Eurofund (2014), *Effects of Restructuring at Regional Level and Approaches to Dealing with the Consequences*, Publications Office of the European Union, Luxembourg. [9]

European Commission (2017), "Reflection Paper on Harnessing Globalisation", European Commission. [31]

François, J., M. Jansen and R. Peters (2011), "Trade Adjustment Costs and Assistance: The Labour Market Dynamics", in Jansen, M., R. Petes and J. Salazar-Xirinachs (eds.), *Trade and Employment From Myths to Facts*, ILO, Geneva. [6]

Haddad, M. et al. (2013), "Trade openness reduces growth volatility when countries are well diversified", *Canadian Journal of Economics/Revue canadienne d'économique*, Vol. 46/2, pp. 765-790. [53]

Hausmann, R. and F. Neffke (2016), "The Workforce of Pioneer Plants". [37]

Henke, J. and C. Zhang (2010), "Increasing Supplier-Driven Innovation", *MIT Sloan Management Review*, Vol. 51/2, pp. 41-46. [52]

Hofer, H., A. Weber and R. Winter-Ebmer (2013), "Labor market policy in Austria during the Crises", *Working Papers*, No. 1326, Johannes Kepler University - Department of Economics. [51]

Humphrey, J. and H. Schmitz (2002), "How does insertion in global value chains affect upgrading in industrial clusters?", *Regional Studies*, Vol. 36/9, pp. 1017-1027. [39]

James, S. (2013), "Effectiveness of Tax and Non-Tax Incentives and Investments: Evidence and Policy Implications", *SSRN Electronic Journal*. [21]

Jensen, N. (2017), "Job creation and firm-specific location incentives", *Journal of Public Policy*, Vol. 37/01, pp. 85-112. [18]

Kline, P. and E. Moretti (2014), "People, Places, and Public Policy: Some Simple Welfare Economics of Local Economic Development Programs", *Annual Review of Economics*, Vol. 6/1, pp. 629-662. [22]

Lederman, D., M. Olarreaga and L. Payton (2010), "Export promotion agencies: Do they work?", *Journal of Development Economics*, Vol. 91/2, pp. 257-265. [5]

Levy, R. (2005), "Les doctorants CIFRE : médiateurs entre laboratoires de recherche universitaires et entreprises", *Revue d'économie industrielle*, Vol. 111/1, pp. 79-96. [46]

Liu, A. (2016), *Remaking Economic Development: The Markets and Civics of Continuous Growth and Prosperity*, The Brookings Institution. [34]

Lorenzini, E. (2011), *Territory branding as a strategy for rural development: Experiences from Italy*, ERSA 2011 - 51st Congress of the European Regional Science Association, Barcelona. [25]

McGee, M. (2015), "The Modern Day Border War: How Kansas Can End Its Economic Development Battle with Missouri in the Kansas City Metropolitan Area", *Kansas Journal of Law & Public Policy*, Vol. XXV/1, pp. 111-130. [20]

Moretti, E. (2012), *The New Geography of Jobs*, Houghton Mifflin Harcourt. [7]

Morrar, R. (2014), "Innovation in Services: A Literature Review", *Technology Innovation Management Review*. [48]

OECD/ILO (2017), *Engaging Employers in Apprenticeship Opportunities: Making It Happen Locally*, OECD Publishing, Paris, http://dx.doi.org/10.1787/9789264266681-en. [33]

OECD/ILO (2017), *Better Use of Skills in the Workplace: Why It Matters for Productivity and Local Jobs*, OECD Publishing, Paris, http://dx.doi.org/10.1787/9789264281394-en. [32]

OECD (2009), *How Regions Grow : Trends and Analysis*, OECD Publishing, http://dx.doi.org/10.1787/9789264039469-en. [11]

OECD (2010), *OECD Innovation Strategy: Getting a Head Start on Tomorrow*, OECD Publisher, Paris, http://dx.doi.org/10.1787/9789264083479-en.. [27]

OECD (2011), *Regions and Innovation Policy*, OECD Reviews of Regional Innovation, OECD Publishing, Paris, http://dx.doi.org/10.1787/9789264097803-en. [44]

OECD (2011), *Demand-side Innovation Policies*, OECD Publishing, Paris, http://dx.doi.org/10.1787/9789264098886-en. [47]

OECD (2012), *Promoting Growth in All Regions*, OECD Publishing, Paris, http://dx.doi.org/10.1787/9789264174634-en. [12]

OECD (2013), *Rural-Urban Partnerships: An Integrated Approach to Economic Development*, OECD Rural Policy Reviews, OECD Publishing, Paris, http://dx.doi.org/10.1787/9789264204812-en. [29]

OECD (2014), *OECD Territorial Reviews: Netherlands 2014*, OECD Territorial Reviews, OECD Publishing, Paris, http://dx.doi.org/10.1787/9789264209527-en. [3]

OECD (2014), *OECD Reviews of Innovation Policy: France 2014*, OECD Reviews of Innovation Policy, OECD Publishing, Paris, http://dx.doi.org/10.1787/9789264214026-en. [45]

OECD (2014), *Job Creation and Local Economic Development*, OECD Publishing, Paris, http://dx.doi.org/10.1787/9789264215009-en. [55]

OECD (2015), *The Innovation Imperative: Contributing to Productivity, Growth and Well-Being*, OECD Publishing, Paris, http://dx.doi.org/10.1787/9789264239814-en. [17]

OECD (2015), *The Future of Productivity*, OECD Publishing, Paris, http://dx.doi.org/10.1787/9789264248533-en. [35]

OECD (2016), *Enhancing the Contributions of Higher Education and Research Institutions to Innovation: Case Studies.* [41]

OECD (2016), *OECD Regional Outlook 2016: Productive Regions for Inclusive Societies*, OECD Publishing, Paris, http://dx.doi.org/10.1787/9789264260245-en. [1]

OECD (2016), *OECD Regional Outlook 2016: Productive Regions for Inclusive Societies*, OECD Publishing, Paris, http://dx.doi.org/10.1787/9789264260245-en. [36]

OECD (2016), *Job Creation and Local Economic Development 2016*, OECD Publishing, Paris, http://dx.doi.org/10.1787/9789264261976-en. [28]

OECD (2017), *Report on the Implementation of the OECD Gender Recommendations - Some Progress on Gender Equality but Much Left to Do*, OECD, http://www.oecd.org/mcm/documents/C-MIN-2017-7-EN.pdf (accessed on 09 January 2018). [30]

OECD (2017), *OECD Territorial Reviews: Northern Sparsely Populated Areas*, OECD Territorial Reviews, OECD Publishing, Paris, http://dx.doi.org/10.1787/9789264268234-en. [15]

Oliveira, E. (2015), "Place branding in strategic spatial planning: A content analysis of development plans, strategic initiatives and policy documents for Portugal (2014-2020)", *Journal of Place Management and Development Planning*, Vol. 8/2, pp. 23-50. [23]

Ortega-Argilés, R. (2012), *Economic Transformation Strategies: Smart Specialisation Case Studies.* [13]

Pietrobelli, C. and R. Rabellotti (2010), "Global value chains meet innovation systems: Are there learning opportunities for developing countries?,", *IDB Working Paper Series*, No. 232, Interamerican Development Bank. [38]

Sala, A., P. Landoni and R. Verganti (2016), "Small and Medium Enterprises collaborations with knowledge intensive services: an explorative analysis of the impact of innovation vouchers", *R&D Management*, Vol. 46/S1, pp. 291-302. [50]

Sörvik, J. and A. Kleibrink (2015), "Mapping Innovation Priorities and Specialisation Patterns in Europe", *S3 Working Paper Series*, No. 08, European Commission. [16]

Tarczynska, K., T. Cafcas and G. LeRoy (2016), *Slicing the Budget: How Three States Allocate Economic Development Dollars*, Good Jobs First, https://www.goodjobsfirst.org/slicingthebudget (accessed on 01 January 2018). [49]

UNCTAD (2013), *Global Value Chains: Investment and Trade for Development*, UNCTAD. [40]

Vallance, P. et al. (2017), "Smart specialisation in regions with less-developed research and innovation systems: A changing role for universities?", *Environment and Planning C: Politics and Space*. [42]

Winter-Ebmer, R. (2001), "Evaluating an innovative redundancy-retraining project: The Austrian Steel Foundation", *CEPR Discussion Paper*, No. 2776, Centre for Economic Policy Research. [10]

ORGANISATION FOR ECONOMIC CO-OPERATION AND DEVELOPMENT

The OECD is a unique forum where governments work together to address the economic, social and environmental challenges of globalisation. The OECD is also at the forefront of efforts to understand and to help governments respond to new developments and concerns, such as corporate governance, the information economy and the challenges of an ageing population. The Organisation provides a setting where governments can compare policy experiences, seek answers to common problems, identify good practice and work to co-ordinate domestic and international policies.

The OECD member countries are: Australia, Austria, Belgium, Canada, Chile, the Czech Republic, Denmark, Estonia, Finland, France, Germany, Greece, Hungary, Iceland, Ireland, Israel, Italy, Japan, Korea, Latvia, Luxembourg, Mexico, the Netherlands, New Zealand, Norway, Poland, Portugal, the Slovak Republic, Slovenia, Spain, Sweden, Switzerland, Turkey, the United Kingdom and the United States. The European Union takes part in the work of the OECD.

OECD Publishing disseminates widely the results of the Organisation's statistics gathering and research on economic, social and environmental issues, as well as the conventions, guidelines and standards agreed by its members.

OECD PUBLISHING, 2, rue André-Pascal, 75775 PARIS CEDEX 16
(85 2018 06 1 P) ISBN 978-92-64-29309-0 – 2018

www.ingramcontent.com/pod-product-compliance
Ingram Content Group UK Ltd.
Pitfield, Milton Keynes, MK11 3LW, UK
UKHW051502290926
15471UKWH00008B/1356

9 789264 293090